UNIVERSITY OF
WOLVERHAMPTON

Writing Women's History

Edited by
Michelle Perrot

Translated by
Felicia Pheasant

From an original idea by
Alain Paire

BLACKWELL
Oxford UK & Cambridge USA

First published 1984
English edition first published 1992

Blackwell Publishers
108 Cowley Road
Oxford OX4 1JF
UK

238 Main Street, Suite 501
Cambridge, Massachusetts 02142
USA

British Library Cataloguing in Publication Data

A CIP catalogue record for this book is available from the British Library.

Library of Congress Cataloging in Publication Data
Histoire des femmes est-elle possible? English.
Writing women's history / edited by Michelle Perrot; translated
by Felicia Pheasant; from an original idea by Alain Paire.
p. cm.
Translation of: Une Histoire des femmes est-elle possible?
Papers from a symposium suggested by Alain Paire and held in
Saint-Maximin (Var) in July 1983.
Includes bibliographical references.
ISBN 0–631–15632–1 (hb). – ISBN 0–631–18612–3 (pbk)
1. Women – Historiography – Congresses.   2. Women – France – History –
Congresses.
I. Perrot, Michelle.   II. Paire, Alain.   III. Title.
HQ1121.H62913   1992
305.4'09 – dc20   92–3229
                                                                         CIP

Typeset in 10 on 12 pt Sabon by Graphicraft Typesetters Ltd. Hong Kong
Printed in Great Britain by T.J. Press Ltd. Padstow Cornwall

This book is printed on acid-free paper

Contents

List of Contributors

Alain Corbin (University of Paris I)

Arlette Farge (CNRS, Paris)

Agnès Fine (University of Toulouse)

Catherine Fouquet (University of Aix-en-Provence)

Geneviève Fraisse (CNRS, Paris)

Christiane Klapisch-Zuber (Ecole des Hautes Etudes en Sciences
   Sociales, Paris)

Yvonne Knibiehler (University of Provence)

Michelle Perrot (University of Paris VII – Jussieu)

Elisabeth Ravoux Rallo (University of Provence)

Jacques Revel (Ecole des Hautes Etudes en Sciences Sociales, Paris)

Anne Roche (University of Provence)

Pauline Schmitt Pantel (Centre de Recherches Louis Gernet, Paris)

Sylvie Vandecasteele-Schweitzer (CNRS – Université Lumière, Lyon)

Danièle Voldman (CNRS, Paris)

Twenty Years of Women's History in France: Preface to the English Edition

Michelle Perrot

This book, which came out of the symposium held in Saint-Maximin (in the Var region) in July 1983, gives an idea of the French historiography of women's history. Modest in comparison with its English and American precursors, this historiography is nevertheless significant, as it reflects the development of a field of research that has proved to be one of the most dynamic in recent years.

In fact, this book can now be seen as marking the halfway stage between the first attempts at women's history in the 1970s and *A History of Women in the West*, currently being published (Italy, 1990–2; France, 1991–2, and translations into six other languages to come) and which is the work of the team that took part in the symposium at Saint-Maximin.

Let us briefly recall the various stages in the development of women's history in France. In 1973 three teachers at the Université de Paris VII (Jussieu), Fabienne Bock, Pauline Schmitt Pantel and myself, held the first course in women's history. This was our own express wish and that of a number of our women students, all of us committed in various ways to the women's movement, which was very active in France at that time. We found it so difficult to construct this course, without adequate material and without a proper framework within which to define our subject, and we were so uncertain as to the validity of the object of our work that we called the course: 'Do women have a history?' The course consisted of a series of lectures. The first semester dealt with the present, and we worked with sociologists, who were ahead of us in terms of reflecting on the relations between the sexes. Andrée Michel, sociologist, friend of Simone de Beauvoir and founder of one of the first laboratories for research on women at the CNRS (Centre National de la Recherche Scientifique) opened fire in a charged atmosphere. She dealt with 'family models'. The course had attracted a great many people, in particular a number of left-wing students (Trotskyists, Maoists, etc.) who, clinging to a rather superficial form of Marxism, considered that the question of women was secondary, a derivative of the real problem of the hour, which was revolution, whether in society or in the third world. They came with the firm intention of arguing, and that is what they did. Andrée Michel was reproached for speaking on 'family models': they said that they did not want to hear about family models; the family was bourgeois. To this the speaker replied that as a sociologist she did not advocate any one model, but was content to analyse them all. Another member of the audience asked her what she thought of orgasm: wasn't this the only meaning of 'the relations between the sexes'?

This recollection of a now distant past will seem amusing (indeed, we found it amusing at the time!). But this was in fact the situation in which we found ourselves, and it brought to mind an atmosphere which, as historians, we had found in the nineteenth century: the atmosphere that surrounded any meeting of women about women. Above all, our interlocutors really wanted to express their disapproval symbolically. After a while the arguments came to an end. After the first semester on sociology, we called on our most brilliant historian colleagues – those who were closely linked with the *Annales* school and were thus open to this type of questioning: Pierre Vidal-Naquet, Jacques Le Goff, Emmanuel Le Roy Ladurie, Jean-Louis Flandrin, Mona Ozouf and others. We devoted one session to prehistory, and even to natural history, looking at the differences in behaviour between male and female baboons. We were haunted by the notorious question of the origin of sexual inequality. These lecture-debates were very successful. They allowed us to break new ground, to collect a certain amount of material and to sketch out a framework for our subject. Over the next few years, we took our fate into our own hands, with courses on 'Women and the Family' and 'Women and Work'. At the same time, a number of research projects began, in the form of *maîtrises* (fourth-year university papers) which were often turned into theses. Among the first subjects to be researched were housework or work in the home, the role of war (in particular the two world wars) on relations between the sexes, abortion and infanticide, debates on maternity, delinquent women and women prisoners, the upbringing and education of girls. A body of specialists began to form, and they took part in the first symposia.

The youthful, militant ardour that underlay this research was little concerned with theory. But what was to be done with all this material? Wasn't there a risk of accumulation without reflection? Hence the desire that arose among many of those undertaking these early pieces of research to compare points of view. Arlette Farge and Christiane Klapisch-Zuber began a series of regular informal seminars based on texts (anthropological or feminist) or themes (for example, women's solitude, a subject on which a collective work was subsequently published[1]). A little later, this group, wanting to open up discussion within the milieu of professional historians, sent an article to *Annales*; after examination the article was published, with the title 'Women's culture and power. A historiographical essay'. It was signed by ten people, giving it the appearance of a manifesto, which caused much surprise![2]

In the meantime, Alain Paire, the chairman of the 'Rencontres de Saint-Maximin', suggested that we should hold a symposium on the theme 'Is it possible to write a history of women?' in that lovely abbey in the Var. This was in spring 1983. Ten years after the first course, we were convinced that women had a history. But could it be written, and how? Although this book contains the papers given at the symposium, it cannot evoke the warm atmosphere and rich debates that were such an important part of our meeting. Nevertheless, it constitutes a record of the state of research and questioning in 1983, and we feel that it has not lost too much of its topicality. Bibliographical details have been updated wherever possible. The journey we undertook all those years ago has in a way found its completion in *A History of Women in the West*, most of whose authors were at Saint-Maximin, and I must say a few words about it.

Following the popularity of the Italian translation of *A History of Private Life* (Seuil, edited by Philippe Ariès and Georges Duby), Vito and Giuseppe Laterza put the idea of a history of women to Georges Duby. Duby, who had published *Le Chevalier, la femme et le prêtre* (Hachette, Paris) in 1981 and given several courses at the Collège de France on women in the Middle Ages, thought the idea an excellent one, but felt unable to carry out the work involved. He therefore called on me. I too hesitated when faced with the scale of the task, and consulted the team that had built up over the years and is at present foremost in this branch of history. Pauline Schmitt Pantel, on ancient history; Christiane Klapisch-Zuber, on medieval history; Arlette Farge, with whom Natalie Davis agreed to collaborate on modern history; Geneviève Fraisse on the nineteenth century; and Françoise Thébaud, on the twentieth century, after some reflection agreed to undertake the project. This team defined the boundaries (the West from antiquity to our time), the axes, the style and the framework (more than a history of women, rather a history of the relationship between the sexes), recruited collaborators (seventy-two in all, from many different countries, though with a strong core of French historians) and supervised the work from start to finish. We began in 1987 and are now in the finishing stages. Publication of the five volumes in Italy and in France (by Editions Plon) was completed in 1992. The first two volumes of the English-language edition will be published by Harvard University Press in 1992, and the remaining volumes in 1993.

Of course it is not for us to say whether or not we have succeeded. The purpose of this Preface is simply to set out the genealogy of our work. It is by necessity incomplete, and is in any case destined to be overtaken fast by the vigorously developing research in new countries, both in the West and in other parts of the world. After the discoveries and achievements of the last two decades, this decade seems, at its inception, more uncertain where relations between the sexes are concerned. We may nevertheless hope that it will see the women of Africa, of the East and of Latin America taking their history into their own hands, in the two senses of the word, both the history that we make and the history that we write, which so often go together.

The possibility of a history of women resides first and foremost in women's awareness of themselves. It depends on feminism in the widest sense of the term and therefore on democracy, of which it is the indispensable and demanding companion.

NOTES

1 *Madame ou mademoiselle? Itinéraires de la solitude féminine en France au XIXe siècle*, ed. A. Farge and C. Klapisch-Zuber (Montalba, Paris, 1983).
2 *Annales Economie Société Civilisation (ESC)* 1986, March–April (3), pp. 271–95.

Introduction

Michelle Perrot

The architects of what we know as 'women's history' today have many questions to discuss. What exactly is the significance of this line of work which already has its own history? What are its roots and why was it necessary? What results has it achieved and what effects has it had? What knowledge has it produced? For what and for whom? In short, where are we? After a period of primitive accumulation, carried on in all directions at once without much consideration of the problems involved, as if discovery was a sufficient end in itself, the time for reflection has come. We must, with Arlette Farge, 'take the time to look back and to retrace our steps' (chapter 1).

First of all, we must recall the banal fact that the word 'history' has two meanings. On the one hand it conveys events, the things that happen or that have happened, and on the other, the account given of these events, written history, history as a discipline. It is this second meaning that we are considering here. Is it possible to write the history of one category of sex – in this case women? This supposes that we give a positive content to the first definition: there are events that are specific to women, and there are some things that concern them particularly.

In the 1970s we were not so sure. Apparently doomed to the silence of reproduction, to the infinite repetition of daily tasks, to a sexual division of the world which sometimes appears unchangeable, so much so that one searches for its origins in the mists of time, do women not belong rather to anthropology? 'Do women have a history?' This was the title of a course given in Jussieu (Paris VII) in 1973–4. The title conveyed our perplexity. This anecdote provides a measure of the progress we have made. We no longer doubt that women have a history or that they produce history, and therefore we do not doubt that we can write that history, although not without facing problems that merit our consideration.

First, a few words on historiography. Since history has existed as a
'scientific' discipline – in other words, more or less since the nineteenth
century – the amount of attention given to women has varied, depend-
ing on men's perception, since up until now, to all intents and purposes
men were the only historians. There is no guarantee, in any case, that
women would have written any differently, since the sex of the individual has only relative importance. Jules Michelet, for example, saw in the
relationship between the sexes one of the driving forces of history,
modulated by the latent conflict between Woman/Nature and Man/
Culture. Woman may be a power for good when her maternal nature
takes the upper hand, but becomes a force for evil when she usurps
political power and steps out of the private sphere. Then history is
disturbed and woman becomes a witch.[1]

In the second half of the nineteenth century, the issue of matriarchy
dominated anthropological debate in Europe. Engels discussed the
theses of Johann Bachofen and Lewis Henry Morgan, wrote *The Origin
of the Family* and subordinated the emancipation of women to a revolution in property. At the same time, positivist history, whose importance
in the establishment of the craft of the historian in the academic domain
is well known, and of which Charles Seignobos was the great master,
succeeded in completely suppressing the subject of women and, more
widely, that of everyday life. It devoted itself to the political, to affairs
of state. Diplomatic and military events took over the stage of public
and national history.

With the increasing influence of the *Annales* school (Marc Bloch,
Lucien Febvre and others) from the 1930s on, prospects certainly im-
proved in the sense that the field of history was considerably extended.
Nevertheless, economic and social concerns predominated. The emphasis was on the study of the economic climate and structures, of social
categories and the class struggle. The sexual dimension was hardly taken
into account; and the family, suffering from the conservative ideology of
Le Play and his disciples, was rather forgotten. Between 1920 and 1960,
the history of women, confused with the history of feminism, was the
work of only a few isolated individuals: Léon Abensour, Jules Puech,
Marguerite Thibert and more recently Edith Thomas (see chapter 11);
and also, very close to us, a few sociologists, such as Madeleine Guilbert
and Evelyne Sullerot, who were forced to sift out historical facts for
themselves. It is significant that a pioneering sector like historical
demography should have so little to say about women, considered
simply as a variable in the reproductive process, and should only take
into account the household, without considering single persons (including those widowed, separated or divorced), although for the most part

they outnumbered married persons, particularly amongst women,[2] and that when it reconstructed family genealogies it only retained male patronymics, thus perpetuating a patrilineal vision of history (see chapter 2). That those in this discipline should, in 1979, have felt the need to organize an exchange of views on 'historical demography and women' indicates a change of direction.[3]

A whole series of factors led to this change: the development of a new historical anthropology which put the study of the family and sexual roles in the forefront of its preoccupations; the development of what we call 'new history', anxious to take account of everyday ideas and behaviour, all subsumed under the rather vague term 'mentalities'.[4] There is undoubtedly a more receptive climate for women's history.

But in France, as elsewhere, this history has come from the women's movement itself and from the many questions it raised. Women expressed themselves with particular forcefulness in the years 1970–5, a period that corresponds to the political breakthrough of the Women's Liberation Movement and the rise of the feminist press.[5] A need for history was felt in many circles, including universities, once there were teachers capable of responding to the demands of female students, and indeed of stimulating this demand. Courses were planned; discussion groups were set up; symposia were held; the first reports appeared;[6] and above all, research was begun at the level of masters' degrees and doctorates. We are now seeing the fruits of this research. The political changes that came about in May 1981 had a stimulating effect in many spheres.[7]

Today women are on the agenda, both inside and outside university institutions. Learned societies devote 'study days' to them. Eminently academic journals publish articles, and even special editions, on their history.[8] Venerable collections (such as Hachette's *Daily Life* series) have 'women's' titles.[9] Several publishers have 'women's' series.[10] Biography in particular is flourishing. Even the television channels have shown a series of portraits of the pioneers of feminism.

Is this simply a fashion? We should no doubt be pleased, as this is a sign of recognition. All fashions are significant. At the same time we should be wary lest the subject be quickly exhausted. Fashion too often creates its own saturation and kills the object of fashion before it has had time to define itself.

For the rest, we must not delude ourselves. Quantitatively, the space devoted to women's studies in scientific publications remains very modest, as is suggested, for example, by Arlette Farge's analysis of the *Annales* and of *Histoire* in chapter 1. Women's history is treated as marginal: an extra chapter to be added without changing the whole. We may doubt whether this work has changed the nature of the historical approach, for the stereotypes continue to reign and silence prevails. But can women's history carry out this questioning of history unless it remains open to question itself? Mustn't it begin by questioning its own content and method?

In the essays that follow we have tried, not to draw up a report on progress so far – this has been outlined elsewhere[11] – but to measure the difficulties, both extrinsic and, above all, intrinsic. There is, in particular, the problem of sources, which applies to any kind of history, and which raises the question of evidence in a most striking manner. In the words of a book that reconsiders the problem of medieval marriage (*Le Chevalier, la femme et le prêtre*)[12] Georges Duby makes the following point: 'Amongst all these men who loudly proclaim what they have done or what they dream of doing, we must not forget the women. They are much talked about. But what do we know about them?' This is indeed an important question. Because their actions and gestures do not generally attract the attention of observers, they are hardly ever recorded in primary sources, though there are great differences from one period to another. Women have constantly been the target of exhortations and normative sermons delivered by moral and religious authorities who, by emphasizing what they ought to be, have helped to obscure what they really were. In the form of images and fantasies, they are at the centre of a literature that is very precious, but which we must approach with extreme caution, as Elisabeth Ravoux Rallo and Anne Roche suggest in chapter 6. More than any other, the image of women has been distorted by the media and we must decipher the nature of this distortion.

These distortions and obstacles explain the enthusiasm on the part of women's historians for oral sources which have generally allowed those who are usually silent in history to speak to us: the workers, those on the edge of society, and indeed women. 'To listen to women, the oppressed majority, talking, would be sufficient to restore them to history: they would then arise, mute and submissive, if allowed one word, one conversation to make up for centuries of silence. Oral history thus becomes a means of demanding justice for oneself in a society organized along masculine lines.' In chapter 4 Danièle Voldman and Sylvie Vandecasteele-Schweitzer describe for us an experiment conducted over three years within the framework of the Institut d'Histoire du Temps Présent, the possibilities opened up and the problems created, for example, by the feeling of complicity between women. They ask: in what sense can one speak of 'women's memory'? Does this signify anything but the expression of a cultural position in relation to the family and private life? They warn that oral documents are not a panacea; like any other documents, they require criticism and elaboration.

In her remarkable study of the trousseau (chapter 10), Agnès Fine tells us that the essential contribution of oral enquiry is to shift the initial question. 'What the old women questioned tell us so strikingly is not simply the composition of their trousseau, still less its economic value. As we listen to them, we begin to realize that the trousseau represented something essential in their lives as women, something that went far beyond the few ritual objects of which it consisted.' It constituted a history, 'a long history between mother and daughter'.[13] These vibrant texts allow us to hear, see and feel the past. They take us through to the other side of the looking-glass. From this point of view they are irreplaceable.

But women's history must also consider the longer time-span, and must necessarily turn to the traditional sources and ask new questions. For the object is defined by the way in which we regard it. Pauline Schmitt Pantel's demonstration with reference to Greek history (chapter 7) is very convincing in this light. We have very little record of what was explicitly said about women in ancient societies. And yet the work of feminists such as Michele Zimbalist Rosaldo and Annette Weiner, by renewing the approach to the problem, has led to a re-examination of iconography.

> Any research into death, food, clothing, war, rituals, possessions, gifts, or production in general allows us to define more precisely the division of masculine and feminine spaces and roles . . . A new reading of iconography is one of the fundamental bases for any enquiry of this kind. It is not enough to collect all the scenes on vases described as scenes from the *gynaeceum*. We must order and study the simultaneous and alternate presence of men and women at moments of great importance for the city, such as the departure or return of warriors, funerals, banquets and certain feasts. (chapter 7)

This method can be extended to any amount of data. Documents taken at face value tell us very little, as we know. It is the viewpoint that we apply to them that extracts something more and reconstructs the information in another way.

Women's history has also changed as regards its content, both in terms of its approach and in the objects it examines. At first it was simply a question of rediscovering and remembering. Women's history was concerned – as it still needs to be – to bring to light things that had been forgotten or lost, or indeed that had never been perceived. Few questions were asked about the reasons for this amnesia, which makes women's history as discontinuous as women's struggles. This kind of simple inventory is no longer adequate today. 'In terms of historical research, to speak of loss and re-appropriation supposes that archive material is an object in itself' comments Geneviève Fraisse (chapter 11), who emphasizes 'the need for work on the reasons why aspects of history are forgotten'. What we need to understand is the way in which memory itself works. Where is the 'seat of memory' for women?

Women's history was preoccupied with the origins of domination and oppression, and drawn to images of woman as victim, beaten, deceived, humiliated, underpaid, alone, prostituted. It was the history of female misfortune. Then, wishing to show women as agents of intrigue, with their own forms of action and expression, their own gestures and words, if not their own culture, which is a more questionable notion, women's history switched its attention to active and rebellious women, women actively present in history. We might describe this method as carnivalesque; it operates by inversion, moving from white to black, and thus requires a cautious approach. Alain Corbin (chapter 9) is surprised, for example, by the concealment of male suffering: an insidious distribution of images reserves grief, tears and vapours for women and forces men into quite unreal virile postures. It is all or nothing, heads or tails, and this masculine/feminine dichotomy leads to an impasse. It is more fruitful to explore the grey areas, where definitions are less precise. Rather than asking whether or not women have power, we prefer to ask what is the nature of their powers.

The objects of this history were first identified as being in the domain of women's 'natural' roles: motherhood, childbirth, prostitution. Then attention shifted towards women's work: in the home, paid work, the occupations of the leisured classes, the question of feminine professions and their evaluation. On the borders of literature and history, work has been done on representations of women. Women's struggles have won attention, but much work remains to be done on feminism, in particular in terms of analysing it in the political dimension that it is ordinarily denied.

Women's history was first of all a history of their bodies. Catherine Fouquet (chapter 5) analyses the reasons for this 'unavoidable detour'. The biological imposes itself as a starting-point. For Yvonne Knibiehler (chapter 3), 'perhaps any chronology of women's history has to take this as its starting-point and map out the chequered progress of a twofold emancipation, from biological constraints and from male domination.' She proposes a new discipline: 'chronobiology'. Because the female body has been denied, repressed, masked by the very cult of which it was the object, it was necessary for women to recapture their bodies and make this rediscovered femininity the source of a renewal of women's writing (see chapter 6). Women must find their identity by claiming, assuming and proclaiming their own sex.

While the history of the female body, dominated by biological factors, is no doubt a necessary step along the way, women's history must, and in fact does, go beyond this. This point is made in most of the following chapters, which reproduce the debate that occupied American historiography for some time, highlighting the opposition between biological sex and 'gender', an infinitely more complex notion defined by roles, cultural practices and symbolic representations. Anne Roche (chapter 6) agrees with Jacques Revel (chapter 8) on this. For the former, the concept of 'women's writing', an expression of women's bodies, only reproduces the old idea of nature, the very notion that was at the origin of sexual domination. 'One cannot deny the existence of a symbolism of sexual difference, but this symbolism is blurred.' If we do not reflect on this blurring, women's writing will become nothing more than 'inverted masculine writing'.

For Jacques Revel, 'the reduction of categories of sex to their biological determination is no doubt the single factor that has, more than any other, prevented us from thinking about their existence or social functions' (chapter 8). To reduce women to their biological nature is to say that 'feminine identity is primarily the product of a particular physiology.' The same could be said of men. It is more important to study social roles in history than to study the 'signs which might constitute a feminine domain'.

We must also beware of describing a feminine culture that would be no more than the rigid designation of a complementary space and, in the end, another formulation of immutable nature, the basis for a heritage and a tradition. This notion of feminine culture has recently given rise to an animated debate in Italy.[14] The risk is that we shall go on for ever reproducing a tautological argument.

The question of the relationship between the sexes and of the difference between them is of prime importance. 'To take the masculine and the feminine into consideration on equal terms in any historical analysis and to believe that the relations between them can be moving forces in history' (Pauline Schmitt Pantel in chapter 7), such is the path chosen by the female historians of the Greek city. To examine social practices, types of discourse, representations and images, and to reject simplistic dichotomies such as 'nature/culture' and 'domestic/public'; to stop brandishing the word 'misogyny' as the explanation of the place allowed women; to reject clear-cut dividing lines in favour of grey areas, interaction between zones, lack of clear distinctions, inversions, and to reject harmonious complementarities in favour of conflicts and contradictions; to accept the ambivalence of things and to reject all stereotypes: these would be the essential features of a methodological undertaking that would also aim to integrate the social levels that cannot be disregarded.[15]

Our goal is not to create a new territory called women's history, a quiet concession where women could work in peace, protected from contradiction, but rather to change the direction of historical attention by posing the question of the relationship between the sexes as central. This is the inescapable price of women's history.

NOTES

1   Thérèse Moreau, *Le Sang de l'histoire. Michelet, l'histoire et l'idée de la femme au XIXe siècle* (Flammarion, Paris, 1982).
2   Farge and Klapisch-Zuber, *Madame ou Mademoiselle?*
3   'Démographie historique et condition féminine', a special issue of *Annales de Démographie Historique* (Editions de l'Ecole des Hautes Etudes, Paris, 1981).
4   *Revue de Synthèse*, special edition on 'Sciences et Mentalités', July–December 1983 (11–112) (articles by R. Chartier, J. Revel, J. Roger and some interesting reflections on a controversial notion, Albin Michel, Paris).
5   Liliane Kandel, 'L'explosion de la presse féministe', *Le Débat*, 1 (May 1980).
6   Remember that *Pénélope. Cahiers pour l'Histoire des Femmes* began to appear in autumn 1979 and reached its eleventh issue in Autumn 1984: *Les Femmes et les associations*.
7   The Centre National de la Recherche Scientifique ran a programme on women and feminist studies in the early 1980s. There have also been historical research programmes, particularly on contemporary feminism, but also on Christian trade unions in Isère in the twentieth century, etc. The Ministry of Women's Rights encouraged the setting up of Feminist Studies posts in universities, and took part in the Flora Tristan Symposium (organized by Stéphane Michaud) in Dijon in May 1984. The Ministry has also supported *Pénélope*. There has, however, been no attempt to annex feminist studies to the socialist cause.
8   For example, there are studies on women in the January–March 1984 editions of the *Revue Historique*, in *Vingtième Siècle*, 3 (July–September 1984) and the *American Historical Review*, 89 (3) (June 1984), which was entirely devoted to 'Women's History Today'.
9   Claude Dulong, *La Vie quotidienne des femmes au Grand Siècle* (Hachette, Paris, 1984).
10 E.g. that produced by Stock, under the direction of Laurence Pernoud, *Les Femmes au temps de . . .* , with Régine Pernoud and Dominique Desanti (*La*

Femme au temps des années folles), E. Ravoux Rallo (*La Femme au temps de Casanova*).

11 See in particular M. Perrot, 'Sur l'histoire des femmes en France', *Revue du Nord*, lxiii (1981); A Farge, 'Dix ans d'histoire des femmes de France', *Le Débat*, 23 (January 1983); Joan Scott, 'Survey articles. Women in History', *Past and Present* (1983) pp. 101, 141–57.

12 Duby, *Le Chevalier, la femme et le prêtre*.

13 On this subject, see a historical analysis of this fundamental relationship by Marie-Françoise Lévy, *De mères en filles. L'éducation des françaises (1850–1880)* (Calmann-Lévy, Paris, 1984).

14 On this subject, see nos. 4 and 5 of the *Bulletin* of the Centre de Recherches et d'Informations Féministes (CRIF) (Winter 1983–4 and Spring 1984), with reference to the principal texts, in particular those by Rossana Rossanda.

15 In this connection one might read Jeanne Peterson's fine article, 'No angels in the house: The Victorian myth and the Paget women', in the *American Historical Review*, 89 (3) (June 1984). Using the private papers of three generations of women, she shows how women are not like the commonly given stereotypes and suggests areas for analysis that will lead away from the masculine/feminine dichotomy. She stresses the need to take account of social levels, even within the middle classes, which do not constitute a homogeneous whole. The model of the angel in the house might be an aristocratic dream for some women, but was a repressive nightmare for others.

1

Method and Effects of
Women's History

Arlette Farge

When what we now call 'women's history' emerged amid the ideological and social upheavals of the 1970s, there was no question of asking whether or not such a history was possible. The need to draw up, and then write, women's history was seen as evident and imperative. Thus, alongside a new theme in the field of history, was born a new way of carrying out work in that area.

This unusual starting-point, rooted in often violent political and ideological debates, has given women's history very specific conditions of existence. The starting-point was ideological, of course, but also existential, and determined one of the most characteristic aspects of its nature. The new field involved a separation of the sexes, since women decided to take charge of this privileged, hitherto misunderstood, object of research, which was themselves. Nothing of the sort occurred at the birth of working-class history, which also took place in an ideological storm, because it was for the most part written by intellectuals and not by the workers themselves. Women's history, however, combined ideological bias with an identification with its subject matter.

Its arrival in the field of learning set in motion a whole chain of mechanisms which are difficult to separate from the very process whereby the content and method of women's history as a subject were defined. The way in which the subject began to be practised led to results that necessitated new positions, new questions and new ways of answering them.

The process of constructing women's history and the results of this process have thus been closely interwoven, producing such a series of echoes and responses that it is now possible to write their history.

It is possible, and at the same time necessary, for we cannot, without running the risk of understanding nothing at all, isolate 'women's history' from the way in which it has constantly been perceived and received, and indeed awaited. Because of its existential nature, it has always given rise to considerable hopes and expectations, even if at first it was seen as no more than the indispensable companion to the blossoming Women's Liberation Movement. Because it was determined to bring a new dimension to official history, it aroused a certain feeling of surprise in academic circles. Because it was in tune with the upheavals of the time, it quickly found an echo in the media, the newspapers, the publishing houses, in radio and in television.

Thus, at a time when it had hardly begun to explore the terrain, sift the evidence or trace its paths, women's history was, as it were, overwhelmed by a multiplicity of sometimes conflicting responses and demands. While many reactions were aroused, both within feminism and without, passionate and not so passionate, the university institution as a whole greeted it with an official silence which itself constituted part of its history.

The ambivalence of responses, and their confusion, thus contributed to women's history. The time has come to try to assess what has been achieved and what lies ahead. There is no denying that we have now built up a primitive body of knowledge about women. What we must do is question this, examine its efficacity, its scope, and ask ourselves whether it represents a definitive achievement or not. If, with the necessary detachment and spirit of criticism, we examine the events that have influenced the material and the results of this research, it may be possible to formulate new criteria, to see new directions, to forestall certain kinds of response or criticism, and to force history to take more account of this research, if only by sometimes modifying the structure of its enquiries.

What I seek to do is not to judge, not to express regrets, not to hand out compliments; I simply want to take the time to look back, to retrace our steps and to set down markers that may help us to develop our thoughts further. This is a very necessary step, for the demands made upon women's history are becoming greater and more insistent every day. The discipline must learn both from its achievements and from its failures; it must also define its field of enquiry more tightly and reflect both on the path it has followed so far and on the way ahead.

What we face is a task that must be tackled co-operatively. It is essential that we, both male and female historians, assess the situation together. The fact that we are able, for the first time, to have meaningful discussions, however difficult, with our male colleagues is undoubtedly an achievement. It must also be a point of no return.

I think that we can divide the years of women's history into two unequal periods – one long period when things were falling into place and when both its basis and its marginal nature were established, while the responses it met with took many different forms. Then, after 1979–80, came another period, in which reactions were speeding up and the scope of the discipline diversified, while the output was no longer solely from authors identified with their subject or motivated by the feminism of the early years.

This means that the theme has achieved almost full recognition: all the more reason why this is the right time to question as sharply and precisely as possible our methods and the range of problems to be solved.

A LONG, EVENTFUL PERIOD OF ESTABLISHMENT: 1970–1980

One of the demands raised by the feminist movement of the 1970s was the chance for women to exist in their own right, free from social and biological constraints, from stereotypes and compulsory functions. This demand spread and set up echoes which came back with a new reply: in order to exist and to stake a claim for oneself one has to have a memory, to find in the dim past the women who came before us and whom history has never taken into account.

This memory is necessary, but in trying to establish it we immediately come up against the reasons why it does not exist. Our search must begin from scratch, because, in its asexual account of the passing of time, history has erased all traces of women and provides female researchers with a long series of male sources, redoubling the problem of women's non-existence. Two groups of figures emerge out of this: on the one hand the forgotten heroines, exceptional women; and on the other the subjugated mass of women who have remained mute throughout history. Both themes run through university research and militant studies and appear both in the feminist newspapers and in published works. Women take up the biographies of those who went before them, our mothers and sisters in oblivion, and stress the apparent silence of the archives in order to reveal all the more clearly the oppression of which women have been victims. In both cases, the vocabulary used makes it clear that they have to be dragged out of oblivion. The metaphors are those of becoming visible and revealing the unseen; they seek to compensate for the secrecy, to break the silence and to prevent future amnesia.

Based at the outset on the idea of negation and neglect, women's history naturally allied itself in its first phase with the history of mentalities and benefited from the development of this field and also that of anthropology. The time was ripe for the omissions of the human sciences to be repaired: the marginals, the deviants, the mad, prisoners, the sick, all became the subjects of history; those who had been 'excluded from history'[1] were rehabilitated by it; so women naturally found their place amongst these groups.

Thus a new field of enquiry was opened up and this initial accumulation of knowledge led to several new questions. For making a subject known leads, to a greater or lesser degree, and most often without one realizing it, towards a kind of positivism. It was positivism dictated by urgency, of course, because not only did we have to work fast, but we had also to open up a virtually unknown territory. The descriptive aspect outweighed the consideration of the problems involved, which itself created problems later when we realized that the emergence of the feminine event was based almost exclusively on the axis of domination and oppression.

Moreover, if we draw up the historiography of those first few years, we realize that the major themes are those that consider the body, sexuality, maternity and female physiology, as if in the first stage it was impossible to move away from the very notion of 'feminine nature' which was being contested by those who were translating it into historical terms. The first studies undertaken in the field of women's work in part took up this functionalist perspective, for they tried at first to describe the jobs closest to what was considered traditionally to be women's identity. Thus we saw books or articles on nurses, midwives, nannies, teachers and domestic servants. It was only later that attention was given to more undifferentiated 'women's work',[2] in other words, work that did not correspond directly to the sexual roles as society had defined them in various eras. This choice of subjects, considered urgent in order to fill in the blanks left by history, was based on the need to consider the history of traditional feminine roles, and as such was also rooted in a certain paradox, for it confirmed the persistent myth of unchanging feminine nature running through our cultures from antiquity to the present day.

At the same time as women's history was emerging, the problem of how it should be written was being raised. Should we claim a specific method for the feminine writing of history? The question goes beyond the discipline and concerns the status of women's writing in general. In history, even those women who do not claim a certain subjectivity in their method or in their writing find themselves asking the question; and their work is often read through this prism.

Here we have to consider the attitude of the academic establishment. Inevitably its reactions influenced the work of female historians, which in turn provoked other responses, and so on, thus giving women's history a rather different tone from that of other types of research.

At this point in our work the attitude of the academic institutions was relatively decisive. The first reaction was surprise – women's history was also a victory – which stiffened into tolerance. Studies on women unfolded in the face of the freedom that was accorded them and had little time to consider the ambiguities masked by this tolerance: a feeling of guilt at not having thought sooner of introducing sexual differences into the study of history, and also a certain dexterity in using the theme as an alibi. The alibi has two facets: some universities are proud of having women's studies, rather as the churches were proud of having their poor; others accept them in the name of modernity and progressive ideology. However this may be, this tolerance, which took the form of consent, and not initiative, fairly soon led to the designation of reserved spaces, of closed territories built in isolation on a basis of almost total silence on the part of male colleagues as a whole. There seemed to be no kind of reaction to what was done or written, apart from personal exchanges between individuals. It is rare to have no feedback in the human sciences where everything is quickly commented upon. But there was no reciprocal influence, as if there were two watertight branches of history which were foreign to one another and would not communicate. Women's history was met with a sort of indulgent shrugging of the shoulders, and this initial attitude was to have certain consequences, and even some rather perverse effects. It was no accident that in the laboratories women who did not have the status of 'confirmed researchers' saw the advent of women's history as an existential and intellectual possibility. By a pernicious process, the difference between their status and that of the male and female researchers finally contributed to weaken still further the influence of their chosen field of study. Certain weaknesses in the approach of those women who were studying women's history, whatever their official status, encouraged reticence on the part of the university institutions which, while operating a policy of tolerance, were sometimes confirmed in their idea that women's history was of very little interest. Nothing like this occurred at the origin of working-class history. Its validity was never questioned on the grounds that some pieces of work might be considered less good than others.

This unsympathetic attitude doubtless reinforced some of the methodological failings (feeling that one's value has not been recognized does not always make one able to work better) and strengthened the career distinctions that so often follow distinctions of sex. The problems were thus compounded.

In universities, as elsewhere, this situation provoked new reflections. The fear of the ghetto set in: to create, as in the United States, independent 'women's studies' would be to risk, in the French context, giving out degrees in feminist courses, which would inevitably carry less prestige and less weight in the job market. After many internal discussions, the wish to avoid separating disciplines outweighed other concerns. Masters' degrees and doctorates on the condition of women took their place in the normal syllabuses and entered the institution from the inside.

As the demand from women students and researchers increased, new fields of study emerged. A certain amount of boredom began to surround the theme of women as eternally humiliated or oppressed. In opposition to this so-called *misérabiliste* current there arose one that emphasized women's presence, triumphantly portraying women as alive, rebellious and active. This was intended to undermine the sterile stereotype of man as misogynist and woman as dominated, for the notion of misogyny was used to link a whole range of theses without there ever being any explanation of how it functioned, but with a moral judgement always attached to it, which placed it in the category of definitive invariants.

While studies multiplied, some had quite a large impact on the publishing houses. Most of the large publishers started Women's collections; the media, newspapers and television stations took up the theme. There was a real public demand. One might almost speak of a social demand, because certain women's professions began a thorough examination of their past, while some sectors of professional activity asked women historians to help them consider the situation of women within them. The demand was greatest and most insistent within the socio-educational area. Colleges for nurses and social workers introduced history into their curricula; workers in the social sector, whether prison instructors, education counsellors, group leaders or marriage-guidance counsellors, began to set up series of conferences on women and the family. So much was expected of a study of the history of private life and of women that it became difficult not only to meet the demand, but also to take on the always questionable role of the social expert, capable of explaining everything.

TWO JOURNALS: *LES ANNALES* AND *L'HISTOIRE*

As a complement to this analysis, it is interesting to examine what was happening at this time in two publications that consider history on very different levels: on the one hand *Annales (Annales Economie Société*

Civilisation), a journal of great prestige and international influence, and
on the other *L'Histoire*, a journal aimed at a very wide audience,
published in 1978 by Seuil, who recognized the great public interest in
history as a discipline that sheds light on the past and holds lessons for
the future.

Between 1970 and 1982, *Annales* produced 71 issues and 751 articles:
139 articles, or 18.5 per cent were written by women, a percentage that
corresponds more or less to the proportion of men and women in
careers in history.

If we set aside the 'Family and Society' issue which appeared in 1972
(no. 4–5), which deserves special study and which, in its twenty-two
articles, considers in particular the structures of kinship and descent,
matrimonial strategies and deviances, without isolating the condition of
women from the rest of its subjects, we find 34 articles (4.5 per cent) on
women, premarital conception, marriage, sexuality, kinship systems,
family communities and deviances. Of these 34 articles, 17 were written
by women and 17 by men. This strict equality shows a shared interest
which reflects the preoccupation of historians as a group with modes of
kinship.

Of these 34 articles, we might (although distinctions are sometimes
difficult to operate and it might be fairer and more convincing to work
also on all the articles as a group) select 13 articles whose principal
subject is women. These 13 articles may be divided up as follows:

> 2 published in 1970
> 1 published in 1972
> 2 published in 1976
> 3 published in 1977 for the 'Medicine' issue
> 1 published in 1980
> 2 published in 1981
> 2 published in 1982

We may note that 7 articles were written by men, of whom 6 were
foreign, and 6 by women, of whom one was foreign.[3]

The choice of themes, which is doubtless partly a result of the sources
available, is significant: 9 out of 13 articles about the body, childbirth,
medicine, nuns and prostitutes;[4] while the others consider the notions
of masculine and feminine. Here we find, in miniature, the same way
of examining women as that described above: close attention to their
'nature' or their most archetypal roles. There are no studies of women's
work, of women's involvement in social or political conflicts or in public
life. Moreover, there is no reference to women in economic life, in

systems of production or consumption; no mention of them in the examination of cultural systems, or even in representational systems; and nothing on women in relation to rural or industrial skills. The fact that the journal as a whole devotes most attention to ancient, medieval and modern history cannot entirely justify these omissions.

It would also be worth making a close study of the articles on family structures to see how often the problem of sexual differentiation seems to be ignored and at what point it begins to appear more clearly.

However this may be, there is a strange link of absence and presence between women's history and *Annales*. Absence, because *Annales* was almost totally preserved from the questioning that was going on elsewhere on the subject of women. The great debates on the family and kinship systems did not consider this new subject. No allusion was made to developments in the United States where journals on women's history and feminist history were being created. This historiographical current is not reflected as such in the journal, or even in the section 'Annales' Choice' which lists recent stimulating publications on two sides of blue paper. The journal's distance from intellectual and ideological turmoil is in keeping with its spirit. *Annales* has always preferred methodological innovation to militant involvement.

Presence, because some of the articles on women that appeared in *Annales* were to have a special fate.

Curiously, the first article to tackle the problem of masculine and feminine space dates from 1970, written by Lucienne Roubin.[5] Almost ahead of its time, this innovative text still remains of great interest because of its method and scope. It was not until 1982 that two articles took up its subject: one by Annette Weiner, returning to the subject of the Trobriand Islands, and the other by Luisa Accata-Levi, investigating the women of the Friuli region of Italy.[6]

There was also, early on – in 1972 – an article by Robert Trexler[7] on celibacy at the end of the Middle Ages and the nuns in Florence, which is an example of the effective use of demography. His study on the flood of very young and older girls into the convents considered in relation to the economic and fiscal situation of the time allows him to avoid the traditional explanations and to tackle the links between economic functions and the assignment of sexual roles.

Two articles seem to have had a symbolic fate within the community of female historians as well as that of feminists. The first, published in 1976 by Jacques Rossiaud,[8] deals with prostitution in France in the fifteenth century in relation to the status of young people and the social structures of that time. For a while this article was considered very feminist and was thus widely quoted and used, but later it was strongly rejected as being more on the side of male chauvinism than on the side of feminism. This about-turn can be explained. As he was also working on social functions, Rossiaud presents the phenomenon of prostitution as an institution for peace between the different age groups and social groups. This tendency to normalize phenomena and stress their social significance doubtless contributed to the criticisms directed against him.

In contrast, Jacques Gélis's work on midwives and male obstetricians in childbirth in modern France[9] has contributed greatly to the dominant theme in women's history, namely that of men's dispossession of women with regard to their traditional roles. At the same time, little attention has been paid to some very significant aspects of this research in which the author raises the importance of political relations during this period and of the debate about the possession of the techniques and tools of medical knowledge.

This is no more than a rapid glance through a journal that merits a rather more detailed analysis. But from this initial consideration it is clear that the absence and presence of women's history give a reasonably faithful picture of the place of this branch of history within the institution as a whole.

The journal *L'Histoire*, launched in 1978, has very different criteria and is aimed at a different audience. It attempts to reach secondary-school teachers and a wide history-loving public, whom existing journals (*Historia* and others) could not satisfy intellectually. Its large circulation, its desire to get professional historians to write, and its ambition to please and convince justify a quick look at it,[10] to establish both its treatment of women's history and the extent to which women contribute to it.

From the journal's first appearance, until November 1982, there were 49 issues. Each issue contained about 120 pages, with 70 pages of in-depth articles, the rest containing articles or columns of various sorts. Of these 3,500 pages, there are 80 pages of substantial articles on women, in other words between 2 and 3 per cent. Of the 2,000 remaining pages, 64 are devoted to works on women.

Two themes seem to stand out: famous women, such as Joan of Arc, Catherine de Medici or Elizabeth I; and women's collectivities: nuns, harems, etc. A few more difficult articles remain in a very small category of their own, such as that on women and the French Revolution, women and the Middle Ages and female workers in the French cinema industry. The best-represented periods are the Middle Ages and the modern period, while the nineteenth and twentieth centuries have scarcely been tackled on this level.

If women's history, feminism and contemporary women are poorly represented in the journal, in contrast we note that women play an active role in its publication. Here the figures relate only to articles of substance: 54 articles were written by women, the breakdown according to period being as follows:

Subject of article	Number
Prehistory	1
Ancient History	9
Middle Ages	8
Modern History	14
Contemporary History	13
Ethnology, Travel	9

Out of 3,500 pages, 540 – in other words, around one-seventh of the total – are written by women. When women write, they prefer the history of behaviour, social history, ethnology, biographies and the theme of 'travels in time'. They write little specifically about women, although there are of course exceptions.

We must not forget that these proportions also relate to the place of women in the history profession. History being a sector that is highly considered by men, there are many men in the field. This latter fact may of course also explain the former. We should make it clear that this journal has often solicited articles on women, and some of the responsibility must lie with those women who could have provided material and results.

WHAT HAS WOMEN'S HISTORY ACHIEVED? THE YEARS 1980–1983

If there has been an increase in the reciprocal links between the methods of creating women's history and the effects it produces, this is because it is now clear that this field of research is at last recognized and accepted. We are no longer at the stage of justification or conversion. Created out of a clearly ideological consideration of the problems and out of existential attitudes, women's history is now carried on by many people without there necessarily being political links between it and its authors.

Despite its apparent tendency to make commonplace, or to normalize, the spontaneous boomerang responses of the media still maintain a special climate of relations with it. When a rebellious, vital woman springs up out of our historical work, the media either announce the death of feminism or start wheeling out clichéd comparisons to Egeria or the Gorgons. When authors and novelists write works of popular appeal, they are either accused of concentrating on the sordid aspects of life or praised as embodying the eternal muse.

What we seem to be seeing in the work of researchers (whether male or female) is an appropriation of the theme without a renewal of the general approach to the problem. Paragraphs are added to articles, chapters are added to theses, a page is added to a book, without any real questioning of the 'concept of the difference between the sexes'.[11]

At the same time, the production of women's history by women is increasing. We can refer to the many research projects being carried out in universities, to courses being given, to research on this theme in laboratories, to the expectations raised by the journal *Pénélope*,[12] to the symposium in Toulouse in 1982, and to the CNRS's efforts to create a framework in which to include research on women. In the face of these expectations, this flood of work and the place made for the subject in the institutions, it is fair to note that so far women's history as a whole has not completely succeeded in drawing up an outline of its approach and its subject matter that is capable of redefining the analysis of sexual differentiation in political and motivational terms.

There remains the underlying and constantly used dialectic of domination and oppression which makes it difficult to construct a social, economic and political history of the confrontation between the sexes and their reciprocal stakes. If we really want to form an accurate assessment of the state of the subject and its future, we must recognize that a good many analyses do not succeed in rising out of tautology, but postulate at the start theses that will inevitably be found intact at the end.

In those works that deal with the eighteenth and nineteenth centuries, the choice of subjects reveals a great predilection for normative speeches and texts. This is understandable if we consider the difficulties of finding sources, and yet we must question this predilection, and particularly the manner in which it is expressed. There is no shortage of treatises on the norm, and women have a privileged place in these treatises from the start. Men of letters, philosophers, doctors, priests and theologians, lawyers and teachers write abundantly on woman and the dangers facing her, her physiology, her illnesses and the role she must fulfil within the family and in society. These texts reveal a vision of the relations between the masculine and feminine worlds and of the constraints one exercises on the other. It is therefore not surprising that this body of literature has been the object of many studies and has captured the attention of researchers. Their work has been marked, most often unconsciously, by a feeling of indignation at what was written in other ages. The analysis contained in such works clearly reflects this, even to the point of making this indignation the basis of the argument. These researchers play on this effect of indignant surprise on the one hand, and, on the other, remain silent on the obvious anachronism that creeps in between the reader and the text. Their work focuses on the spectacle of statements that should never have been made. The body of the text gradually becomes a sort of denunciatory gloss of the earlier text, and slips imperceptibly into an attempt to go further.

The need to make known what has been written about women, and to convince readers of the fate meted out to women, outweighs analysis, producing curious effects of repetition, and leads authors to forget that it is necessary to ask other questions about the texts: the forms taken by the argument, the manner in which it was received, the similarities and differences over various periods and its social and political functions. Rather as if they had been caught in a looking-glass, these authors have become prisoners of the works they study and endlessly repeat what has already been said, without managing to focus on the actual results of these texts – whether they created distances between groups, encouraged wrongdoings or indifference – and on their constructive and destructive results in the social context of the time. When the commentary becomes thus far subservient to its object, it sometimes seems to become inverted. Indignation gives way almost imperceptibly to a strange fascination, as if the text studied were more powerful than the tools with which the commentator tries to tackle it, as if the images it creates had not ceased to have an effect, as if the mirror were somehow too powerful.

We must question this fascination, reflect on the reasons why it exists and, as a counterbalance, we must devote more attention to the normative texts on the subject of men. There is probably a methodological and intellectual weakness in always analysing aspects of women's lives (whether real or as written about by men) without comparing them with men's lives.

Women's history has an ambivalent relationship with the past. It would probably be fruitful to discuss this. Some works have advanced the idea of progress in women's condition over time, others have put forward the notion that their devalued status has been permanent and unchanging – as if history were necessarily linear, and not subject to advances and retreats; as if the present arose intact out of a frozen past. In restoring the history of women's cultural, social and political identity, we must avoid limiting it to two unchanging, unrealistic images: that of a past which is gone for ever and that of a present paralysed by tradition. History is full of contradictions, of alternating currents, of overlapping events where consistency and inconsistency both have a place. Nothing lasts for ever in history.

In recent years, studies by men on the theme of women have seen the light of day – and this is undoubtedly one of the more spectacular effects of women's history. These have not been the work of students or young researchers, but of mature men with important posts in institutions and reputations throughout France and elsewhere. This is an important new fact: it means that the question first raised in the early 1970s has finally been accepted and the theme has become part of the historical field. The domination of men over women can be mentioned and written about, even by those who stand accused because of their sex. Two fine books, by Georges Duby[13] and Maurice Godelier[14] make this clear in very different ways. The style of one is withdrawn and modest, haunted by the fear of never knowing, and the other is coloured by feelings of guilt and a desire for reparation. Whatever we may think of the justifications, the styles of writing or the ways in which data are put forward, all of which, we may say, are to one degree or another existential, we must now reflect on the effects of this recognition and ensure that the debate between male and female historians evades none of the problems.

A word about work produced by other less eminent male researchers. Sometimes the fascination felt by women for some of the normative texts, which we denounced above, ensnares men too. When they set out to expose the misogyny of certain texts, sometimes a curious alliance (or even complicity) becomes apparent. The writer begins to sound as if he is enjoying the excessive vocabulary, and the reader is no longer quite sure whether the author is denouncing or accentuating the effects of the texts, slipping surreptitiously towards the very misogyny which he began by holding up for blame.

It is also interesting to analyse the importance given to the theme of the masculine and the feminine in anthropology and in the history of ancient and modern societies, because here too method and effects can be considered together. The research techniques envisaged are effective and can help us to restructure the knowledge that has so far been accumulated. Examination of our societies through the prism of the masculine and the feminine has uncovered the themes of private and public space, and of domestic, social and public power. One may wonder if the success of these approaches was not due to the impossibility of widening the enquiry into the political field and of working on masculine/feminine relations within the global, social and political system. The study of the family and of domestic spheres, considered as a satisfactory counterbalance to the masculine forms of political power, or as a symmetrical power, should at the same time lead to new research into asymmetry, conflicts and struggles for influence. As Pauline Schmitt Pantel said in a seminar on women's history at the Centre de Recherches

Historiques, 'We must not allow an examination of masculine/feminine relations to become a new denial of women's history.'

It would be an important achievement to establish finally a history of the tensions between masculine and feminine roles and to show how their conflicts and complementarities are a thread running through the whole account of history. There can be no question of constituting a closed field of knowledge, but on the contrary, historians must ask new questions, introducing the notion of the difference between the sexes and tracing the successive, and often simultaneous, moments when relative strength, indifference, power struggles, hatred and desire between men and women not only produced the social and political tissue of society, but divided the cultural system and the whole sphere of social imagination between them. Again, there is no question of establishing definitive invariants on one side or the other, but rather of making a meticulous record of the changes and differences, bringing out the importance of social divides and economic tensions within the very division between the sexes. The nature of relations between masculine and feminine has not only varied over the centuries and according to social class, but has, at each moment in history, fulfilled a certain number of functions. It is the task of historians, both male and female, to discover these functions and the way in which they arose and came into conflict with one another.

NOTES

1 *Cahiers Jussieu*, no. 5, 'Les marginaux et les exclus dans l'histoire', col. 10/18, 1979.
2 *Le Mouvement Social*, no. 105, Oct.–Dec. 1978, 'Travaux de femmes dans la France du XIXe siècle' (Paper by Michelle Perrot).
3 The articles are as follows: L. Roubin, 'Espace masculin, espace féminin en communauté provençale', *Annales ESC*, 2, 1970; S. Pembroke, 'Femmes et enfants dans les fondations de Locre et de Tarente', ibid. 5, 1970; R. Trexler, 'Les religieuses à Florence au XVe siècle', ibid. 6, 1972; J. Rossiaud, 'Prostitution, jeunesse et société au XVe siècle', ibid. 2, 1976; Y. Knibiehler, 'La nature féminine au temps du Code Civil', ibid. 4, 1976; J. Léonard, 'Religieuses et médecins au XIXe siècle', ibid. 5, 1977; J. Gélis, 'Sages-femmes et accoucheurs dans la France moderne', ibid. 5, 1977; M. Laget, 'La naissance aux siècles classiques', ibid. 3, 1977; A. Rousselle, 'Le corps de la femme d'après les médecins grecs', ibid. 5, 1980; E. Shorter, 'Les règles en 1750', ibid. 3, 1981; R. Trexler, 'La prostitution à Florence au XVe siècle', ibid. 6, 1981; L. Accata-Levi, 'Masculin, féminin, aspects sociaux d'un conflit affectif', ibid. 2, 1982; A. Weiner, 'Echanges entre hommes et femmes dans les sociétés d'Océanie', ibid. 2, 1982.

4   Four articles on nuns and prostitutes. Five articles on the body, childbirth
    and medicine. The distant and antithetical eternal feminine figures (virgin–
    whore) are better represented than the traditional figures of maternity or
    the female body.
5   Roubin, 'Espace masculin, espace féminin'.
6   Weiner, 'Échanges entre hommes et femmes'; Accata-Levi, 'Masculin,
    féminin'.
7   Trexler, 'Les religieuses à Florence'.
8   Rossiaud, 'Prostitution, jeunesse et société'.
9   Gélis, 'Sages-femmes et accoucheurs dans la France moderne'.
10 I should like to thank Michelle Perrot and Pauline Schmitt Pantel for
    permission to use the results of a study they carried out of the journal
    L'Histoire, on which they reported at a seminar held in 1983 at the Centre
    de Recherches Historiques.
11 G. Fraisse.
12 *Pénélope. Pour l'histoire des femmes*, Centre de Recherches Historiques,
    54 Boulevard Raspail, 75006 Paris.
13 Duby, *Le Chevalier, la femme et le prêtre*.
14 M. Godelier, *La Production des grands hommes* (Fayard, Paris, 1982).

2

The Medievalist: Women and the Serial Approach

Christiane Klapisch-Zuber

The history of women in the Middle Ages has for long been confined to the laws of the period – to women's rights. This field, which was intensively cultivated by the positivist historiographers of the nineteenth century, appeared to be the only ground solid enough to allow the passive, silent shadows of the women of the past to take shape. All that has been said, and is repeated even today, about the women of the Middle Ages comes to us often directly from this history. As Régine Pernoud has written, 'It is to the law, and more precisely to the history of the law, that we must turn if we wish to know about customs.'[1] It is therefore worth considering the reasoning behind, and the implications of, such a difficult approach.

In this type of work the description of women is limited entirely to the laws governing their existence. All the various phases of their lives are described by the law, which is not the case with the other categories of the population also known primarily through the law that applied to them – serfs, freeholders, vassals, etc. Thus enclosed within a sort of ghetto of category, medieval woman is scarcely able to take on any social reality in the eyes of the historian. The figure drawn by the juridical approach is all the paler, as she is portrayed as confined in a straitjacket of irrefutable normative texts and never as an actor in history. She is the plaything of these norms, reduced quite simply to the law applied to her, yet without constituting a legal entity in her own right. She is confined to a statute and thus definitively reduced to 'a woman's condition'.

This condition is nevertheless a historical object in so far as it evolves with the law that governs it. And here historians, with all their ideological presuppositions, intervene to assess the direction of this evolution. For some it is positive, considered, since Burckhardt, to be leading from the darkness of the Middle Ages to the light of the Renaissance.

Rodocanacchi is a good example of this progressive vision of the feminine condition 'before, during and after the Renaissance', according to the title of his work,[2] which sees women as attaining equality with men in the Renaissance period. In reaction to this, many studies since the 1930s have blackened the juridical regulations governing women in the late medieval period and in modern times, citing the deterioration of women's status, which went hand in hand with the rise of the bourgeoisie and misogyny in university and clerical circles, and stressing in contrast the freedom of action enjoyed in the central medieval period by 'women at the time of the cathedrals'.[3] The most positively established juridical facts thus gave rise to completely opposite interpretations of the nature of the evolution, until finally, moving from theory to practice, historians decided to look for more concrete clues as to the lives led by a good half of humanity.

This more direct approach was made first through biography. Here, it was no longer the rigidity of normative prescriptions that contributed to confining women's history within its traditional failings, but rather the anecdotal, hazy nature of the exceptional. Isolated from the mass, to be grouped together in a more or less arbitrary fashion, individual female lives were examined in a sort of collective biography of women, whose only point in common was the exceptional nature of their existence. Women's history tends to consider only women deemed as 'without equal', and the semblance of unity or cohesion it sometimes claims for its disparate troop is based, despite all the denials, on their unrepresentativeness. These shining women are viragos, strong women – Eleanor of Aquitaine, Joan of Arc or Christine de Pisan – or else women isolated simply by reason of their social status as abbesses, queens or courtesans.[4] Once again, their status raises them above that of ordinary women and reduces to irrelevance the patient notations of legal historians.

It is clearly easier to describe a group of women notable for their social position or their exceptional activities, since the medieval narrative sources favour the dominant classes and decisive events. But this attitude is not found only in medieval history. It reappears whenever the subject is women (even the feminists of the nineteenth century) and I think that it is important to note how literal and uncritical their biographies tend to be. Any famous woman is a candidate for this treatment, and this naïve conception of collective biography in the end takes as its sole criterion in constituting the corpus of material, apart from sex, the exceptional nature of the women concerned. But these women who are exceptional by their status or by their actions leave their sisters not fortunate enough to be chosen by this type of hagiography to a flat, unchanging type of history, or rather to non-history.

The latter fall into the third traditional historiographical type of women and are found in the categories of daily life and of domestic and private life – in short, of 'customs'. In the many histories of daily life or histories of lifestyle inspired by the Middle Ages, a chapter on women almost inevitably comes next to those devoted to festivities, food, the house and its contents, and entertainments. Women are no longer simply a juridical category; nor are they stars in an empty sky. They become a reified category of historical objects.[5] Women are thus assigned to daily life and the domestic sphere – we need hardly say it – in a totally ingenuous fashion, without any analysis of the ideological justifications or representational systems that attribute such a place to women in the societies in question – both that of the historian and that in which the object of study lived. Shrouded in the erudite fog of daily life, which they are said to dominate, women are described through the repetitiveness of their acts and their dealings with objects. The other domain, that of men, is open, enlivened by a third dimension – that of time. In this sphere is unfolded the noble history of politics and creativity, and also the history of productive techniques. The daily, domestic life of women has no historicity, even though some, with the laudable desire of reasserting the value of women, see in the primary position they occupy in this sphere one of the 'elements of feminine domination'.[6]

Thus the history of women in the Middle Ages is above all characterized by its juridical formalism, the unrepresentative nature of the examples eternally cited and discussed and the unexplained acceptance of the traditional roles judged as natural. Historical research has set out to remedy these obvious weaknesses, not simply by defining the object of study more ambitiously and more rigorously, but also by resorting to methods, rather too quickly seen as a panacea, that had been proved elsewhere. With the constitution of quantifiable corpuses of material and a serial approach, an attempt has been made to restore to genuine scientific and objective research a population hitherto classed with the vague masses, and at the same time a poorly regarded sector of historiography. To the simplicity of the juridical norms that established the status of women and regulated their condition has been opposed the diversity of their actions, and an attempt has been made to discover, for example in wills, in land transactions, marriage agreements, fiscal records, etc., the margin for manœuvre enjoyed by women, whether protagonists or witnesses to these acts, their own strategies and the networks of affiliation they recognized and sought to perpetuate.[7] Anomic behaviour with regard to masculine practices may thus be traced, enabling us to arrive at a more serious and more refined study of the feminine condition, since it rejects the immobility and inertia of this condition and restores autonomous historical roles to women.

But it is above all at the level of biographical data[8] that the introduction of the serial approach can lead to new results, beginning with changes of methodological perspective. It is obviously difficult to assemble the individual variables for the Middle Ages in consistent corpuses. This applies even more to women than to men, less as a result of the nature of the sources themselves than as a result of the way in which they have generally been handled. Thus prosopography and collective biography have been used to aid the study of power, of the formation of, and the role played by, the elite who had power.[9] And the individuals who have been gathered together to form this corpus are men, united by the social appurtenances received at birth and by the skills or material tools of power acquired in the course of their education and career. Such an approach and its corresponding analyses appear at first sight of little relevance to the female half of the population, excluded from power, which was officially designated by registrations, professional roles, titles or public office. The only feminine careers mentioned are those of nuns within the walls of their convents; and these are admittedly rather limited careers. The only other careers are those of women who became exceptional by accident (criminals known through legal records) or by profession ('public' women, thus found within a very narrow framework). Here, then, is a method of historical enquiry that has little cause to focus on women, because it sets out to meet the demands of a study directed solely towards the description of the mechanisms of power, an approach that excludes women from its very citeria and from the means of fulfilling them.

In these circumstances, a corpus of individual data on women is liable to be limited to their biological life and their family career – at best, to their role as demographic agents. So is this return to demographic history, which has led to so many calls for the renewal of historical enquiry over the last few decades, neutral with regard to women's history? For demographic history, which treats men and women with apparent equality, does not escape certain preconceptions which introduce considerable distortions into the analysis. The following remarks point to some of these.

We might begin with choice of vocabulary, which is not always innocent when it repeats, and gives scientific approval to, common prejudices. Thus an expression as ambiguous as 'the marriage market' is used without question. The term may appear neutral if one defines it with reference to the imperatives of supply and demand which apply equally to the male and famale pools of potential spouses. But the expression takes on a derogatory connotation as soon as the choice of spouses, far from operating mechanically as a function of the balance between these two groups, brings into play strategies by which men are always seen by demographers as taking the initiative and by which women are the stakes, or indeed merchandise sought and traded on the 'market'.[10]

These are slightly caricatured aspects of the possible distortions, but there are others, probably more insidious, which affect the very processes of constituting the corpuses of demographical and biographical data. These distortions arise because the terms of reference are generally male, because the vanishing-points at the horizon of women's history are determined on the basis of the non-female. Corpuses of female material are assembled not at random, but quite simply by taking the wives of a particular group of men – a process that in the final analysis subordinates the female characters studied to criteria of selection relating to another population.[11] In our society, use of the husband's family name in establishing the history of family lines generally amounts to ignoring female lines and thus the permanent features, the traditions passed on from one woman to another, since wives bearing another name, coming from elsewhere, and girls married into other families, fall outside the investigation if the researcher adopts our patrilateral vision of family links without further examination. Couldn't we reconstitute female lines, which would reveal different strategies as soon as we considered the hypothesis that women were actors in their own right?[12]

Another example of these male vanishing-points: the control of fertility and contraception, that old battle-horse of the demographic historian of the modern period, armed to the teeth with statistics. The results are there, pointing to the precise period when the French repressed their sexuality sufficiently for the figures to begin to show this clearly. These are modern, male practices. Everything that preceded them, covered in a reprobation not very different from that attached to them by the Church in the Middle Ages, is thus discounted as women's magic, doubly useless, because it was magic and because it was carried out by women. Even if it is difficult to measure the influence of spells, herbs and traditional recipes against conception statistically, they still need to be studied in relation to other practices, and we need to examine, for example, the links between the repression of sorcery, which began at the end of the Middle Ages, at a time of vast demographic decline, and the accusation made against witches of bringing about sterility, abortions and infanticides. In other words, it would be useful to consider the fact that all this knowledge and the primitive control of the birth-rate, which were fiercely condemned, were attributed to women, while as soon as men took charge of the regulation of births, the practice was viewed with a large measure of indulgence.[13]

One last example: the analysis of the domestic structures, of the household, the starting-point for so much research into the functions of the family, roles within the family and attitudes and affects.[14] In spite of the many warnings given by sociologists and anthropologists, the yard-stick against which we measure and compare the forms observed still remains the good old conjugal family with its couple of parents. All that surrounds this is covered by the term 'extension', and becomes a sort of excrescence or residue which must inevitably be absorbed into the orig-inal, basic nucleus. By following categories that are dominant today and applying them to the systems of organization of another era, we ignore widows, unmarried women, isolated women, those who are the excep-tion in the typologies and analyses, even if at the end of the day these women emerge as the pivot and cement of a family group. The model of the couple and the conjugal family and the models of authority that derive from them and are automatically transplanted into the past, contradict the data and relegate to subgroups formations that, if not in the majority, were at least much more frequent than such classifications would lead us to believe.

The serial approach, quantification and numerical routine thus shelter no prejudices. Statistics are not so stubborn. Rather it is the minds of the researchers that remain obstinately attached to ancient divisions. There is clearly no point in taking refuge in the serial approach if one does not question frankly and constantly the unconscious choice that guides the selection of variables and rules out phenomena judged to be in the minority. The serial has the advantage of drawing average profiles and overall developments. It has the disadvantage of crushing the secondary and the accidental. This is no small danger for the history of women, who have been beavering away within systems they do not dominate, deviant with regard to the masculine norm. How can we define the historical specificity of women if the way in which corpuses of material are constituted, the typologies adopted, the references chosen, depend invariably on masculine moulds which remain undiscussed? A consid-eration of the categories of masculine and feminine within history cannot avoid questioning the most solidly established methods that have served men's history very well.

NOTES

1   Pernoud, *La Femme au temps des cathédrales*, p. 19. I shall cite only a few titles from this enormous body of work: F. L. Ganshof, 'Le statut de la

femme dans la monarchie franque' and René Metz, 'Le statut de la femme en droit canonique médiéval', *Recueils de la Société Jean Bodin (La Femme)*, 12 (1962), esp. pp. 5–58 and 59–113. We must also remember the many studies on marriage, among them, A. Esmein, *Le Mariage en droit canonique*, 2nd edn by R. Genestal and J. Dauvillier (Paris, 1929–35). For feminist considerations of legal problems, cf. Jo Ann McNamara and Suzanne F. Wemple, 'Marriage and divorce in the Frankish kingdom', in *Women in Medieval Society*, ed. S. M. Stuard (The University of Pennsylvania Press, 1976), pp. 95–124; also by the same authors, 'Sanctity and Power: The dual pursuit of medieval women', in *Becoming Visible. Women in European History*, ed. R. Bridenthal and C. Koonz (London and Boston, 1977), pp. 90–118, with full bibliography.

2 See Jakob Burckhardt, *La Civilisation de la Renaissance en Italie*, French trans. and ed. by R. Klein (Plon, Paris, 1958). E. Rodocanacchi, *La Femme italienne avant, pendant et après la Renaissance* (French trans., Hachette, Paris, 1922). Cf. the forceful article by Joan Kelly Gadol, 'Did women have a Renaissance?', in *Becoming Visible*, pp. 137–64.

3 Pernoud, *La Femme au temps des cathédrales*. Ruth Kelso, in her seminal *Doctrine for the Lady of the Renaissance* (Urbana, Ill., 1956) concludes that this period did not see equality for men and women.

4 On the nuns, see the old work by Lina Eckenstein, *Woman under Monasticism* (Cambridge, 1896); Eileen Power, *Medieval English Nunneries* (Cambridge, 1922); the collection *Medieval Women* by the same author (Cambridge, 1975) includes a series of essays and lectures from the period 1920–30. See also the collection edited by Derek Baker, *Medieval Women* (Oxford, 1978), and in particular the articles by S. Thompson, Brenda Bolton and Joan Nicholson. Brenda M. Bolton, 'Mulieres sanctae', in *Women in Medieval Society*, ed. S. M. Stuard, pp. 141–58. Christine de Pisan has been the subject of a number of studies, the latest being that by Pernoud, *Christine de Pisan* (Calmann Lévy, Paris, 1982), which gives the traditional view and a bibliography of old texts on this figure. For a feminist consideration, see Susan G. Bell, 'C. de P.: Humanism and the problem of a studious woman', *Feminist Studies*, 3 (Spring 1976), pp. 173–84.

5 Thus E. Faral, in *Vie quotidienne au temps de saint Louis* (Hachette, Paris, 1938), Part 2, includes a ch. VI entitled 'La condition des femmes' and a ch. VII, 'Le mariage'. The more recent *Vita privata a Firenze nei secoli XIV e XV* (Olschki, Florence, 1966) contains no chapters on women, but has contributions on weddings and clothing.

6 Robert Fossier, 'La femme dans les sociétés occidentales', Introduction to the symposium *La Femme dans les civilisations des X–XIIIe siècles*, Poitiers, 1976 (Poitiers, 1977), pp. 3–14 (pp. 93–103 in *Cahiers de civilisation médiévale*, xx (1977), nos. 2–3). The problem of feminine power in the Middle Ages is well expressed by Jo Ann McNamara and S. Wemple, 'The power of women through the family in medieval Europe, 500–1100', in *Clio's Consciousness Raised: New Perspectives on the History of Women*, ed. M. S. Hartmann and L. W. Banner (New York, 1974), pp. 103–18.

7   Cf. David Herlihy's stimulating article, which remains a milestone despite
    the controversies, 'Land, family and women in continental Europe, 701–
    1200', *Traditio, xviii* (1962), pp. 89–120; reprinted, with other work, in D.
    Herlihy, *The Social History of Italy and Western Europe, 700–1500* (Vari-
    orum Reprints, London, 1978); cf. id., *Cities and Society in Medieval Italy*
    (Variorum Reprints, London, 1980); M.-Th. Lorcin, *Vivre et mourir en
    Lyonnais à la fin du Moyen-Age* (Paris, 1981) and Stanley Chojnacki,
    'Dowries and kinsmen in early Renaissance Venice', reprinted in *Women in
    Medieval Society*, ed. S. M. Stuard, pp. 173–98, are two successful attempts
    to individualize feminine strategies in relation to masculine strategies
    through their wills.

8   A genre illustrated by Eileen Power, *Medieval People* (London, 1982); cf.
    also her works mentioned in n. 4 above.

9   On prosopography, see the symposium 'Prosopographie médiévale et
    informatique', Bielefeld, December 1982, and the bibliography discussed
    there, published as *Medieval Lives and the Historian. Studies in Medieval
    Prosopography*, ed. N. Bulst and J.-A. Genet (Kalamazoo, 1986).

10 Cf. also the comments by Martine Segalen, 'Quelques réflexions pour
    l'étude de la condition féminine', *Annales de démographie historique*, 1981,
    pp. 9–21, and in particular p. 19, on 'the figures and the vocabulary of
    the demographer/historian which implicitly convey ideological statements.
    When one speaks of a widow's "chances" of remarriage, it is clear that the
    statistical and common meanings are combined, making assumptions as to
    whether the widow considered she was fortunate or not in remarrying.'
    [Translator's note: the French word *chance* means both 'chance' and 'good
    fortune', 'luck'.] One might also question the implicit hierarchies regularly
    observed in the numerical codes attributed to the sexes etc.

11 Noëlle Moreau-Bisseret, 'Surmortels et sous-mortelles. La surmortalité
    masculine: objet des sciences ou outil idéologico-politique?', *Pénélope. Pour
    l'histoire des femmes,* 4 (Spring 1981), pp. 61–7. See also the forceful
    reflections of a sociologist, Martine Chaudron, 'Les approches statistiques,
    biographiques et généalogiques sont-elles exclusives (l'une de l'autre) ou
    complémentaires?' (Paper read at the 10th World Congress on Sociology,
    Mexico, August 1982); and 'Les transformations des problématiques de
    recherche sur le travail des femmes en France (1960–1980)' (Paper read at
    the Colloque annuel de la Société Française de Sociologie, Nantes, June
    1980).

12 This is what Martine Chaudron proposes to do (see n. 11 above) by
    reconstructing female social lines through successive generations of women,
    mothers and daughters, and comparing them to the male lines of the male
    members of the families to which these women belong. So the point is to
    take women as the starting-point and not simply be content with 'a critical
    and sex-oriented reading of the existing categories'.

13 On infanticide, see Emily Coleman, 'Infanticide in the early Middle Ages',
    in *Women in Medieval Society*, ed. S. M. Stuard, pp. 47–70. R. C. Trexler,
    'Infanticide in Florence: New sources and first results', *History of Child-*

hood Quarterly, 1 (1973), pp. 98–116. Barbara Kellum, 'Infanticide in England in the later Middle Ages', ibid. 1 (1974), pp. 367–88. On women's crimes, Barbara Hanawalt, 'The female felon in fourteenth century England', *Viator*, 5 (1974), pp. 253–68. On good and evil witchcraft, see Carlo Ginzburg, *Les Batailles nocturnes* (Lagrasse, Ed. Verdier, 1980).

14 Structures whose typology was proposed in 1969 at a symposium in Cambridge and diffused by the book that came out of it, *Household and Family in Past Time*, ed. P. Laslett and R. Wall (Cambridge, 1972).

3

Chronology and Women's History

Yvonne Knibiehler

Factual history was scorned for a long time. The loss of favour it suffered is linked to the dramatic expansion of the human sciences, in
particular the work of anthropologists and the powerful philosophical
movement they have fostered – structuralism. In Lévi-Strauss's view, all
human science must be brought into line with the logic of structural
description. Roland Barthes (In *Le Discours de l'histoire*, 1967) speaks
of 'the chronological illusion', and denounces historians' narratives as
being as fictional as novels. Are we still intimidated by this? Georges
Duby's *Le Dimanche de Bouvines* (1973) appears to have contributed to
the rehabilitation of the event, and thus of chronology. We have always
known that one of the distinctive features of the human being, both the
individual and the species, is memory, the basis of identity. Although
memory is not the same as chronology, it could barely exist without it.

The chronological method poses formidable problems, particularly
epistemological, which become all the more formidable when one
attempts to express them from a feminine standpoint. I do not claim to
solve these problems, but simply wish to submit a few thoughts which
are as much the result of a woman's experience of life as of the work of
a historian of women.

Drawing up a chronological account of history involves three stages:
picking out dates – in other words events; placing them in sequence; and
dividing the sequence into periods. So is it necessary to select dates, facts
and events in order to write the history of women? Put another way, are
there such things as feminine events and masculine events? If this absurd
hypothesis were carried to its logical conclusion, it would inevitably lead
to the eternal opposition between woman, the natural being, and man,
the cultural being, between private and public life, between biological
time and historical time. The 'feminine' events would be those that

involved the body and family life: births, marriages and deaths – those expected, repetitive events, which can be superimposed on one another and which each social group is able to deal with and fit into a cultural environment, but which have long been considered as too individual and too unchanging to become the subject of history. At the other end of the scale, so-called historical events are in a sense unique and, above all, they affect an entire group and are retained in the collective memory. But how can we say that the events of private life are the preserve of women, or have more to do with women than other kinds of event? Men are born, they marry, they die, they take part in baptisms, marriages, funerals and so on. And it is hard to think of any dates in public life that concern only men. Every political, economic and social fact has consequences for women. Can we say that military reform concerns men only? The army makes war, and war produces widows and bereaved mothers. Events do not respect the difference between the sexes. Indeed, it would be ridiculous to formulate such a truism if, in the name of the opposition between private and public life, women had not, for so long, been placed outside time, and kept out of history.

The true opposition lies elsewhere. It lies in the sexes' share of initiative. The traditional division of tasks and roles has allowed women, if not to bring about the events of private life, at least to impose on them their presence, their will and their desires. At the same time, women remained for a long time without political rights, distanced from decision-making, and were almost always reduced to passive experience of the events of public life, 'historical' events. Note that I say 'almost always'. For there are a few exceptional dates, all the more interesting to consider, when the event was *brought about*, and not simply *experienced*, by women. In most cases this was a protest, an act of resistance, a demand, an insurrection – in other words, a more or less violent form of revolt.

But let us make no mistake. When we begin to put together these facts, what we are building up is not a history of feminism, but rather a history of the suffering of women and their children. The demand, or the explosion, is prompted by an increase in their anguish. It is interesting to observe the way in which traditional history deals with such events. It considers or ignores them, according to whether or not they fit into a masculine perspective. For example, the events of October 1789 have been classed as a genuine historical event. The women of Paris went to Versailles to find the King and brought him back in the midst of his people. They were demanding bread. They contributed in fact to the weakening of monarchical authority and the rejection of the influence of the Court. Historians of whatever camp stress this. In contrast, Olympe de Gouges's *Declaration of the Rights of Women* (1791) was immediately forgotten. Until now it has never counted as a historical fact.

To dig up events that have been regarded as insignificant or neglected,[1] to give them importance and to explain why, is not simply to repair an omission, it is to change the criteria and to overturn the hierarchy of values.

Clearly, no fact exists in crude form. All are judged, classified and hierarchized by the historian, which poses the problem of the selector and of selection. It is recognized that in any chronological work the subject is chosen before the relevant dates are selected, and the choice of subject defines the way in which the sequence is drawn up. Michelle Perrot makes the point in her Introduction that the object is defined by the way in which we regard it. And our viewpoint is never neutral, but always profoundly subjective. Should this worry us? I believe that we should rather regard subjectivity as the sap that nourishes the human sciences. Those who deny this are blinded by false rationalization. It is right that women's history should contribute to the anti-positivist current which puts us on our guard against quantitative history. Statistics appear to be neutral; sometimes they are only an alibi, a way of reassuring us in the face of realities that are not quantifiable.

Masculine chronological sequences have their own coherence, their orientation, their perspective. Feminine chronologies propose another perspective which might at first have appeared disconcerting or meaningless in the high places where history is written. This is doubtless the reason for the initial ghetto. The 'institution', it was said, allowed women's history to develop separately, outside the established centres of research. But it is clearly not possible to maintain the ghetto. A purely 'feminine' chronology is unthinkable. It only becomes intelligible if we draw up synchronous tables to show the correlations with political, economic and cultural history. These correlations confirm women's dependence and lack of initiative. But they also reveal one other fact: that feminine sequences of events are not synchronous with masculine. This is perhaps one aspect of what Louis Althusser, in his book *Lire le capital*, called 'differential temporality'. Women achieve emancipation of all kinds later than men, whether it be access to education, the right to vote (among other rights) or unionization. On the other hand, women are often ahead of men when it comes to undergoing any kind of repression. In any revolutionary crisis, reaction always begins by the closing of women's clubs, the curtailing of women's rights, their space and their movements.

The most noticeable discrepancy concerns the very emergence of feminine events and chronologies in official history. Why this suppression of the feminine? Was the aim to deny or refuse feminine identity? The word 'suppression' belongs to the vocabulary of psychoanalysis. Women's history may indeed appear to be a device for analysing the male psyche. It should lead men to ask themselves questions about this suppression. The fact remains that for a long time women accepted this suppression of the feminine. Why did they accept it and why do they no longer accept it? If history is the search for identity, it must be accepted that women were able to survive without this identity for a very long time. What else did they rely on? A child psychiatrist from Marseilles recently stated that for a long time motherhood was an adequate justification and identity for women. What, then, is happening today? Why is motherhood no longer enough for us? And what about men? Why has fatherhood never been adequate for them as a justification and an identity?

Before we leave the issue of sequences of events and their many implications, we must mention the usefulness of chronologies over a long period. They alone allow us to get beyond the permanent features of a society – features that are the domain of ethnologists and that tend to mask change.

Nothing is as important to the historian as good periodization. If the series of events expresses the choice of subject, periodization reveals the meaning of history. It allows us to interpret and explain events. To try to define periods is to locate the points of change, to pinpoint the different stages, to reveal a process of development or to construct one.

Written history is delivered to us divided into periods: antiquity, the Middle Ages, the modern period, the contemporary period; and also into reigns and regimes. Do these divisions have any significance for women? The question is surely worth asking, but its answer has yet to be found. Let us limit ourselves for the moment to a few comments which may help us to arrive at an answer. The traditional division of history, often based on great political and economic upheavals, is no longer sacred. The subjects dealt with by the 'new history' often claim specific periodizations. Historians prefer to speak of short periods of time, of long periods and of medium-length periods. This is particularly true in historical demography. The decline in the number of births in France in the eighteenth and nineteenth centuries may be dissociated from political history. The revolutionary crisis does not fundamentally affect the general trend in this domain.

Can women's history claim new periodizations? Progress in obstetrics has allowed more and more women to live their adult lives more fully. Shouldn't this be the basis for a new periodization? In the same way, the

decline in births, which we have just mentioned and which transformed
the maternal role so significantly, could constitute another periodization. We may ask other questions. The increase in a girl's age on
marriage in the classical period transformed the notion of a young girl.
In the sixteenth century, fathers would still marry their daughters before
the age of sixteen and could dictate their future quite freely. By the end
of the eighteenth century, girls were almost always married after the
age of twenty. A new social being had been created, whose upbringing
and establishment in society posed certain problems, as is shown by the
drama of that time. This represents a change in women's fate. In the
same way, the increase in life expectancy meant that there was a larger
number of mature women available for new activities. There is scope
here for a definition of periods, which may well prove new and
significant.

But, one may say, these remarks bring us back yet again to women's
bodies and biology, as if any chronology involving them must start from
this point. Well, why not? If history is the search for identity, it is also
the search for freedom. Women's freedom encounters first and foremost
the obstacle represented by inescapable biological factors. It is because
the 'weaker sex' is constrained by certain biological phenomena that
male domination was able to establish, justify and perpetuate itself.
Perhaps any chronology of women's history has to take this as its
starting-point and map out the chequered progress (the times when
advances were made, the times of stagnation, the reverses) of a twofold
emancipation: from biological constraints and from male domination,
the evolution from female to woman, and from woman to a human
being who happens to be female. In spite of appearances, we in fact
know very little about the biological factors governing women's lives.
They have been described by doctors who were all male. Keen to define
the difference between the sexes, and to prove male superiority, anxious
too to protect some women from exploitation and abuse, doctors have
stressed the fragility and susceptibility to disease of the female of the
species. In the nineteenth century this fragility served as an excuse for
male power, and justified all kinds of exclusions. Historians of both
sexes can, with the methods of their discipline, call into question these
medical definitions. A new discipline, chronobiology, is perhaps what
they need to help them in this task. Women's bodies go through various
time sequences, with monthly hormonal flows, the phases of childbirth
and breastfeeding, and then the onset of the menopause. We need to
know how the women of the past managed their lives and their freedom
against the background of these cycles of the sexual body. An American
historian, Edward Shorter, is trying to discover the age of young girls at

the onset of menstruation in the classical era. He feels that this would be a good indicator of the standard of living of people at this time. Above all, it would be a good indicator of the health and development of young girls. But where can we find this information? Where such subjects are concerned, doctors were, for the most part, content to repeat what the ancients said and undertook little methodological investigation until the end of the nineteenth century. Biographies would be precious, but they would need to be a new kind of biography, which attempted to bring to the fore what is usually hidden from view – namely, physiological events. Individual examples drawn from different periods and different social milieux would doubtless help us to a better understanding of the history of women. Biography gives us a vast amount of information and many hypotheses, as can be seen in Natalie Davis's *Martin Guerre*[2] or Carlo Ginzburg's *Menochio*. Biographies are, in effect, individualized chronologies and, as such, help us to see in what circumstances a female human being is able to find free time for anything besides simple biological reproduction. This is what is now called micro-history.

In conclusion, one might ask whether, from a feminine point of view, chronology does not entail changes in the epistemology of history. Not being a philosopher, I am not sure that I really know what epistemology is. But I have given the question some thought. I began my career as a researcher with a thesis on François Mignet who was, in 1825, the first great historian of the French Revolution, and who revealed that class struggle was an essential driving force of history. Historical research was profoundly shaken by this, in its objectives, its sources, its methods and its function. Instead of being a chronicle of monarchs, it became an investigation and an evaluation of social factors. The history of the people took over from the history of the princes. I felt that it was legitimate to ask whether this constituted an epistemological change. The jury of assessors who considered my thesis did not take up this question.

The history of women, in my view, raises a similar problem. Until now, history was asexual (as are all the human sciences). Male researchers naïvely believed that they were writing *History*, in its unique and true form. It may be that the sex of the researcher is of no importance when it comes to setting out the laws of the expansion of gases or the laws of the strength of materials; but when it comes to analysing the functioning of human societies, the sex of the historian is a variable of great importance. Is it an epistemological innovation to introduce the sexual dimension into the human sciences?

Apart from the changes already mentioned – the new importance attached to the subjective, to oral sources, psychoanalysis and micro-history – it must be realized that chronology from a feminine standpoint may well upset the order of importantce of facts. Contraception, which gives women the power of life and death over our western societies, draws attention to demographical facts, which are supplanting political and economic facts as factors of change. One might also question the 'scientific' nature of history. What should we think of a human science that had hitherto ignored the feminine viewpoint and still suppresses it in many areas? There is no question of renouncing the rigorous discipline of scientific procedures. It is an asceticism which at least acts as a safety mechanism, for our investigations might otherwise succumb to worse aberrations. But we must not be fooled by it. In the midst of this fog, what becomes of epistemology?

NOTES

1   It must be remembered that this is difficult. The archives are almost always poor, since they only contain what men have seen fit to keep; and the few documents that survive are sometimes not even listed. Until official archives take more account of women generally, we can only approve the setting up of specific banks, collections and libraries, such as have recently appeared in the United Sates in particular. We must hope that this is only a temporary segregation.

2   N. Z. Davis, J.-C. Carrière and D. Vigne, *Le Retour de Martin Guerre* (Laffont, Paris, 1982).

4

The Oral Sources for Women's History

Sylvie Vandecasteele-Schweitzer and Danièle Voldman

As a focus for research and discussion, the series of seminars on the relationship between oral history and women's history, held at the Institut d'Histoire du Temps Présent from April 1982 to June 1983 had a threefold nature. It was the result of an explicit social demand from women who came from various disciplines and who wanted to take women as their subject, and it brought to light several of the implications of women's history, and in particular the possibility and the necessity of this history. The historical field of this study was deliberately restricted. Not spread over a long time span or fixed on a contemporary period rooted in the nineteenth century, it was defined as 'the history of the present time'. Leaving aside the 'long-term memory', the focus was upon the changes of the previous forty years, a period during which women's history was characterized by militancy. Finally, the work was based primarily on oral sources, the use of which, as we know, has reinforced the hypothesis that a group can be constituted by means of its memories.

THE APPROACH

The history of the present cannot be written without oral sources. The absence of written sources, the closed nature of the archives, the opportunity to talk to those involved, imposed oral sources as a palliative and a complement before they reached the status of archives in the classical sense of the term.[1] For women's history it is even more essential to use them, since women have committed much less to writing than have men. They have used speech much more widely than the written word. Even if a large number of works have shown the degree to which such propositions reflect prejudice and stereotype, this remains true.[2] More-over, as they belong – whether by tradition, by right or by nature – to the intimate or private sphere, their history consists more of oral vestiges than written ones. Collecting their verbal accounts thus becomes a priority and the oral mode becomes the most important form of their history. Yet, despite the great importance accorded to listening to oral accounts, we have always thought that oral sources are not an 'oral his-tory' in the English sense, nor a history that collects popular traditions, nor indeed an active type of history in which the historian participates in a psycho-historical reconstruction of the individual questioned.

The seminar on the 'Oral sources for women's history' involved a kind of research based on, and justified by, the simple term 'woman', which seemed enough to bring together the various fields of work and justify the procedures. Thus, research into the evolution of the mid-wife's profession from 1900 to 1965 was placed alongside research into the voting habits of female shopkeepers under the Fifth Republic. And despite the different methods used, from the examination of profes-sional registers to the use of opinion polls and electoral analyses, the fact that researchers had collected oral records seemed a sufficient reason to allow us to attempt comparisons. So we tried first to isolate the domain of the history of women by and for themselves.

The priority given to oral sources allowed us to put forward an axiom – that of 'sisterhood' – and gave credibility to an absence of distance between the object of research and the subject who carried out that research.

Since the female historian felt a sense of 'shared sex' with the interviewee – a feeling modelled on the Marxist notion of shared class – it was supposed that a kind of complicity would be established, that deeper or more sincere truths would emerge from the interview and that the distance between subject and object would become blurred. Other questions then arose which affected the analyses presented. They related more to the relationship between the historian and her witness than to the supposed complicity between women, for many variables besides sex – social position, links with the events reported, age, etc. – had a role in the reception given to the researcher.[3]

Indeed, the very richness of the expression 'oral history' entails ambiguities. It is at the same time a means of constructing life histories, of researching the factual, of working on the functioning of memory and of understanding the way in which the historian constructs his or her source. The multiple meanings of the term may cause hesitatation and loss of the sense of direction, perhaps especially in the area of women's history. To listen to women, the oppressed majority, talking would be sufficient to restore them to history. They would then arise, mute and submissive. Oral history thus becomes a means of demanding justice for oneself in a society organized along masculine lines. By using this particular type of source, female historians hope to invert the dominant order, to allow women to speak to women at last, without an intermediary. And they are not ashamed to claim the inherent and acknowledged subjectivity of this method. Within the framework of the exclusive, dangerous relations the historian enjoys with the witness he or she is questioning, oral history in the area of women's history might lead one to expect the exaltation of a world without men, where widows are queen.[4] But this exclusive approach denies reality. Whatever liberating value women may find in them, oral sources in the first place call for a reflection on the forms and working of memory.

WOMEN'S MEMORY

Studied from a philosophical, a sociological or a psychological point of view, the process of historical memorization has held very little interest for historians, who have been more interested in the study of its content than its form. In the field of women's history, however, the problem of memory is central, because women still remain an oppressed group, whose history is denied. To give them back their memory is to give them back their past, their history, because one specific sphere (that of private life) is assigned to them and it is assumed that they are good at retaining the memory of this. A complement to autobiographical memory, the study of the 'historical' memory of social groups allows us to define them. But recognition of this process, in which the individual is abandoned in favour of the group, forces us to stop considering women exclusively as martyrs excluded from history. They cease to be simply part of the group of those oppressed by masculine power and join not only all the other marginalized categories, but the whole of humanity and its history. We can then abandon the hypothesis of a memory specific to women, a hypothesis that rests on a sophism. It coincides – both at the symbolic level and at the real level – with the division of tasks and social roles. This reasoning has contributed to two types of exclusion: the exclusion of women from the political, public sphere and the exclusion of men from the intimate, private sphere. We find this twofold exclusion as much on the male side in traditional historiography as in the work of certain radical feminists.

Beyond the historians' quarrels as to choices of words and concepts, the militant implications of which can clearly not be denied or underestimated, it seems to us rather that – for men as for women – memory is marked and structured by social roles. The comparison of the memories of two women deported to Birkenau is interesting in this context.[5] The first of these women, a Jew, had a survival strategy which was entirely based on the affirmation of her femininity taken to the point of caricature. What allowed her to survive was her knowledge of cosmetics. Her skill in making up the female guards and her determination to retain an elegant appearance saved her. The second woman, also a Jew, who had been arrested for taking part in the Resistance, was imprisoned as the 'head of a family' and then deported. She had a masculine image of herself, partly no doubt as a result of the fact that she was a doctor, a very unfeminine profession at that time. The memories of these two women are very different. The 'feminine' respondent is very precise as to chronology and daily events, places and names, so that we may call hers a concrete memory. In contrast, the doctor's memory is determined by world events, by moral and political condemnation of the Nazi phenomenon. It is linked with her involvement in associations of those deported, organized around their memories. Hers is an abstract memory, logically restructured. In the same way, within the French Resistance movement *Franc-Tireur*, married women who were not working have a memory based on private life and anchored in personal chronology. But unmarried women, or those who had a 'masculine' social function have a memory that is based far more on collective time.[6] These examples show that memory is not based on the individual's sex, but varies according to the events of the individual's life. To work on the functioning of memory therefore implies drawing up a typology, according to social milieu and level of education, of the habit of abstracting and manipulating models. The way in which an individual's life fits into the historical context, his or her political commitment and age group are all elements that interfere with the reconstruction of the past.

Structured by social roles, memory and its various forms should therefore be conceived and analysed as an element in the war of the sexes, the sexualization of memory being one aspect of the debate on the socio-historical determination of masculine and feminine.

VALUES AND STEREOTYPES

How should we define 'masculine' and 'feminine', beyond the biological level? This question of the difference between the sexes, familiar to anthropologists who have found very different ways of answering it,[7] runs through the whole of history, including the history of women. But the contemporary period, because it has seen new developments in this sphere, hesitates to give an answer. For a long time history had its markers, its established modes of living, its domains attributed, and spheres reserved, to one or other sex; but what is the position today, after the changes of the 1960s, the advent of female ministers and 'new fathers'?

There are, for example, many cracks in the stereotypes based on the body. Women's bodies, mentioned in male speech, attract much more research than men's bodies do. Women are caught between the representation of evil seduction and terrifying power (the power of giving birth), allied to a constitutional weakness. Today these images are becoming blurred and the use of oral sources reveals contradictory forms of discourse, in which images are confronted with tradition and different types of reality (women's reality, that of the social group to which they belong, etc.) Thus physical weakness remains women's handicap, even for their exclusive social and biological role, motherhood (and more particularly childbirth). Women think that they are – and say that they are – weak, contrary to all the evidence. And yet this statement often goes hand in hand with another, which may seem inconsistent. When a woman in childbirth says that she is 'tough' in the face of pain, is it because she resists pain, because she can overcome the biblical command, or because she is proving herself the equal of man, of the male, in this notorious physical test?[8]

Outside the realm of maternity, women also use their bodies in contexts very far from their traditional role of seduction.

Thus the deported Jew discussed above maintained her seductive appearance in order to survive; and she succeeded because she did not abandon women's most traditional precept: to make one's body an object of pleasure for others. Called 'Hollywood Dolly' by her companions, the feminine woman became an impulse for survival. This analysis is of a totally anti-heroic safety device. The researcher who carried out the research met with hostile reactions on the part of feminist readers. The question is to determine where the stereotype lies. Discussion remains open on the possibility of overturning an order by the use of one's own laws. Should one die refusing to give in to the notion of feminine seduction or survive, thanks to lipstick?

The dividing line between stereotype and its corruption is just as difficult to evaluate where the values of the social order are concerned. Here, too, oral sources have shown up two points of view. On the one hand, women's comments on their own social behaviour, and on the other, their actual behaviour. First accounts often reproduce the dominant theme. Even women who have been very active in history (for example, in the Resistance) will take a secondary role in relation to male heroes, who are spoken about because they have spoken. In subsequent interviews, however, these women will talk about their own exploits, almost apologetically, stressing the banality of their involvement. Thus, women who belong to an association of those deported to concentration camps place more emphasis on the solidarity and mutual help of the soldiers than on their own actions.

These analyses were first undertaken in the traditionally feminine domains of the body and the emotions. But, in parallel to the recent revival of political history, women's history has moved towards research more closely focused on these areas. The obtaining and use of the right to vote has allowed us to measure and analyse behaviour in this context. Contrary to certain persistent ideas, it is clear that electoral choice (like memory) is less determined by sex than by lifestyle. Among active voters – both men and women – voting patterns reflect, in order of decreasing importance, religious practices, social position and sex.[9]

FROM THE PUBLIC TO THE PRIVATE

The attention given to the political sphere within studies on women is always timid. Historians continue to separate, even if not with absolute rigidity, the spheres of the private and the public. Is this in order to give themselves a basis in 'reality'? Should we see in this an honest description of the facts, pure mental habit or a simple reference to the masculine view of society, which does in fact separate the two spheres? Certainly, the oral sources record that women find it difficult to speak of their public life, unless they belong to a profession that confers prestige.

If midwives are willing to talk about their profession and their careers, they are nevertheless much less open about their own motherhood, which belongs to the private sphere.[10] It is possible, of course, that this difficulty is due to an inability or a desire not to separate two domains that would form an inseparable whole. In a society based on division, the affirmation of the undivided self causes discomfort.

In any case, the public is never put forward as a fundamental motive for behaviour. Among the women of the Resistance, even if they speak of their love for their country, one notes a total absence of nationalist talk to justify their actions.[11]

This is all the more spectacular at the present time, since we are living through a period of upheaval on several levels. The 1980s saw a tendency in western Europe to redistribute the traditional social roles, or at least an attempt to rethink them in relation to economic, social and cultural developments. The status of men and women is becoming more complex, with the overlapping and inversion of the roles attributed to the sexes. The spheres that sociologists call the spheres of production and reproduction are no longer as rigidly assigned. For so long confined to the private sphere (the role of reproduction), women are now participating vey widely in the public sphere (productive work and social responsibilities). At the same time, masculine roles are being redefined.

The divisions of private and public, of production and reproduction are thus of less significance in immediate history than in the nineteenth century or even in the first half of the twentieth century. Their use often leads to ambiguity or to failures which many studies have brought to light. When one questions female shopkeepers about the difficulties of their job and their demands, they mention first the factors that concern the masculine element of the profession: long hours, heavy taxation, etc.; and their answers are identical to those of their husbands.[12] Paradoxically, it is the husbands who introduce the problems specific to women in the trade, criticizing, for example, the injustices of insurance policies for shopkeepers' wives. The idea of problems linked with both their social situation and their biological nature, as female shopkeepers and women, seems to have been difficult to formulate both for the researchers and for those questioned.[13]

In this way the use of oral sources, which liberate speech and reveal daily life, allows relations between the private and the public to be made clearer and more refined, and permits us to take a new look at supposedly well-known areas. As a result, these areas are enriched by elements that have traditionally not been taken into account very much. For example, the work on the women of the French Resistance during the Second World War has shed light on aspects of the way in which clandestine groups worked. It has stressed the fact that women were involved as well as men in these movements, both as operatives and as officials, and it has led to a deeper understanding of the reasons for the active commitment of militants of both sexes. Alongside moral, philosophical and political choices, the women of the *Franc-Tireur* movement talked about the sentiments that influenced them, whether it was a taste for taking risks or the desire to share in the cause defended by their husband.[14] And, using the same type of questioning for men, the historian heard accounts in which intimate feelings (of family life, fear, sentimental reactions) were present in a very real way.

WOMEN'S HISTORY: ONE FIELD OR SEVERAL?

Women and their history thus take their place in the much wider consideration of the differentiation between the event and the daily happening, without either having a sex – or rather, because both are experienced by a population made up of both men and women for whom it is false to think of the event as being masculine or the daily happening as being feminine. In this respect, if the rejection of 'factual' history facilitated the development of the history of mentalities, with the return of the event perhaps political historians will not forget the fruit- ful discoveries made while they were exploring societies' images and the commonplace. According to François Lebrun's expression in one of our seminars, all history benefits from the results of those who ventured 'beneath the bedclothes'.

If we accept the hypothesis that women's history belongs to the history of the oppressed, it constitutes a field of its own in the same way as working-class history, the history of the towns or the history of health. But can we, without hasty assimilation, group together research into women, feminist studies and the specific approach of women to history? To separate them totally would be to ignore reality, without distinguishing areas that are close, though not congruent. The feminism of the 1970s, by opting for a radical separation of the sexes, favoured the view that men should be excluded. Every woman who studies women finds concordance, resonance and echoes between the object of her study and herself. And female historians, because they are women, have been interested in new historical objects, and so they have broadened the male approach. Thus, when women began to study women and their voting behaviour, they devoted as much attention to female electors as to those few women who had been elected, and they sought to define the attitudes of a population that was, officially and effectively, not concerned with electoral problems.[15] In the same way, to study women in war is deliberately to attempt to bypass a sexual division of the social roles. When men are at the front, what do women do? How do they produce goods? How do they carry on resistance? In short, where are they? And if it is true that wartime operations remain, in spite of everything, a man's business, perhaps these new ways of looking at things may renew historiography. Study of the behaviour of women prisoners in Nazi camps made it possible to reappraise the strategies of survival which, since the work of Bruno Bettelheim,[16] had above all been thought of in terms of masculine values.

What we are talking about is not one field – women's history – but several, indeed all fields, in which women are considered an element, once minimized, in history as a whole. We may not need new tools, new concepts or a new methodology in order to investigate and identify these fields, at any rate at the historical level, but perhaps we need to use existing tools and concepts in a new way.

This break with the past affects the method of reasoning of historians, both male and female. Perhaps we may find more useful divisions – or more pertinent ways of thinking of the difference between the sexes – when we have carried out a certain number of historical studies on the mental and social representations of feminine and masculine roles. Thought needs to be given above all to the distinction between the public and private spheres, for it leads almost inevitably to allocations. It is not so much a question of placing women in the public sphere (and perhaps men in the private sphere) as of seeing social structures and social life as one whole. What we do not need to do, after demolishing a masculinized historical object, is to construct a feminine historical object.

The difficulty in defining feminine identity shows a certain confusion in the face of all these data (stereotypes, redefined social roles, the difficulties of working on the present time, especially when we are looking at changes and breaks with the past). Everyone agrees that, as a matter of priority, in the 1970s it was necessary to affirm and confirm the presence of women in history. Now it remains for us to reinstate them and to redefine their position without falling into hagiography or confining women to one single field of research. If we take the example of the historians of the working-class movement, who gradually rejoined the field of wider social history, we do not want to construct a history of women, but rather many histories, without dispensing with the masculine environment. We do not want to fall into the same trap that has too often caught traditional historiography, even in reverse.

The historian, of either sex, does not need to argue for a change in the social status quo – that is not our role. But we must change our approach. Not only must we no longer write history without women, but we must no longer treat men as the universal human gender. If we stop writing history in which the actors are asexual (men, people, masses and so on), perhaps we shall see the emergence of identities, both masculine and feminine. We would thus be able to compare social beings on an equal footing (whether as similar, identical or complementary) and we could work on their memories, their oral accounts and their place in time and the evolution of history with its pauses, its accelerations, and sometimes its retreats.

NOTES

Some of the notes refer to papers given at the series of seminars described at the beginning of the chapter. These papers were not published.

1   On these questions, see P. Joutard, *Ces voix qui nous viennent du passé* (Hachette, Paris, 1983); *Questions de méthode en histoire orale* (CNRS–IHTP, 1981), and D. Voldman, 'L'invention du témoignage oral', in *Questions à l'histoire orale, Les Cahiers de L'IHTP*, no. 4, June 1987. See also D. Voldman, ed., *La Recherche historique et les sources orales: bilan d'expériences, Cahier de l'IHTP*, Spring 1992.

2   E.g. A. Farge, 'L'histoire ébruitée', in P. Werner, ed., *L'Histoire sans qualités* (Galilée, Paris, 1979). See also G. Duby, M. Perrot, eds, *History of Women in the West*.

3   Cf. S. Vandecasteele-Schweitzer and D. Voldman, 'Historiens et témoins', *Actes du IVe Colloque international d'histoire orale* (Aix, 1982).

4   C. Auzias, 'Les femmes anarchistes', *Histoire orale et histoire des femmes* (CNRS–IHTP, 1982).

5   See the work of M. Pollak, 'Survivre dans un camp de concentration', *Actes de la Recherche en Sciences Sociales*, no. 41, 1982; 'Paroles des déportées' (Paper given at one of the seminars, and *L'Expérience concentrationnaire, Essai sur le maintien de l'identité sociale* (Paris, Métailié, 1990).

6   See D. Veillon, 'Mémoire de résistantes et de déportées' (Paper given at one of the seminars); 'L'ADIR, Association nationale des déportées et internées de la Résistance', *Mémoire de la seconde guerre mondiale* (Metz, 1984).

7   E.g. Margaret Mead, *Male and Female: A Study of the Sexes in a Changing World* (Gollancz, London, 1949); Aline Rousselle, *Porneia* (PUF, Paris, 1983; trans. Felicia Pheasant, Basil Blackwell, Oxford, 1988).

8   Papers given at the seminars: D. Tucat, 'Sages-femmes et accouchées, 1876–1970'; M. Dubesset, F. Thébaud and M. Zancarini, 'Mères entre les deux guerres'.

9   J. Mossuz-Lavau and M. Sineau, 'Une enquête sur les femmes et la politique' (Paper given at one of the seminars).

10 See n. 8 above.

11 See n. 6 above.

12 N. Mayer, 'Les choix politiques des petites commerçantes' (Paper given at one of the seminars).

13 See n. 9 above.

14 See n. 6 above.

15 See n. 9 above.

16 B. Bettelheim, *The Informed Heart*.

5

The Unavoidable Detour: Must a History of Women Begin with the History of their Bodies?

Catherine Fouquet

It is now accepted that the history of the human body is a study worthy of attention in universities. Various study groups have been set up, and are exploring this terrain which, we may recall, was first defined in France by two articles. The first text, produced in 1972 by Jacques Revel and Jean-Pierre Peter,[1] considered the origins and problems of the history of health. The second, six years later, broadened the range of this branch of history from the body to its gestures, manners and techniques.[2] At no time did these authors appear to suggest that there might be any question of introducing a sexual variable into this work. The body they describe belongs simply to the human species. In this chapter I shall ask why it seems that women's history goes hand in hand with an insistent, many-sided effort to analyse the history of the female body. At the same time, I cannot hide the anxiety I feel each time a consideration of this kind seems to bring us back to a bland definition of 'feminine nature', a concept that seems to resist development.[3] Is it really legitimate, useful or safe, within the field of research into the history of the body, to isolate this theme of the female body, which appears at first sight to imply inferiority and exclusion? In fact, is this really a new subject? By following these paths, are we not, despite ourselves, helping to reinforce the old attitudes whereby woman was intrinsically tied to her body, prisoner of her biological fate?

Before debating this, I should like to stress a point of chronology. At what point in our history did this new question arise? Roland Barthes noted that Simone de Beauvoir's *Le Deuxième Sexe*, which appeared in 1949, only found an audience in 1970. The 1960s, in France, marked the beginning of what Jean Baudrillard has called *corporéisme*.[4] This came after the three decades in which the demographic upheavals caused by the war, the baby boom and the use of antibiotics gave women a permanent numerical advantage in France.[5] From then on, young people and women exercised a physical pressure within French society which has perhaps not been without effect on the emergence of these new fields of study. This observation fills me with anxiety. Is my interest in the body and its history obeying the dictates of fashion? By asking questions about women and their bodies, am I only reflecting the times?

Without nourishing too many illusions about the intellectual independence of one researching into the human sciences – indeed, rather the opposite, duly warned by recent historiography of the researcher's dependence on topicality – I shall reject this objection. The fruitfulness of new enquiries stimulated by involvement in the contemporary world proves that history is alive. To reject them would be to demonstrate sclerosis.

Nevertheless it is quite true, if one considers the treatment given to the female body by historians of the old style, that their approach is defined by traditional values. Briefly, we can say that as woman was strictly contained within the roles fixed by the dominant ideology – that of a masculinist society – the description of the female body in the work of different authors was limited to a reflection of its subordination to the necessities of the time. In Orderic Vital's *L'Histoire ecclésiastique* in the twelfth century, women are considered above all as brood mares. When speaking of a woman, he would mention her fertility, her sterility or her beauty, which helped her to corrupt men.[6] This monastic model is not very far from the epic model. In Homer, too, women – Helen, Penelope – are defined in terms of the use made of them by men. The list of companions or Egerias could go on for ever. And let us note that when these ancient chronicles refer to a woman, she always has some remarkable attribute, whether physical or genealogical. Queens and famous mistresses all hold their position as a result of a matrimonial or genital link, as a result of the sexual use made of their body. In the same way, the 'Mata Hari effect' is used to describe those women who devote their body (and its erotic uses) to a particular cause. From Judith onwards, in history the female body has served as an instrument of seduction in the service of politics. But, as they are told to us, these tales show us heroines who do not make use of their bodies for their own purposes. All the women, whether wives or spies, are subservient to the species.

Romantic history has of course embellished and exalted this model. And the nineteenth century carried a certain definition of the female being to its paroxysm. Let us think, for example, of Jules Michelet who feminized history to the utmost and called for the Assumption of woman.[7]

As for the heroines whose great deeds are reported by this deliberately legendary history, it is by the unusual use of their bodies that they appear as heroines, even in the historical imagery of our own century. Jeanne Hachette,[8] Joan of Arc, and murderous virgins such as Charlotte Corday are also mythological figures just as much as real ones. They have their counterparts now in the figure of Geneviève de Galard, whose calm heroism as an army nurse in the Indochina war magnifies the caring role traditionally attributed to women. The wonder they arouse, their ability to generate a golden legend around themselves, stems from the fact that they have managed to rise out of their condition because they have shown themselves to be driven by a virtue traditionally reserved for men: warlike ardour, the courage of arms. There is no place in the gallery of heroines for women who simply obeyed the laws of their sex. In a society whose written culture is essentially masculine – in the learned treaties, in the laws by which the subordination of women is confirmed – the accent is firmly on the stereotype of feminine nature: woman fulfils her role by giving birth to children, bringing them up, and giving pleasure to men. These tasks are so far taken for granted that they merit no attention. For the majority of the men who wrote history, until very recently, the feminine condition sprang out of that part of history that they liked to consider unchanging: just as the earth is round, women work for the continuance of the species. Feminine roles continue through the centuries without apparent change. A familiar expression reminds us of this: the whore carries on 'the oldest profession in the world'. Since the beginning of time, from mother to daughter, in blood and pain and death, women have given birth to the world, men's world, which belongs to *them*, the world *they* dominate. Men are on the side of intellect, power, war, history. Women give birth to warriors and workers, they feed them, restore their strength and give them pleasure. What reassuring images! As far as women are concerned, the comfort of tradition and no change! With the constant return of their cycles, women create a regular rhythm in which inevitably, without surprise, life and death recur. From mother to daughter, nature's cycle is accomplished. How could it have a history?

Of course women's bodies sometimes represent a crucial element in this old-fashioned history. From the rape of the Sabine women to the belly of Marie-Louise,[9] the question of reproduction has been intimately related to that of power, has led to negotiations, political transactions, even to wars (Oh Eleanor of Aquitaine!) as preserved for us in chronicles and treaties. They thus become events. And yet in these cases women appear as intermediaries rather than as actors. Assigned to their bodily status, they can act in history only in so far as their bodies have served them well, by serving their master and the dynastic interest.

To reduce women to their bodies, in this respect, is thus to exclude them from history. Everything is changed once it is shown that the female body itself has a history, through even its most humble functions. None of the functions that have traditionally been assigned to the female body escapes this rule. Giving birth, bringing up children, working in the home, making oneself attractive, these are all acts that have changed over the centuries in their forms, their intentions and their consequences for women's health and longevity. The carefully perpetuated illusion of unchanging feminine nature masks these profound differences, in time and place and according to the social group considered. It helps to maintain the cliché'd opposition between man as a being of the outside world and woman as a creature of the interior, the domain of private life. But this illusion has been gradually dissipated by an increasing number of studies. Demographic research has led to research into the family and sexuality. Wet-nurses, seamstresses, mothers, prostitutes and female workers have all had their histories written. The roles women fulfil by using the specific nature of their bodies have changed over time. The female body itself has been put to different uses; it has been transformed by them.[10] The illusion that nothing has changed has been fostered to serve the ideology that seeks to maintain men in the dominant position.

But is there not a basic symmetry between men and women? One might reply in response to my argument that up to the 1950s no one had written the history of the male body either; that, as it did for women, the renewal of history by historical demography and its numerous offshoots put the history of the male body on the agenda. It might also be argued, above all, that this 'new' history that was being created had as its object the human race as a whole and that this must not be altered unless one wishes to run the risk of binding women once again in the bonds that tie them to everything that is biological. Wouldn't 'old-fashioned' history cite the metamorphoses of the male body? This is true only in part. And what I wish to stress first of all is the differences in the treatment of the two sexes. Masculine roles are no doubt just as stereotyped as feminine roles. There is a 'natural' vocation that assigns certain functions to men. As a result, both men and women have their places in a scheme of human nature that is frozen and almost unchanging.

But this is not quite correct. The roles traditionally attributed to men, in masculinist society,[11] centainly involve, as in the case of women, a 'natural' or 'primitive' use of the specific nature of their bodies. Thus warriors win because of their strength; workers are more successful, and thus prosperous, if they are physically strong. If they are ill or infirm, workers – whether industrial or peasant – sink into an undesirable condition, in earlier times the condition of poverty, nowadays that of someone on social welfare.[12] Illness and poverty are linked (in all cases, whether applying to men or women), at least when one is talking about the poorest groups in society. We may recall the name given to the old charity institutions devoted to the 'sick poor'.

In this context we may make one comment which divides the masculine fate from the feminine: for men at least, the higher the role in society, the less importance the body has. It is peasants and soldiers, the humbler groups, who earn their sustenance by pressing their bodies into service. Baldwin of Jerusalem was a leper, but he was King nevertheless. A barren queen was soon repudiated. Josephine, who was sterile, had to give up her position. Louis XIV's fistula did not detract from his power.

The men whose bodies receive particular attention are those whose commercial value is judged on the basis of physical characteristics. The dwarf or the giant may make use of their strangeness, but their situation has no prestige. The monster, whether male or female, has been known throughout history.[13] In former times the poor made a living by exhibiting prodigies. Beggars traded on this. But in general terms, in our civilization since the end of antiquity,[14] hiding one's body has been the norm. Those who show their bodies and use them for commercial purposes are inferior. To sell one's body, as the prostitute does, is to sink to the level of a slave. In ancient Greece, in classical times, the victors of the arena were those chosen by the gods. In Rome, gladiators were the dregs of the masses.

Perhaps we may cite an exception to what seems to be a rule. Under the Third Republic it was considered fitting for generals to be physically impressive. Jean Estèbe, who has studied their files at the War Ministry, tells us of the more or less flattering reports made by their superiors.[15] Reading them, one realizes that for these leaders service, according to the army's ideal, involved something approaching the servitude that characterized most of those whose profession or social role included an aspect of showmanship. So it was considered an advantage if a soldier was a 'fine-looking officer'; not, as Jean Estèbe tells us, as a sign of latent homosexuality, but because at that time it was 'an established expression which did not surprise contemporary people, for whom the contemplation of a handsome military man dressed up in his finery was a customary pleasure.'[16] In any case, at a time when the practice of war still frequently involved hand-to-hand fighting, an officer was expected to possess charisma, which might be a result of his physical appearance. Moreover, at the end of the nineteenth century slimness and an elegant bearing were also linked with aristrocratic blood. But physical beauty was of no use if these men entered politics. On the physical level, the advantage then passed to the members of the bar, who possessed both the gift of eloquence and a good voice. The voice was all that counted: 'the orator's physique might, without disadvantage, present imperfections that today would not be acceptable on the television screen.' This is a significant point. The decisive change in public life brought about nowadays by the power of the image is reflected in these comments from a contemporary historian about men of past times, for whom the same values were not in force. But are they any less interesting?

After centuries of secrecy about the body, our society indulges in the exaltation and worship of the functional body. One might speak of a new ethic in relation to the body. A return to gymnastic exhibition began at the end of the nineteenth century with the new Olympic Games. Sport rehabilitated the male body first; women followed later. We are experiencing this phenomenon very consciously today: we are aware of witnessing a reversal in trends. But when did the secrecy surrounding the body, its exclusion from the domain of subjects worthy of study, its elimination from the mainstream of education begin – if we accept that for the Greeks physical and intellectual education went hand in hand?

Aline Rousselle places this revolution between the second and fourth centuries AD. *Porneia* gives a detailed analysis of this move 'from mastery of the body to sensory deprivation'.[17]

Christianity is usually blamed for this state of affairs, but in actual fact several forces contributed to bring it about. Among them were the adoption of a new style of hygiene whose rule was to observe abstinence in order to preserve *pneuma*, the vital spirit; social and legal conditions of marriage in Rome, which made it, for girls, an ordeal; and the decision made by eastern solitaries to deny all the body's desires in order to help the perfection of the soul. The treatises written by the bishops of the time 'to convince women to remain virgins and families to remain chaste' met with a favourable response from men already won over to the idea that continence was a form of asceticism necessary in order to make full use of one's mind and from the women of Greece and Rome who were already fulfilling their conjugal duties, without pleasure, in honourable frigidity.[18]

Although actual behaviour in periods such as the Middle Ages did not always bear out this rejection of the body, and although nakedness was readily accepted, the Church nevertheless maintained the continuity of doctrines valuing modesty and chastity. Churchmen thus contributed to this rejection of bodily realities which, after several vicissitudes, culminated, in the nineteenth century, in the bourgeois world we know today. They achieved this with the aid of concepts and beliefs accepted between the second and fourth centuries. After the doctors of antiquity and after Plato – whose *Timaeus* was, according to Aline Rousselle, bedtime reading for all the learned people of the Graeco-Roman world – clerics wanted to contain the excesses of the human body in order to prepare for the reign of the Spirit. And the female body seemed to be particularly rebellious to these wishes. The Church-dominated culture that emerged from the Middle Ages thus allotted the body a very small role.

The male body's return to history in the 1960s took place in the wake of demographic history. First it was family behaviour and life expectancy that inspired research, then came studies of the massive amounts of source material made more accessible to analysis, thanks to the computer. This source material itself oriented the work of researchers. Because they were far more numerous than women in large institutions, men were the subject of in-depth studies before women were. The army and the hospitals provided a satisfactory series of conscripts and workers. But we cannot really say that (apart from the conscripts) they were studied because they were male or because they fulfilled a specifically male role. The pathology of the working class concerns women to the same degree as men. Indeed, the scandalous plight of female workers in the nineteenth century gave rise to the first important work in this area.

So it seems to us that this approach – to the male body – came about as a rebound effect or as a complement. The history of the female body is essential to those who want to study a society in which femininity has been deliberately linked with the body, while the male has been seen as being on the side of all that is intellectual. But soon the same questions are raised symmetrically in connection with the male body, but almost apologetically. There is no doubt that men are much more reluctant than women to speak about such things (although there are a few brave pioneers), particularly as they are convinced, and want to believe, that this domain belongs to women. Their old-fashioned upbringing hangs over generations of researchers who are ill at ease with their own bodies. They try to hide their embarrassment by describing as futile all studies that set out to explore this side of reality. Male nudity remains much more shocking than female nudity.

In 1975, the publisher Balland published an album of photographs called *Portraits of Famous and Unknown Male Nudes*. These frontal portraits, arranged in alphabetical order of the men's names, were to be part of a exhibition in the Nikon gallery which in the end gave up the project. The Preface explains the photographer's intentions as follows: 'These men have been photographed as they are. They are not "posing", and they are not hiding their identity. They are relaxed, natural, real. They accept their bodies.' This is clearly what the photographer wanted to show: everyday male nudity, without affectation. But in reality, when one examines the variety of poses and the number of men who contrived to appear like *Antinoüs pudicus*, one is far from convinced. The desire for the portraits to appear 'natural' doubtless explains the fact that, unlike what one finds in shops specializing in the exaltation of the male body, here are no ephebes, or beautiful young men, no emulators of Hercules. We find some bearded figures, a few pot-bellied men. Three are posing with children who serve to hide their private parts. Some of the pictures remind one of classical poses – there is, for example, one 'thinker' à la Rodin.[19] This is, in fact, one way of depersonalizing and disguising oneself. By copying the artistic archetype, the nude loses its erotic or shocking power. The attempts of some sculptors to symbolize work by means of a male figure met with the same fate. Their creations were so far from realistic that they prompted this protest in poetic form from Jacques Prévert: 'Human effort is not this handsome young man smiling as he stands on plaster or stone leg . . . Human effort wears a truss and the scars of the battles fought by the working class . . . '[20] The academic tradition of the representation of the body no doubt partly explains this phenomenon, as we have indicated. I myself see something more in it. I see the eternal reluctance to represent the male nude as anything but a symbol. The taboo concerning male bodiliness has been so strong for centuries that male dress, restricting and neutral in colour, has finally fitted in with it. Many are the men who think they are being 'natural and real', whereas they are in fact conforming to the dress of their class.[21] Showing an interest in problems such as this lays one open to accusations such as that of futility, and men fear these accusations even more than women.

Histories of the body are thus thought of as being above all 'women's subjects'. To devote onself to this area is to run the risk of being confined to a ghetto. But is it enough, in order to break this curse, to call for the 'breaking up of the usual structures of thought'?[22] Simone de Beauvoir, in 1949, in her Introduction to *Le Deuxième Sexe*, wrote: 'The subject is irritating, particularly for women, and it is not new.' This sentence summarizes the problem rather well. But should we agree to abandon a field of work before we have explored it fully? We are far from having exhausted this one.

The family and sexuality still have a great deal to tell us, and reconstructing the past does not necessarily lead to a glorification of the past – far from it. On the way, generally accepted ideas are demolished or confirmed. A-priori ideologies fall by the wayside. Books based on militant hypotheses do not often constitute good history. Our rule must remain subservience to the facts, however feminist we may be. It may well be that anyone who wants to succeed in her career today must undergo a 'feminine deconditioning'. The fact remains that it seems to me to be essential to make a thorough exploration of this area, which for a long time was the only one entirely left to women. And as male–female interrelations are innumerable, a study of this apparently re-stricted area must necessarily lead to new questions about 'masculine reality', just as his study of essentially female prostitution in the nine-teenth century has led Alain Corbin to carry out research into male sexual misery. Aline Rousselle's *Porneia* also gives an account of both the male and the female body.

Our questioning of the masculinist order of things has already given rise to new subjects for research. It is after all logical that researchers should have begun by investigating the areas traditionally considered to be feminine. This in turn led to the profusion of works approaching women's history via the history of their bodies. In the area of health, for example, hysteria has already prompted many historical works, often written by women. Should we interpret this as an indication that women are subservient to generally accepted ideas (*tota mulier in utero*, there is a hysterical creature dormant in every woman), or rather as an indication that we seek not to miss any aspect of the problem in our examination of received ideas in the light of the human sciences?[23] Fortunately, in most cases this attempt results in healthy demystification. In turn, the idea of the 'eternally feminine' has become blurred and, in parallel, a new 'grid' has been applied to research into the masculine. As an example of this I shall cite some studies of anorexia, an affliction which for the most part affects contemporary western women. These studies have led their authors to ask questions about the significance of masculine food-related behaviour and men's attitudes to their own looks.[24]

It would be absurd to claim that in allowing our interest to fix on these subjects we are not following the spirit of the time. Since the emergence of a new ethic concerning our relations with our bodies, it has become possible to say things that were unthinkable in the culture of the clerics. While it began with the feminine domain, research can now turn to the masculine, and the whole picture can be reconstructed. But only after what I consider to be an unavoidable detour.

NOTES

1 Jacques Revel and Jean-Pierre Peter, 'Le corps, l'homme malade et son histoire' in *Faire de l'histoire*, vol. 3 (Gallimard, 1974, pp. 169–91).

2 J. Revel, 'Corps' in *La Nouvelle Histoire*, ed. J. Le Goff et al. (Retz, 1978).

3 Yvonne Knibiehler and Catherine Fouquet, *La Femme et les médecins*, a historical analysis (Hachette, 1983).

4 Jean Baudrillard, *Le Système des objets* (Gallimard, 1968).

5 'Démographie historique et condition féminine', a special issue of the journal *Annales de Démographie Historique*, 1981.

6 Catherine Fouquet and Yvonne Knibiehler, *La Beauté, pour quoi faire?*, *Essai sur l'histoire de la beauté féminine* (Temps Actuels, 1982).

7 Jean Borie, 'Une gynécologie passionnée' in *Misérable et glorieuse, la femme au XIXe siècle* (Fayard, 1980).

8 A French heroine who, at the age of about sixteen, took up a hatchet to defend the town of Beauvais which Charles the Bold was besieging in 1472.

9 Napoleon's second wife, who, unlike Josephine, was able to give him a son.

10 Fouquet and Knibiehler, *La Beauté*.

11 See the definition of *masculinisme* in Knibiehler and Fouquet, *La Femme et les médecins*.

12 Henri-Jacques Striker, *Corps infirmes et sociétés* (Aubier, 1982).

13 Ibid.

14 Henri Irénée Marrou, *Décadence romaine ou antiquité tardive?* (Seuil, 1977).

15 Jean Estèbe, *Les Ministres de la République* (Presses de la Fondation des Sciences Politiques, 1982).

16 Ibid., p. 139. Note the convergence of two tendencies: while military uniforms were shedding their rich trimmings and gold and becoming less exciting to look at, civilians were attaching increasing importance to their clothes and physical appearance. For men, the notion of parade was changing its meaning.

17 Aline Rousselle, *Porneia*.

18 Ibid., p. 198.

19 Photographs by Jean-François Bauret, Preface by Gabriel Bauret.

20 Quoted by Maurice Agulhon in 'Propos sur l'allégorie politique', *Actes de la recherche en sciences sociales* (in reply to Eric Hobsbawm), June 1979.

21 Pierre Bourdieu, *La Distinction*, a social critique of taste (Minuit, 1979).

22 A. Farge, 'Dix ans d'histoire des femmes', *Le Débat*, vol. 23 (Gallimard, January 1983).

23 See the bibliography which appears as an appendix to vol. 8 of *Pénélope*, 'Questions sur la folie', Spring 1983.

24 Erika Apfelbaum, 'Kilos ou Q.I.: un enjeu pervertissant pour l'anorexique', *Pénélope*, vol. 8, Spring 1983; Véronique Nahoum-Grappe, 'Beauté et pouvoir: une réflexion sur la pathologie de certains comportements sociaux', ibid.

6

Body, Remains and Text

Elisabeth Ravoux Rallo (Part I)
Anne Roche (Part II)

'The female body is no more than a metaphor of the generations of women that went before it.'
Antoinette Gordowski, Chaussée d'Antin

Women's history entails the history of their bodies. This is because they are (or perhaps because for a very long time they were?) no more than bodies. The following words by a psychoanalyst deserve our attention:

> What is the relationship between woman and death? Does it flow from the special nature of her relationship with her body? Doesn't she feel even more the injustice and irrefutable fatality of death which in the end makes her body – *a non-place or non-event whose language she does not herself understand during her lifetime*[1] – a place of the flesh henceforth devoid of speech; that is, devoid of the language incarnated by her body although she never possessed the key to this language as the third dimension of a possible symbolism.[2]

Yet this body, imperfectly known by women themselves, has been celebrated, listened to, invented, questioned and decoded by the male mind for centuries, above all in literature. This non-place for women is precisely the subject of men's language. To examine this masculine language is of course to contribute to the history of the female body – in other words to the history of women – if women exist first and foremost, as we are convinced they do, through their bodies.

We can make no claim to deal with this subject exhaustively. What research could ever sum up all the representations of female bodies in literature? This is something that remains to be done. And why not? But here and there a few things have been written, and we do possess that invaluable tool, memory coupled with intuition. Here we shall use it as a tool: we shall call up some well-known and less well-known texts that support a few thoughts that may help to pave the way for the research that needs to be done.

Prévost and Stendhal: two styles, two beings, two men with radically different ways of looking at women and writing about their bodies. Both show the restraint of their time, certainly, and also delicacy. There are things that remain unsaid, subjects that are out of bounds, but the body is still discussed over and over again. As we remember, as few of Prévost's readers could forget, Manon is 'Love itself'. Madame de Chasteller is the only one who seemed 'a woman' in Lucien's eyes. But if we look a little closer – which is what men do when it comes to women's bodies – these bodies appear and disappear in the closely woven fabric of the text.

Prévost *(Manon Lescaut)*

Manon always crying, her face covered by tears, her eyes closed, her unusual pallor, Manon, 'Love itself', but a love that is already dead at the beginning of the book. Jacques Proust has shown brilliantly in his article 'Le Corps de Manon' that she is already absent, already lost at the start of the book.[3] Although she is a woman given up to sensuality, she is in fact no more than a ghost, Des Grieux's double, his sister dead and divided, a corpse about which one no longer knows what to say ... 'Love itself'! A 'place of the flesh henceforth devoid of language' which Des Grieux constructs and reconstructs at leisure without ever tiring of repeating the same words which give nothing but death to his beloved, and which celebrate only her remains.

Stendhal *(Lucien Leuwen)*

Lucien desires only Bathilde, who is dressed in a gown which comes 'up to her neck' and always hides what other women around him are constantly showing off. And what is it exactly that she hides and other women display? A shape: 'Madame d'Hocquincourt in an elegant state of undress ... was lounging on a sofa two steps away from him'; shapes: 'pretty shoulders, the light camisole which had arrived from Paris the previous day, her plump arms shining under the gauze'; parts of the body which had no sexual appeal: 'He kissed this forehead, these cheeks, this neck, but was not for a moment distracted by her beauty'; a hand resting on Lucien's arm. Only Bathilde awakens his senses, even though the young dancer Raimonde quenches the young man's sexual torments: 'Morality has so little to do with my relations with Mlle Raimonde that I feel almost no remorse on her account, and yet (you will laugh at me) I do often feel remorse when she is kind to me . . . But when I am not courting her . . . I am too gloomy and I keep thinking of suicide, for nothing amuses me.' This is a strange confession about sexual desire, which for men is so close to the desire for death itself. In any case Bathilde, as seen by Lucien, as seen by Stendhal, covers her body with a virginal little dress of white muslin, but cannot master the signs of sexual desire; trembling, the beating of her heart, fainting, blushing right up to her eyes (Stendhal notes in the margin: 'The womb, my dear'!), which are always flitting from one thing to another, unco-ordinated, condensed into the gaze, the most disembodied area of the body's features: 'How I believe you and I am yours', Madame de Chasteller's eyes seemed to say.

Antoine Compagnon (Le Deuil antérieur)

Why do they all think me so strong? Why won't they see that I can't go on? As soon as I contradict the image they have of me, they take flight. As soon as I falter, they all fall on me. Can't I be allowed to waver too, occasionally? (I'm not speaking only for Cléopâtre, nor for all the women to whom I have been intransi-gent; I'm speaking for the female body which gives such sensual delight when I love so much that I moan as if I were going to die).[4] [The body faltering, wavering, the female body falling apart; when it is alive, it is never seen as a whole.] I haven't a single photograph of Cléopâtre . . . All [those that I have loved] are strangely absent, for they are indescribable. A picture would be a contradiction. I examine the other's body in detail when I'm making love . . . The blazon is no longer fashionable.

The living female body is no more than a blazon, one part is as good as another, little bits that are nibbled, or places that bleed ('my penis ringed with your blood'), suffering in the body, 'drawn features, jerky movements, thinness'. But once it is dead, the female body – silent at last – can be seen: 'I took a photograph of my mother on her deathbed when I found myself alone with her for a moment.' Because 'you can do what you like with a dead woman.' A dead woman, a dead female body is finally univocal, unified, at last perceptible, unveiled, whole, a body which becomes a person? At the moment when it is deprived of language, because one no longer has to give it meaning or to listen to its meaning . . . In *Le Deuil antérieur* Compagnon is like both Stendhal and Prévost in this male obsession with decoding female bodies, constructing and destroying them, in order to reconstruct them in a different way, in their own way, according to their way of looking at them. So that women's bodies should not remain an 'area whose language is not understood, a non-place', women must speak of them themselves, they must break these old images, and they must find the words to mould men's bodies to which they thus give birth twice. Perhaps the time has come when the female body will take its place in women's speech. Will it be any different? We shall find out – or our daughters will.

PART II

In *Rome, le livre des foundations*[1] Michel Serres discusses the seminal role of violence, and in particular the importance of the body as object, the piece of body, in the establishment of a collective order. The body shared out is at the origin of the empire and of peace, as he illustrates with the example of Romulus put to death and torn apart by the crowd. It is striking how many myths, both ancient and modern, have as their starting-point a dismembered male body: Orpheus, Osiris, several heroes in the Scandinavian legends, Pentheus (in *The Bacchae*), Achilles (in *Penthesileia*), the father in Freud's *Totem und Tabu*. Apart from this last example, all the bodies were torn apart by women; but all these texts, as far as we know, were written by men – the first expression, perhaps, of 'male mourning'.

If a city is founded on the violence done to a sacred body, what about story-telling as a genre? We find two similar models: the Othello model (telling stories in order to seduce, in other words to gain access to another's body) and the Scheherazade model (telling stories to put off death, to save one's own body). Could this be one origin of the sexual distribution of roles in stories? It would doubtless be bold to make this claim categorically. We shall be rather more prudent, and try to define an area for enquiry as follows: the body is a new epistemological object, but while historians have equipped themselves with tools to study it, in the domain of literary analysis this object, with very few exceptions, has given rise to a vast number of stereotypes, which may be summarized by the equation 'body-text', without any critical reflection on the relationship between these two. In an attempt to shift this massive corpus of evidence, one might begin by examining the implications of 'sexualizing' writing. Isn't the only way to tackle the problem honestly to talk of the desire to write without ignoring the difference between the sexes, but admitting that it is a problem?

Before we turn to the representations of women in texts written by women – for texts written by men Elisabeth Ravoux-Rallo's analysis above is confirmed by any number of modern authors, as different as Pierre Drieu, Paul Nizan and Michel Leiris – it is necessary briefly to recall the relation of the woman writer to her text. Women today, at least in the West, have a theoretical access to all levels of the symbolic, which raises the problem of the choice of subject in their writing. Theoretical discussion of anything other than 'women's domains' is still relatively rare. A book such as Blandine Barret-Kriegel's *L'Etat et les esclaves*,[2] in which the author's sex does not seem pertinent, is the exception rather than the rule nowadays,[3] compared with a text like Noëlle Châtelet's *Le Corps à corps culinaire*:[4] men eat too, of course, but in this text sex is relevant (and is not restricted to the traditional division of roles). But whether or not a woman's body constitutes an obstacle in her own writing, theoretical discussion remains the prerogative of a restricted minority. In other types of text, women writers seem most often to restate accepted ideas to which male criticism traditionally restricts them: they restrict themselves to accounts of families (husbands, children, other partners). While the presence of the body in these texts may be a relatively new departure, sometimes successfully achieved,[5] as long as it remains simply a theme, it represents very little threat to the essential status quo.

In the case of most of these texts (many of which are written as analyses) the major referent remains the psychoanalytical horizon, even though the writer may express her mistrust of Freud's misogyny. Social, historical and political levels (men's domain) arouse suspicion, if not outright rejection. The woman writer takes as her starting-point her own personal oppression, but seems unable or unwilling to link it to any collective factor other than the feminine. Is the body (understood simply as belonging to one sex) operating here as a block, an obstacle? This is what Julia Kristeva suggests.[6] She feels that one cannot legitimately speak of women's writing, since this is only a way of masking the radical weakness that constitutes the being who is speaking (whether man or woman). It is certainly possible to identify a set of themes (in which the organic body, exhibited and no longer hidden, has a place, along with love and all the plans to 'reformulate' love), and also a style, but it would be misleading to conclude from this that there is a 'sexuality' of the written text. Hélène Cixous opposes this notion.[7] In her view, we must not erase the difference between men and women, but must work on it; we must not cut ourselves off from male writing, but deconstruct it, displace it, 'point out, denounce and undo the area of transgression', and perhaps also the culture, since 'culture is only constructed as a weapon against me.'

Of these two conceptions, the second, because of the active proposals it makes, seems at first sight the most dymanic. Nevertheless, it also supposes that the problem is resolved by the argument that the difference between the writing of the two sexes is based on the difference (biological, historical and cultural) between the sexes. One cannot deny the existence of a symbolism of sexual difference, but this symbolism is blurred (or over-determined) by what Kristeva calls 'self-enslaving sulkiness'. (We may add that the formula, 'culture is only constructed as a weapon against me', which has two registers, the theoretical and the emotional, is in fact contradicted by Cixous's method of writing, in which intertextual links with male writers (Kleist, Kafka, Rimbaud and others) abound.) We shall therefore devote our attention to the first conception, and go beyond its apparent negativeness. It has the advantage of envisaging writing as something radical, as a questioning of sense and of the speaker, and not as a regional practice. In the same way as writers in exile speak of separation which has nothing to do with geography (e.g. Hölderlin, Celan, Jabès), or the writers of the former colonies speak of breaking away, which is not simply related to history (e.g. Kateb, Farès), women's writing probably has to do with things other than sex – and the writing of the difference-ghetto, even, or indeed above all, by women, serves to clear out whatever different writing can shake loose by 'regionalizing' it.

'There is something feminine about writing... The writer is not necessarily "woman", but writing leads to becoming a minority'. Virginia Woolf goes further, and suggests that creativity perhaps only exists when one forgets that one is a woman: 'she writes like a woman who has forgotten she is a woman', and, in particular, 'that curious sexual nature which is only apparent when sex is no longer conscious of itself...'[9] Because they fail to try to imagine this limiting point, most considerations of so-called women's writings fall into typologies, which are nothing but inverted masculine categories – from which men suffer as much as women. Let us quickly give an example of this. A female author[10] will define women's writing by a series of criteria: genre ('the predilection of women for letters and diaries') or the rejection of genres (a taste for informal or unfinished texts, 'in the image of women's bodies', *sic*), both incidentally being described as failures (for example,

Woolf's *Orlando* is a badly written historical novel). When we move from genre to work on language, we learn that in women's writing language ceases to be functional and informative and becomes autonomous – which defines the poetic, and not the feminine style, unless we wish to reopen the file on Shakespeare's sister. The only solid element in this analysis lies in the identification of organic metaphors, dear to men when they were describing us (see the writing of Michelet, for example) and taken up again by women: writing as body fluid, milk, blood, placenta, saliva, lymph, amniotic liquid. In *Le Corps lesbien*, by Monique Wittig,[11] the metaphor is taken further and becomes no less than a function of the text: it is an attempt to solidify the female flow on the page with a break in the text every ten pages and a 'menstruation of words coagulated together'.

It would be absurd to deny all specificity, but what we need to do is to stop asserting its existence and seek to question it instead of immediately closing it off. In order to do this, we need a vast amount of research into a whole range of texts (and we should doubtless not limit ourselves to so-called literary texts). Let us briefly give two possible examples. In her novel *Retable/Rêverie*, Chantal Chawaf describes the sexual act in terms that clearly fit a masculine model (speaking of the woman as being kneaded like dough or clay). One thinks in particular of Michel Leiris, who, in *L'Afrique fantôme*, describes Emawayish, the Abyssinian woman, as having 'a crotch moist as the earth of which golems are made.'[12] But the difference is that in Chawaf's writing things are moving. The woman narrator of the text describes herself as dough etc., but she also describes her desire, her activity *vis à vis* the man's. One might put forward an initial hypothesis: it is not the representations that differentiate men's and women's texts, but the way in which they move.

We find a similar, though more complex, phenomenon in an older text, *Ces plaisirs qu'on appelle à la légère physiques* (also called *Le Pur et l'impur*), by Colette. The universe she evokes (opium smoking, a homosexual milieu, etc.) which makes one think of Drieu's *Gilles*, is apparently marked as deviant, atypical and full of neurosis (for example, the anorexic and suicidal behaviour of Renée Vivien). The female narrator, whom one of the protagonists refers to as a '*bonne petite bourgeoise*', is trying, in these anomic circles, to forget a classic broken heart, and one of the ways in which her devaluing of herself as an abandoned woman is conveyed is by the textual treatment of male homosexuality (the radical inadequacy of the female body poorly imitating the male being in the story of May and Jean; the horror of the transvestite, because the beauty of the male body is corrupted by female clothes in the story of 'Vercingetorix', and so on). All this seems to spring from female masochism (accidental or structural), in which the body of the female narrator, who is brooding over her abandonment, makes things worse because of her acceptance of the traditional view of men, of herself and of others.

This level of reading, while it is not incorrect, nevertheless proves to be inadequate when one tries to use it. Colette's text achieves, in a way many more modern authors might envy, a generalized circulation of bodies (of both sexes), a sort of deterritorialization, a 'rhizome', in which specifics are exchanged and finally end up floating and disintegrating altogether. It might be thought that the risk would be that this kind of writing might erase the difference. It seems to me, on the contrary, that it reduces or destabilizes it, which in my view is the aim we should set ourselves.

We have moved from the body torn to pieces by violence or the courtly blazon to the breaking down of categories. Texts like those of Chawaf or Colette, which work on representations of the male and the female, are equally far from the negation (which was predominant for a long time) and from the hysterical affirmation of frontiers (which tends to be the rule today, but fortunately no one really agrees on their exact position). Are we seeing in texts like these the emergence of a new type of subject, a new way of thinking of the self, or rather the bringing up to date of constants that up to now have been obscured? The (literary) history of female representations seems to be hesitating today between culturalism and the rejection of history. On this point, theoretical advance has not followed the forays achieved in practice. There are two possible types of reason for this. The invitation (whether 'feminine' or feminist) to an open, unstable and polysemic style of writing may very well harden into a rhetorical command if it mistakes the constraints that it too must obey. Moreover, the attempt at theorization in this area, which remains prisoner to a closed concept of the body (and a concept of the body as being closed), while affirming the presence of the body at a superficial level, has in fact allowed it to become what is not thought about in the text – in other words, its 'remains'.

NOTES TO PART I

1 My emphasis.
2 Antoinette Gordowski, *Hiéroglyphes du Corps, Chaussée d'Antin* 10/18, vol. 2, p. 139.
3 J. Proust, 'Le corps de Manon', *Littérature*, no. 4, 1971, pp. 5–21.

4   The male narrator is trying to imagine the thoughts of Cléopâtre, the woman
    he loved, who has killed herself, and also those of other women. It is in this
    sense that he is 'speaking for' them. (Translator's note.)

NOTES TO PART II

1   Michel Serres, *Rome, le livre des fondations* (Grasset, 1983).
2   Blandine Barret-Kriegel, *L'Etat et les esclaves* (Calmann-Lévy, 1979).
3   There are, particularly in university circles, a number of theoretical works
    produced by women in which the speaker is masked or neutralized. This
    situation is changing, but there is a risk that it will move in the opposite
    direction (so that the body becomes obligatory).
4   Noëlle Châtelet, *Le Corps à corps culinaire* (Seuil, 1979).
5   Annie Leclerc, *Au feu du jour, Parole de femmes*. Hélène Cixous, *Le Livre
    de Promethea*. Chantal Chawaf, *Retable/Rêverie*. Or the contributions of
    Christiane Verschambre, Catherine Weinzaepflen, Jeanne Hyvrard to the
    book *Manger* (Yellow Now, Chalon-sur-Saône, 1980). These texts all go
    beyond the thematic and succeed in mobilizing writing.
6   See in particular Kristeva, *Révolution du langage poétique* (Seuil, 1974)
    p. 614.
7   Cf. *Revue des Sciences Humaines*, no. 168, 1977-4.
8   Gilles Deleuze, 'Dialogues avec Claire Parnet', published in *Le Nouvel
    Observateur*, March 1983.
9   Virginia Woolf, *L'Art du roman* (Seuil, 1963).
10 Irma Garcia, *La Promenade femmilière* (Editions des Femmes, 1981).
11 M. Wittig, *Le Corps lesbien* (Editions de Minuit, 1973).
12 M. Leiris, *L'Afrique fantôme* (Gallimard, 1934).

7

The Difference Between the Sexes: History, Anthropology and the Greek City

Pauline Schmitt Pantel

'A new paradigm will only appear when we have begun to take seriously what women and men are in the societies we are studying. This does not mean that it is enough to complement studies on men with studies on women, but that we must refocus our attention on what is 'culturally constituted' rather than on what our traditional analytical categories dictate to us . . . We must place analysis of the relations between masculine and feminine domains on the same level of theoretical abstraction as kinship, politics or economics.'

Annette Weiner, 'Plus précieux que l'or'

'A history of women that consists of an account of their little-known victories or their all too well-known humiliations doesn't really interest me. I don't want another form of truncated memory and I don't want, on the pretext that the time has come, to set myself just to write the history of women . . . What is becoming not only fascinating, but urgent, is to take the historical field as a whole, without restricting it to the feminine domain, by examining it in a different way, by bringing out as often as possible the sexual division of roles. It is precisely with regard to this division of the masculine from the feminine that history has so wrongly been silent.'

Arlette Farge, 'L'Histoire ébruitée'

The two texts above, written by an American anthropologist and a French historian, echo the current transformation in the approach to women's studies. An examination of the lines each society draws between the masculine and feminine domains is a response to new methodological preoccupations and to the theoretical perspectives of contemporary feminism. This new direction of research has come about simultaneously in all the human sciences and has even reached the far-flung realms of classical studies. To place it better in context, I have chosen examples of its origins in two fields, anthropology[1] and history, both of which seem to me to raise equally pertinent questions in relation to the study of the Greek city.

Many women anthropologists have noted that the male approach to primitive societies has almost always led to a minimization of the role of women in the functioning of these societies. They have frequently been surprised when they have gone over the ground already covered by their male colleagues. Such was the case, for example, of Annette Weiner who, returning to one of the 'holy places' of the discipline, discovered and demonstrated the importance of the role of women in the matrilineal society of the Trobriand Islands (Papua New Guinea), by studying the distribution of bunches of banana leaves and grass skirts by women at funeral ceremonies.[2] Observation of these exchanges of objects belonging to women enabled the questioning of previously established 'facts' concerning on the one hand the possession of wealth, exchanges and reciprocity – phenomena hitherto considered solely a masculine preserve – and on the other, the symbolic values attached to kinship, death and the reproduction of the social body. For these bunches of leaves and skirts had both a material and a symbolic significance. They legitimized filiation, they served to measure the importance of relationships between individuals and families and they expressed the principles of decomposition and death. In short, in Trobriand society, the circulation of women's wealth ensured reproduction and the regeneration of the matrilineal system. This whole body of feminine values, recognized through the cultural symbols of wealth represented by the skirts and bunches of banana leaves, was taken over by men in marriage.

So while the starting-point was to take seriously the exchange of bunches of leaves between women, the end result was a thorough reconsideration of all the relationships between men and women, and even the revision of a number of the systems of explanation advanced in connection with Trobriand society.[3] The concern to achieve a better understanding of women's position in primitive or archaic societies, which we find in this book, as in other studies, is not aimed at rehabilitating women and substituting the description of omnipresent feminine power for that of masculine power. The aim is simply to analyse all the roles assumed by the two sexes in any society, to study the links between these roles in any particular culture and to draw from this all the necessary conclusions for an overall interpretation of the social system.

In history, studies on women have followed a similar pattern to that seen in anthropology. By treating society as a male collectivity, historians have always given history a sexual dimension, but it was one-sided because it was based on the rejection of women. The bisexual dimension of history is a recent discovery. The scientific, not to mention ideological, reasons for this long-term orientation of historiography have been analysed.[4] They have to do with the nature of the dominant movements in history (Positivism and Marxism) and with the areas favoured by historians for the last fifty years or so (historical demography and serial history). Anthropological history and the renewed interest in the history of mentalities have prepared the way for history to analyse the sexual roles. But it was the explosion of the feminist movement that provoked a great deal of questioning by creating a demand for militant research and writing. The writing of women's history was a contribution to the spread of awareness of the contemporary women's movement. It was a necessary first step, and today we can make a qualified assessment of it.

An examination of recent writing in the historical domain will enable us to point out the difficulties and ambiguities raised by the notion of 'women's history', a history that has been 'forced to take the place allowed it', a history of everyday behaviour, of everyday life (women's bodies, feminine roles, from that of mother to that of nurse and so on – in short, a history which remains 'in the direct line of reserved spaces'.[5] Many women historians have made the same point, and have simultaneously stressed the need to find a definition of the subject that allows us to give an account of the relations between the sexes in all areas of history.[6] This task, which goes beyond the question of specific gender, allows women's history to avoid the risk of the ghetto and of lonely isolation and brings out the subject on which history has wrongly kept silent, namely 'the sexual division of roles'.[7] If we go a step further, the study of the relations between masculine and feminine also enables us 'to transcribe the history of the tensions between masculine and feminine roles', the history of the debate, of the conflict even between women and men, 'a long-lasting conflict whose consequences historiography has always ignored, and which has been forgotten by historians when they worked on forms of social tension'.[8] What is needed here is thus the same as in anthropology: equal consideration of the masculine and the feminine in any historical analysis and an awareness that the relations between them may be important historical factors.

This new critical direction in anthropological and historical research presupposes the re-examination, and indeed the questioning, of a whole series of pre-established notions that have been, and are still, used in the study of the place and function of the sexes in society.

Anthropologists have launched two successive debates. The first concerned the validity of the association of woman with nature and of man with culture; the second, more recent debate concerns the assignation of woman to the domestic world, and of man to the public domain. I do not propose to go over the now well-known arguments in the debate, on natural woman and cultural man,[9] but I shall take the example of the system of opposition, so often used, between a feminine domestic world and a masculine public world. The categories 'domestic' (or 'private') and 'public' are now so familiar, so prevalent in our contemporary culture that we find it extremely difficult to question the validity of their application to other cultures. It is only very recently that the anthropologists have begun to be wary of this opposition between public and domestic which is 'too easy and too clear'.[10]

In order for the debate to be opened, it was necessary to take this model of opposition to its extreme. An article by Michelle Zimbalist Rosaldo generalizing the public/domestic opposition in order to make it the key to the difference between the roles and the status of the sexes in the whole of society,[11] provoked a very critical response and led scholars to reflect on the ethnocentric nature of these notions. They demanded a better definition of each of the terms of the opposition within each society studied. Field research was begun in order to verify and qualify the validity of these notions. It became clear that they were contingent. They were inapplicable in some societies and their importance varied greatly in different social groups, and even within the same group considered at different stages of its development. The use of the concepts 'domestic' and 'public' in a study of sexual roles aroused the same criticism as the use of the concepts 'nature' and 'culture'.[12] This opposition appears to be a new variant of the 'reduction of the categories of sex to their biological definition'.[13] Rosaldo herself questioned the heuristic value of the dichotomy she had contributed to, maintaining:

> By linking one sex to the existence of a domestic sphere, we tend, I fear, to think that we know the essence of what each sex has as its share, and to think first and foremost of the sexual hierarchies in terms of function and psychology, to minimize the sociological causes of inegality and power ... In any human group sex needs to be understood in political and social terms, not in relation to biological constraints, but in relation to local and specific forms of social relations and social inegalities.[14]

Moreover, in anthropology, the domestic-woman/public-man dichotomy has been taken as a description of social reality, whereas it is often an ideological construct which must be studied as such.[15] This series of points can have consequences for ancient history, as we shall see. Let us simply note, to conclude this section, that the feminist support that was given for a while to this opposition between domestic woman and public man enchanted many authors naturally inclined to find everywhere a division of roles that was all too familiar.[16]

One of the consequences of this system of opposition was to favour the study of the social role of woman. Many anthropological and historical works have analysed this role and stressed the existence of a certain power held by women, a social power.[17] But we must not confuse social power with public power. Women have always held a certain social power, but they have rarely had access to political power. Social power is no compensation for the absence of any other form of power. Describing it should not end with an attempt to analyse it, but should go on to question the consequences of the division of roles in all societies in political terms.[18]

Criticism of the domestic-woman/public-man model is only one example of the effort to rethink all the categories used in the study of sexual roles and to rid ourselves of the dualisms of the past which held that the relations between women and men were those of separation and opposition, always based, in the final analysis, on the respective nature of each sex.

At a time when the sexual division of society is on the way to becoming a favourite subject in anthropology and history – its success revealed by important seminars and increasing numbers of articles and works on the subject – we must recall the progress, sometimes too quickly forgotten, of a feminist line of thought that has refused to allow the study of the relations between the sexes to become a new denial of women's history (as were, for example, the studies of historical demography carried out on the family or certain studies of kinship) by following the familiar path of academic rehabilitation. In feminist studies, this research into sexual division has a history. Its genesis was the constitution of an anthropology and a history of women brought about by the contemporary feminist movement. As the example of the Trobriands reminds us, taking account of women in the analysis of any social system forces the anthropologist and the historian to arrive at radically different analyses of society. The search for sexual spaces and roles, the discovery of overlaps and interference between the masculine and the feminine, but also of the tensions and conflicts between men and women, leads to the clarification of a social and ideological structure, specific to each culture, which has allowed, and still allows the society to function. 'We must place the analysis of the relations between masculine and feminine domains on the same level of theoretical abstraction as kinship, politics or economics,' as Weiner writes;[19] 'It seems to me that a new orientation in feminist epistemology needs to be based on the conceptualization of the difference between the sexes' (G. Fraisse)[20]. These two quotations show how similar the thoughts of feminists in anthropology and history are today. I shall take up Fraisse's phrase, 'the difference between the sexes', in order to give an abstract name to this structure which must henceforth be taken into account in the analysis of any society. Can we begin this process with a study of the Greek city?

There is perhaps a certain paradox in seeking to find this type of social and ideological structure in the Greek city, so often defined as a 'men's club'. How have recent studies and current research led us to consider this problem?

Research into women in the Greek city has long been bogged down either in the search for origins or in the description and evaluation of the feminine condition in the famous debate as to whether the Greek woman was free or a recluse.[21] Today the theme of origins, and with it the myth of the matriarchy, are no longer objects of research or polemic. The time has come to write a historiography of the subject.[22] There also seems to be growing agreement as to the description of the status and condition of the Greek woman in the classical period, a description that attempts to avoid value judgements by basing itself on texts considered, perhaps wrongly, as documents that the historian can trust.[23] Research is now focused on the historical explanation of the status or statuses of Greek women[24] and on the study of the changes that affected them over a period of time and in different cities.[25] In the process, the different systems of explanation proposed reintroduce the question of the degree of freedom and power enjoyed by women, which is not far from the debate carried on at the start of the century, even though it has been resituated in historical evolution, in answer to radically different ideological preoccupations. A look at the vast body of work produced over the last ten years proves, to my mind, that any separate study of Greek women leads to a methodological impasse and that, in order to get round this, we must reopen the file on the masculine/feminine division in the city. In this way we can ask new questions and launch new enquiries, whose results will perhaps enable us to stop referring to the same models or projecting onto the ancient city our contemporary vision of the sharing of roles and the value judgements that go with this vision.

For example, we should study the distribution of masculine and feminine roles in a whole series of social practices, considered no longer from the solely feminine point of view or the solely masculine point of view, but from both at the same time, without prejudging the dividing lines. Any research into death, food, clothing, war, rituals, possessions, gifts, or production in general,[26] enables us to define more precisely the division of masculine and feminine space and roles and to qualify the traditional views, as current anthropological reflection invites us to do. A wider theme, that of the organization of space within the city and of its function, by considering a variety of social practices, enables us to form a clearer picture of the articulation of sexual roles and to put to the test our model, opposing a feminine domestic space by a masculine public space, a model so deeply rooted that we refer to anything that falls outside it as 'exceptions'.[27] A new reading of iconography is one of the fundamental bases for any enquiry of this kind. It is not enough to collect all the scenes on vases described as scenes from the *gynaeceum*. We must order and study the simultaneous and alternate presence of men and women at moments of great importance for the city, such as the departure or return of warriors, funerals, banquets and certain feasts.[28]

This study of the distribution of the masculine and the feminine in social practices is at the same time a study of the different ways of considering the division of the sexes in the city at a given moment. Pictures, texts, archaeological documents, each of these types of source has a language of its own, and none allows an immediate reading of reality, but each is to one degree or another a transposition of reality. We must not give preferential treatment to one type of source in order to draw up a reference model that would be the 'real' relationship between the masculine and the feminine in the Greek city (in the same way as we sometimes think these days that we can describe the 'real' condition of the Greek woman). But we must be able to compare the messages that all these sources give us without wishing at all cost to make them say the same thing.[29]

In this consideration of the division of the sexes that has begun, ana-lysis of forms of thought, of the world of the imagination, has been carried out earlier and has progressed further than analysis of forms of society and social practices. Indeed, although the study of the division of the sexes has not been the main theme of research, the analysis of myths, the first to be carried out, has not only shown the importance of the place occupied by women in the Greek view of the world, but also identified the dividing lines in different areas between the masculine and the feminine and, for example, defined the respective positions of men and women in relation to the fundamental city institutions such as sacrifice, marriage and initiation.[30] The question of the division between the sexes then found its way into very different studies of representations.

Research programmes on women, but also on subjects at first sight further removed from this area, came up against this question and had to take account of it. For example, analyses of classical Attic tragedy and comedy have shown very clearly how the division of the sexes and the representation of the feminine on stage helped to focus thought on problems that were fundamental for the city, such as political criticism, the limits of power, war and the reproduction of the civic body.[31] Thus this area of enquiry emerged in ancient history as much from recent methodological renewal in the study of the preoccupations of the ancients as from the problems encountered by research into the history of Greek women. The two aspects are inseparable, which may well be specific to ancient history.

More and more, and increasingly finer, analyses of the feminine in man, the masculine in woman, and the overlap and grey areas – never completely reciprocal[32] – between the two sexes, will enable us to describe the multiple facets of Greek discourse on the division between the sexes and to explain the role, the function, of this discourse in the city. Why this discourse? How was it used? What were its functions? These are so many questions we are not yet in a position to answer adequately, which is why I prefer to say that we are still at the stage of research rather than that of synthesis.

One of the pitfalls of this research is the over-systematic and insufficiently critical application of grids drawn up on the basis of examples taken from a historical context quite different from the Greek city. Several approaches have already been analysed and the contribution of their method evaluated. Helene Foley has convincingly shown the inefficacy of the psychological approach, at least as adopted by Philip Slater, studying the symbolic role of women in Greek literature.[33] The same author has criticized the sometimes too systematic use of certain oppositions in structural analysis – the dichotomies nature/culture and domestic/public do not always coincide with the separation of masculine and feminine roles as presented in classical Greek drama. On this point Foley takes up the anthropologists' analyses and backs up her argument with a number of articles recently written on tragedy.[34] The contribution and questions that psychoanalytical readings of the division of the sexes raise for the 'historian of the thoughts of another era' have been set out by Nicole Loraux, who has also criticized the use of the notion of misogyny to characterize masculine Greek thought. This notion acts as a screen and does not stand up to a precise analysis of exchanges between masculine and feminine.[35] In short, methodological caution is essential in an area in which the weight of ideologies, often undeclared, is particularly great.

Another pitfall lies in giving too much weight to a study of the unchanging aspects of the division of the sexes instead of charting its history. While it may be true that from Homer to Plutarch the division of the sexes was for the Greek man a way of defining himself, before the city and then within the framework of the city, and while we may also point to constant themes such as the blame reserved for the 'race of women',[36] this structure of the world of thought also has a history in the same way as any theory, any system of thought has. It is the result of given social, economic, political and intellectual conditions, and an anthropological interpretation must leave room for this historical dimension. Otherwise juggling with the masculine and the feminine might become a never-ending game. From Hesiod to Plato, Greek questions on the division of the sexes change direction although it is impossible to say that one period favoured this theme more than another. One of the directions current research needs to take is to write the history of this way of thinking about the Greek city and the Greek world, and, in this context, I should like to submit a hypothesis for discussion.

The starting-point is my observation that texts by Xenophon and Attic orators of the fourth century on the question of the division between the masculine and feminine have been wrongly used. Most modern authors consider these texts to be scrupulously accurate descriptions of the feminine condition and masculine activities and value them as concrete eyewitness reports.[37] They are not treated in the same way as Plato and Aristotle's theories, and no one questions their status as privileged historical documents.[38] But if we were to place these texts in the context of fourth-century writing as a whole, we would see that the different ways of looking at the division of the sexes constituted a coherent and articulate whole. If Xenophon's writings give the impression of real-life observations rather more than those of Plato or Aristotle, they are none the less attempts at ordering the world, and just as theoretical.

These writers were not the first Greeks to theorize on the division of roles between the sexes. In the archaic period we find similar attempts in Hesiod[39] or Semonides[40] which are just as systematic. But no one would claim that the behaviour of bees in Hesiod depicts the attitudes of the men and women of ancient Boeotia,[41] or that the sow described by Semonides is meant to be an accurate representation of the wives of the citizens of Amorgos.[42] The distribution of space and values between the masculine and feminine domains, presented by Hesiod and Semonides in their different, and indeed polemical, styles, is one way of reflecting on the division of the sexes (whether in positive, negative, complementary or opposing terms is of little importance here) and not a way of describing the reality of the sharing of tasks and roles between the two sexes. The writing of the fourth century is exactly the same: a theoretical essay on the same theme. The value of Xenophon's texts should not be that they allow us to write a chapter on the daily life of women in the *oikos* and men in the *agora*, as has been the case. Their value is rather that they allow us to see how the representation of the division between the sexes has changed in relation to earlier constructions.

The theories of the fourth century, and those of Xenophon in particular, in their efforts to classify and oppose masculine and feminine spaces and roles, do away with the idea that there exists a polarity within each of the sexes. The possible ambivalence of each sex, which is sometimes a source of ambiguity, was recognized by the archaic period in certain religious practices and in many social practices.[43] Fifth-century tragedy still reflected this. This aspect of Athenian tragedy has been strongly emphasized by research into the lack of clarity in the categorization of male and female characters in tragedy and comedy.[44] The ambivalence of the sexes was presented on the stage in Athens. It is important to remember that all the subjects in the Athenian theatre drew some of their significance from the fact that they were contributing to a current debate within the city,[45] so surely this is the case with the respective status of the masculine and feminine? The tragic questions and comic situations[46] constructed around this theme perhaps indicate that while the question of the division of roles, at least political roles, in the democratic city was already decided, and while the separation of the sexes was actual practice within the city, the public was still more sensitive to the polarity of the values that exist in men and women than to their radical opposition.

Greek thought on the problem of the division of the sexes evolved. The possibility of an ambivalence in each sex, recognized in the archaic period and perhaps in the fifth century, gave way to a definition of the masculine and feminine which allowed for no grey area between the sexes. The fourth century introduced a logic of separation and opposition in this area in place of a logic of interrelatedness, ambivalence and ambiguity. It placed the feminine and the masculine firmly within specific roles and justified this classification by referring to the notion of nature.[47] In this we can attribute to Xenophon and his contemporaries the merit, if not of inventing, then at least of theorizing, a distribution of sexual roles which is familiar to us today.

One hypothesis, among many, can take account of this change. At the end of the fifth and the beginning of the fourth centuries the private sphere, which had gradually emerged during the fifth century in opposition to the public domain, increased in importance to the point at which some of its values penetrated the political domain. It might be interesting to place the theorization of the radical distribution of masculine and feminine domains by authors of the fourth century within this general movement which was redefining the public and private domains and to interpret the words of Ischomachos as an attempt at a systematic clarification of sexual roles and the difference between the sexes, made necessary by the importance assumed by private values within the city. This example, which needs to be developed further, points to a whole new direction for research.

There are studies that attempt to take account at the same time of both the constant reflection on the division of the sexes, which seems to be one of the structures of Greek thought, and also of the respective social roles of the sexes. They consider all the evidence provided by the Greek city on the division of the sexes without attributing to one set of data more reality than to another. Such a wide analysis leads one, of course, to reflect on the relationship between the social world and the world of thought, a dimension that was not present in the studies that tackled either solely social problems or solely questions of the representation of reality. But the problem of this relationship cannot be formulated in the terms that are used – for example, in relation to Athenian women of the fifth century.[48] By opposing 'Medea' (taken here as the symbol of women's place in the world of representations) to a 'real' Athenian woman, who is in fact constructed on the model of the nameless gentlewoman whom Xenophon describes as having been Ischomachos' wife, we are not taking account of the fact that all literary texts put forward a point of view, whether they are texts from the fifth century, such as those declaimed in the theatre or from the fourth century, like those written by the theoreticians of Greek society.[49] We must be aware that we are comparing two works, one of which is no more real or concrete than the other, and we must remain critical of everything that we believe reveals the masculine and feminine conditions and roles. Only after this, and perhaps never, given the specific nature of our sources, shall we be able to examine from another angle the relationship between social practices, the representations of these practices and the whole area of the thoughts and preoccupations of the members of the society of the city.[50]

The distribution of roles, the division between the masculine and feminine: these are research goals that anthropological history and the history of the world of thought can set themselves without necessarily taking up a feminist position. We can perhaps take the first step in this direction by pointing out that what I have called 'the difference between the sexes' – in other words, both the existence of two different sexes and the relationship between them – is an essential dimension of Greek society and of the Greek way of seeing the world, whether one is describing the effects such a social and ideological structure has on all levels of civic life, or whether making a political interpretation within the framework of the city. This is possible, but only within certain limits – those imposed by the constraints specific to the history of the Greek city. Greek writing is entirely male[51] and we cannot return to Athens in the way that some researchers return to the Trobriands or to the villages of Burgundy. Some questions will never be answered: for example, did each sex have a different perception of the world?[52] What conflicts were there? What acts of violence between men and women? What forms, if any, did female resistance take? How far did women submit or consent to their condition? We are provided with a few furtive, fleeting glimpses of these aspects of the society by the plays (for example, the sexual strike carried out by women in Aristophanes) or by historical accounts (for example, the epidemics of suicide that afflicted a whole age group of the female population of one city and gave rise to the learned comments of the Hippocratic doctors). These very real limits are increased by the current lack of detailed studies, for the examination of the distribution and relations between the sexes is recent, and little research has yet been carried out along these lines. All this explains the caution with which any conclusions must be drawn. The time for great syntheses has not yet arrived. But if we have as our aim an overall consideration of the subject, this can help to give meaning to research projects that might otherwise appear dispersed and unrelated.

So it is no paradox to examine the Greek city, that 'men's club', in this light. By thinking of himself as a man in relation to women, as a free man in relation to a slave, as a Greek in relation to a barbarian, the Greek man forged his identity as a citizen. The difference between the sexes had a certain status in this society which was so preoccupied with the production of men: it was one of the aspects of *politeia*. To seek to make research into the division of the Greek city one link in a wider consideration of the difference between the sexes in history is to recognize how much this investigation owes to the questions of the present.

NOTES

This article owes a great deal to the group of women historians who, in Paris in 1982–3, attempted to draw up a critical appraisal of women's history. The first epigraph is taken from A. B. Weiner, 'Plus précieux que l'or: relations et échanges entre hommes et femmes dans les sociétés d'Océanie', *Annales ESC*, March-April 1982, p. 222, and the second from A. Farge's article in Pascale Werner, ed., *L'Histoire sans qualités, essais* (Galilée, Paris, 1979).

Pauline Schmitt Pantel

1 Several works set out the methodological advances of the last ten years in anthropology: E. Bourguignon, 'Introduction and Theoretical Considerations' in E. Bourguignon, ed., *A World of Women*, Anthropological Studies of Women in the Societies of the World (New York, 1980), pp. 1–13. C. P. MacCormack and M. Strathern, eds, *Nature, Culture and Gender* (Cambridge, 1980); N. Quinn, 'Anthropological Studies on Women's Status', *Annual Review of Anthropology* 1977, 6, pp. 181–225; R. Rapp, 'Anthropology-Review Essay', *Signs* 4, 1979, pp. 497–513; M. Z. Rosaldo, 'The Use and Abuse of Anthropology: Reflections on Feminism and Cross-cultural Understanding', *Signs* 5, 1980, pp. 389–417; S. W. Tiffany, 'Theoretical Issues in the Anthropological Study of Women' in *Women and Society: An Anthropological Reader* (Montreal, 1979), pp. 1–35; A. B. Weiner, *Women of Value, Men of Renown*, New Perspectives in Trobriand Exchange (Austin, Texas, and London, 1976) (French tr. *La Richesse des femmes ou comment l'esprit vient aux hommes, Iles Trobriand*, Paris, 1983), and Weiner, 'Plus précieux que l'or'; and *L'Homme* XIX, July–December 1979, on categories of sex in social anthropology.

2 Weiner, *Women of Value*. The expression 'one of the holy places' comes from Weiner, 'Plus précieux que l'or', p. 222.

3 Weiner, 'Plus précieux que l'or'.

4 See C. Dauphin, 'Femmes' in *La Nouvelle Histoire*, ed. J. Le Goff, R. Chartier and J. Revel (Paris, 1978); Werner, *L'Histoire sans qualités*; C. Fauré, 'L'Absente', *Les Temps Modernes*, Sept. 1980; Perrot, 'Sur l'histoire des femmes en France'.

5 Fauré, 'L'Absente'.

6 See n. 4 above. See also *Réflexions sur l'état des recherches féministes en France*, published CRIF, April 1982; *Bulletin* no. 1, Autumn 1982; and A. Farge, 'Dix ans d'Histoire des femmes en France', *Le Débat* 23, Jan. 1983, pp. 161–70.

7 Farge, 'L'histoire ébruitée'.

8 A. Farge, 'L'Homme et la femme, un conflit qui traverse la bibliothèque bleue', Introduction to selected texts, *Le Miroir des Femmes* (Paris, 1982), p. 25.

9 On this debate see N. C. Matthieu, 'Homme-culture et Femme-nature?', *L'Homme* XIII, 1973, pp. 101–13. Also E. Ardener, 'Belief and the Problem of Women', in J. S. Lafontaine, ed., *The Interpretation of Ritual: Essays in Honour of A. I. Richards* (London, 1972), pp. 135–58; S. B. Ortner, 'Is Female to Male as Nature is to Culture?' in M. Z. Rosaldo and L. Lamphere, eds, *Women, Culture and Society* (Stanford, Calif., 1974), pp. 67–87; and many other articles up to the collection published by MacCormack and Strathern, eds, *Nature, Culture and Gender*.

10 Bourguignon, 'Introduction and Theoretical Considerations', pp. 7–9. On the same subject, see Quinn, 'Anthropological Studies on Women's Status'; Rapp, 'Anthropology-Review Essay'; Tiffany, 'Theoretical Issues'.

11 Rosaldo in 'Woman, Culture and Society', pp. 17–42.

12 Matthieu, 'Homme-culture et Femme-nature?', p. 106: 'Thinking more or less implicitly of sex in terms of reified categories, closed on themselves, refusing to see that they are defined anew by each of a whole system of social relations, leads firstly to conferring on them general attributes and speaking of them in terms of content: models, representations, symbolism particular to each. Then it leads to defining these attributes and contents as different, indeed opposite, for each of the categories, with reification being based on the model of biological difference. Men and women will "naturally" have different behaviour, different ways of reasoning, different views of themselves and of the world.'

13 According to the expression used by Matthieu, ibid., p. 106.

14 Rosaldo, 'The Use and Abuse of Anthropology', p. 400. This article shows rare intellectual integrity by calling into question the first results of a research career that constantly grew in richness up until early 1982 when this young American anthropologist died in an accident.

15 Rapp, 'Anthropology-Review Essay', pp. 508–10. According to Rapp, the ideological model of the domestic–public opposition comes from the contradictions arising out of social relations, contradictions that may differ according to the society. For the author, who uses the example of Mediterranean societies, these contradictions appeared when the relationship between households and larger economic and political groups became one of conflict. She also develops this analysis in R. Rapp Reiter, ed., *Toward an Anthropology of Women* (New York and London, 1975), pp. 11–19 and 252–82.

16 In Greek history this was the case, for example, in J. P. Gould, 'Law, Custom and Myth: Aspects of the Social Position of Women in Classical Athens', *Journal of Hellenic Studies* 38–59, 1980, p. 48, n. 75, who quotes Rosaldo's thesis in 'Woman, Culture and Society' in support of this statement: 'In ancient Greece as in modern, the woman's orientation is domestic: *of the house* as against *of the road*.' (The author had not seen Rosaldo's article, 'The Use and Abuse of Anthropology'.)

17 For the anthropology of traditional rural societies see in particular Y. Verdier, *Façons de dire, façons de faire. La laveuse, la couturière, la cuisinière* (Paris, 1979), and M. Segalen, *Mari et femme dans la société paysanne* (Paris, 1980). In history, see the appraisals of Perrot, 'Sur l'histoire des femmes en France', and Farge, 'Dix ans d'histoire des femmes en France', and their articles in this book.

18 G. Fraisse, 'Les bavardes' in *L'Histoire sans qualités*.

19 Weiner, 'Plus précieux que l'or'.

20 G. Fraisse, 'Sur l'utilisation du concept de "rupture épistémologique" dans le champ des recherches féministes', *Contribution au Colloque de Toulouse: Femmes et Recherches*, Dec. 1982 (Toulouse, 1983).

21 For a summary of this debate, see S. Pomeroy, *Goddesses, Whores, Wives and Slaves, Women in Classical Antiquity* (New York, 1975). Among the most famous protagonists, Rostovtzeff linked women's restriction to the

house with the strengthening of democracy in Athens. Gomme, in a famous essay, held that Athenian women were as free as the 'ladies' of his time, while the partisans of a middle way, like Ehrenberg, stressed both the fact that women were shut away (a form of protection) and the undisputed sway they held over the domestic world. (See M. Rostovtzeff, *A History of the Ancient World*, I: *The Orient and Greece*, London, 1930; A. W. Gomme, *Essays in Greek History and Literature*, Oxford, 1937, pp. 89–115; V. Ehrenberg, *Aspects of the Ancient World*, New York, 1946, pp. 65–6).

22 See the excellent work of B. Wagner, *Zwischen Mythos und Realität, Die Frauen in der frühgriechischen Gesellschaft* (Frankfurt am Main, 1982), with a full bibliography of previous works on the subject.

23 Gould's article, 'Law, Custom and Myth', is the most recent synthesis on the subject. This article claims to be an attempt to show the real complexity of what men call briefly the social position of women (p. 58) and to explain the complementary nature of law, custom and myth in order to appreciate this complexity in its entirety. Gould calls for research to be carried out in various areas. In particular he paints a picture of the condition of women, in law and in customs, based on the texts of the fourth century, without any methodological precautions, because he does not perceive the ideological nature of these texts. This picture is still generally accepted today.

24 Pomeroy, *Goddesses, Whores, Wives and Slaves*, stresses the existence of different statuses according to social category.

25 M. B. Arthur, 'Review Essay-Classics', *Signs* 2, 1976, pp. 383–403, considers these studies. Arthur herself has written several articles studying the changes in the status of Greek women (Arthur, 'Early Greece: The Origins of the Western Attitude Towards Women', *Arethusa* 6, 1973, pp. 7–58; 'Liberated Women: The Classical Era', in R. Bridenthal and C. Koonz, eds, *Becoming Visible: Women in European History*, Boston, Mass., 1977, pp. 60–89; 'Cultural Strategies in Hesiod's Theogony: Law, Family, Society', *Arethusa* 15, 1982, pp. 63–82. On some of her hypotheses, see Appendix 1, to this chapter.

26 Most of these pieces of research are still being carried out. On death in this context, see N. Loraux, 'Le lit, la guerre', *L'Homme* XXI, 1981, pp. 37–67; and 'Le corps étranglé', *Actes du Colloque sur le Châtiment*, Rome, 1984. On gifts: Evelyne Scheid, 'Étude sur le vocabulaire du don et de l'échange chez Homère', thesis, University of Paris IV (1988). On women's economic position: D. M. Shaps, *Economic Rights of Women* (Edinburgh, 1978) does not share this view. See I. Savalli, *La donna nella società della Grecia antica* (Bologna, 1983, Pisa, 1979); and H. C. Van Bremen, 'Women and Wealth', in A. Cameron and A. Kuhrt eds, *Images of Women in Antiquity* (London, 1983). On grief: H. Monsacré, 'Les larmes des guerriers dans l'Iliade', *History and Anthropology* I, 1984, and *Les Larmes d'Achille: Le Héros, la femme et la souffrance dans la poésie d'Homère* (Paris, 1984).

27 'Exceptions': this is the term used, for the most part, to explain the presence of women in a space that is not theoretically their own. According to

this argument, they are slaves, foreigners, young girls, wives of poor citizens; the list goes on so long that it may well include most of the women of Athens!

28 F. Lissarrague tackles many of these points in *L'Autre Guerrier: archers, peltastes, cavaliers dans l'imagerie attique*. (La Découverte/Ecole Française de Rome, Paris, 1990). Bibliography and presentation of some of these themes in *Hommes, dieux et héros de la Grèce*, Exhibition catalogue of the Musée départemental des Antiquités de Rouen, 23 Oct. 1982–31 Jan. 1983, (Rouen, 1982), and P. Schmitt Pantel and F. Thelamon, 'Image et histoire: illustration ou document?', in F. Lissarrague and F. Thelamon, eds, *Image et céramique grecque* (Rouen, 1983).

29 See the comments on method in P. Vidal-Naquet, *Le Chasseur noir* (Paris, 1981), Avant-propos, pp. 11–20 (trans. *The Black Hunter*, Baltimore, 1986).

30 M. Detienne, *Les Jardins d'Adonis* (Paris, 1972; *The Gardens of Adonis*, trans. J. Lloyd, Sussex, 1977) and *Dionysos mis à mort* (Paris, 1977; *Dionysos Slain*, trans. M. and L. Muellner, Baltimore, 1979); J.-P. Vernant, *Mythe et pensée chez les grecs* (Paris, 1965, new edn 1971; trans. *Myth and Thought among the Greeks*, London, 1983) and *Mythe et société* (Paris, 1974; trans. *Myth and Society in Ancient Greece*, Atlantic Highlands, NJ, 1980; repr. New York, 1988); J.-P. Vernant and P. Vidal-Naquet, *Mythe et tragédie en Grèce ancienne* (Paris, 1972; trans. *Tragedy and Myth in Ancient Greece*, Atlantic Highlands, NJ, 1981); Vidal-Naquet, *Le Chasseur noir*.

31 The following are some of the many books and collections of articles: nos 6 (1973), 11 (1978) and 15 (1982) of the journal *Arethusa*; *Les Cahiers de Fontenay*, 17 (Dec. 1979): 'Aristophane, les femmes et la cité' (articles by M. Rosellini, 'Lysistrata: une mise en scène de la féminité'; S. Said, 'L'Assemblée des femmes: les femmes, l'économie et le politique'; D. Auger, 'Le théâtre d'Aristophane: le mythe, l'utopie et les femmes'; Preface by P. Vidal-Naquet 'Aristophane et la double illusion comique'); H. Foley, ed., *Reflections of Women in Antiquity* (New York, 1981); N. Loraux, *Les Enfants d'Athéna* (Paris, 1981); C. Segal, *Tragedy and Civilisation* (Cambridge, 1981); Cameron and Kuhrt, eds, *Images of Women in Antiquity*; *La Femme dans les sociétés antiques, Actes des colloques de Strasbourg* (May 1980 and March 1981) published by Edmond Lévy (Strasbourg, 1983); C. Mossé, *La Femme dans la Grèce antique* (Paris, 1983); S. Campese, P. Manuli and G. Sissa, *Madre materia, sociologia e biologia della donna greca* (Turin, 1983).

32 As shown by H. Foley, 'Reverse Similes and Sex Roles in the Odyssey', and C. Segal, 'The Menace of Dionysus: Sex Roles and Reversals in Euripides' *Bacchae*', *Arethusa* 11 (1978).

33 P. Slater, *The Glory of Hera: Greek Mythology and the Greek Family* (Boston, Mass., 1968). Criticism by H. Foley, 'Sex and State in Ancient Greece', *Diacritics* 5.4 (1975), pp. 31–6, and 'The Conception of Women in Athenian Drama', in Foley, ed., *Reflections of Women in Antiquity*.

34 Foley, ibid.

35 N. Loraux, 'Héraclès: le surmâle et le féminin', *Rev. Franc. Psychanal.* 4–1982, pp. 697–728. Criticism of the notion of misogyny: Loraux, *Les Enfants d'Athéna*, and 'Le lit, la guerre', p. 67.

36 Loraux, *Les Enfants d'Athéna*: 'Sur la race des femmes', and 'Le lit, la guerre', p. 66.

37 Gould, 'Law, Custom and Myth', reflects what is almost unanimously accepted.

38 On all these problems regarding the text in ancient history, see N. Loraux, 'Thucydide n'est pas un collègue', *Quaderni di storia* 12 (1980), pp. 57–81.

39 Hesiod, *Theogony*, and *Works and Days*.

40 Semonides of Amorgos 7, in M. L. West, ed., *Iambi et elegi graeci*, II (Oxford, 1972).

41 Hesiod, *Theogony* 594ff. See J.-P. Vernant's analysis, 'A la table des hommes' in M. Detienne et J.-P. Vernant, eds, *La Cuisine du sacrifice en pays grec* (Paris, 1979, trans. *The Cuisine of Sacrifice among the Greeks*, London, 1983), pp. 110ff.

42 See Loraux's article, 'Sur la race des femmes'.

43 Vernant, *Mythe et pensée chez les grecs*: 'Hestia-Hermès' (1971 edn, pp. 124–70). In this chapter the author studies the religious representations surrounding the couple Hestia–Hermes and many 'social practices that were in keeping with them', several of which embodied the masculine/feminine division. In these social practices the polarity between the two spaces (interior/exterior, mobile/immobile) is to be found within the definition of each sex. Woman can express at the same time permanence, stability and change; man expresses openness, external space and immobility, as shown, for example, by marriage. In this sense we can speak of ambivalence and polarity within the feminine and the masculine.

44 Foley, ed., *Reflections of Women in Antiquity*: 'The Conception of Women in Athenian Drama'; F. Zeitlin, 'Travesties of Gender and Genre in Aristophanes' *Thesmophoriazousae*' in Foley, ed., *Reflections of Women in Antiquity;* Loraux, 'Le lit, la guerre'.

45 Vernant and Vidal-Naquet, *Mythe et tragédie en Grèce ancienne*.

46 It must be remembered that the overlap between tragic and comic discourse and social practice within the city lies in the effect the text is expected to have, in the relationship between stage and audience, and in the degree to which the play's meaning is clear to the spectator.

47 See, e.g., Xenophon, *Oeconomicus* 7, 22, where Ischomachos, a family man in discussion with Socrates, says: 'Now, as these twofold functions of the interior and the exterior demand activity and care, the divinity has, in my view, suited the nature of woman to the tasks of the household and the nature of man to those of the external world.'

48 Emphasis is laid on the discrepancy between the 'real status' of Athenian women (a status that was in all respects inferior to that of men) and the dominant role played by female heroines on stage, and an attempt is made to take account of what appears to be 'a distortion': thus Foley, 'The

Conception of Women'. See my review of this book in *Annales, ESC 1982* (5–6), pp. 1014–19.

49 A problem already discussed above; and see Appendix 2 to this chapter.

50 On this area of study, see M. Augé, 'Présentation – Dieux et rituels ou rituels sans dieux' in J. Middleton, *Anthropologie religieuse, textes fondamentaux* (Paris, 1974), pp. 15–16.

51 With one exception, namely Sappho. This aspect – masculine literature – is often discussed. See most recently S. Humphreys, 'Women in Antiquity', in *The Family, Women and Death, Comparative Studies* (London, 1983), pp. 32–57.

52 A question studied, for example, by S. Rogers, 'Espace masculin et espace féminin: essai sur la différence', *Etudes rurales*, 74 (1979) pp. 87–110. Here again, studies of Sappho are the only ones that can raise this type of question in relation to Greece. I am thinking of the chapters by E. Stehle Stigers, 'Sappho's private world', and J. Winkler, 'Gardens of Nymphs: Public and Private in Sappho's Lyrics' in Foley, ed., *Reflections of Women in Antiquity*.

FURTHER READING

G. Arrigoni, ed., *Le donnne in Grecia*, (Laterza, Rome–Bari, 1985).

J. Blok and P. Mason, eds, *Sexual Asymmetry*, (Gieben, Amsterdam, 1987).

G. Duby and M. Perrot, eds, *A History of Women in the West* (Harvard University Press, Cambridge, Mass., 1992).

D. M. Halperin, J. J. Winkler and F. I. Zeitlin, eds, *Before Sexuality* (Princeton University Press, Princeton, 1990).

R. Just, *Women in Athenian Law and Life* (Routledge, London, 1989).

M. Lefkowitz, *Women in Greek Myth* (Duckworth, London, 1986).

N. Loraux, *Les Mères en deuil* (Seuil, Paris, 1990), and *Les Expériences de Tirésias*, (Gallimard, Paris, 1990).

M. Skinner, ed., 'Rescuing Creusa. New methodological approaches to women in antiquity', *Helios*, 13, 1987.

APPENDIX 1: WOMEN'S STATUS AND HISTORICAL EVOLUTION*

In her writings M. B. Arthur (see n. 25 above) attempts to explain the status of the Greek woman in the classical period in terms of historical evolution. Her theory is as follows. After a tribal society in which woman played a secondary role came a society based on the *oikos* in which the role of woman – as the producer of

* Reference is made here to M. I. Finley in *Revue internationale des droits de l'antiquité*, 3 (1955), 167–94; L. Gernet, 'Mariage de tyrans', *Anthropologie de la Grèce ancienne* (Paris, 1968); J.-P. Vernant in *Mythe et société en Grèce ancienne* (Paris, 1974), 57–81; E. Scheid in *Dialoghi di archeologia* i (1979), 60–73.

legitimate children and economic goods – became primordial. Thus the male reaction was to shut women away and keep wives more firmly subordinate to their husbands, in the interests of the *oikos* which were also those of the *polis*. This hypothesis is of course very different from the evolutionist view often expressed which gives more power and autonomy to women in the Homeric and archaic periods, because they were closer to the so-called matriarchal period than to the classical period. Indeed the two theories are practically diametrically opposed. But I find several elements of Arthur's hypothesis questionable.

In the first place, Arthur explains the small place occupied by women in aristocratic or 'feudal' societies by the fact that aristocratic solidarity was based on a system of exchanges between men. Women were certainly the object of exchanges, but stayed outside the social group and were not vital to its survival. This seems to me to contradict all the analyses carried out by anthropologists of the position occupied by women in societies in which matrimonial exchanges welded social links between families, and, in relation to Greece, this seems to me to contradict various authors' analyses of Homeric marriage (e.g. those of M. Finley and E. Scheid) or archaic aristocratic marriage (e.g. those of L. Gernet and J.-P. Vernant). Aristocratic solidarity is maintained by links between men certainly, but women, and all that they possess in the way of wealth, are at the centre of these links. So I would not thus minimize the position of women in the aristocratic groups of archaic societies.

The emergence of the 'small household' as a productive and civic unit, in Arthur's view, gave women a new importance. From this point on they were necessary to the survival of the *oikos* by producing sons and supervising the daily activities. The nuclear family became a political and economic reality. The laws of the new democracy imposed restrictions on women's freedom in order the better to ensure their subordination to the interests of the city. One might object that it is not clear whether, at the start of the classical period, the *oikos* meant a much more restricted unit than before. And whatever the definition of the *oikos*, we are reduced to conjectures when it comes to considering the importance of women as an economic element. It is necessary to give a precise description of the feminine tasks that were essential to the survival of the family and to show that their importance was different in aristocratic and democratic society. On the other hand, it is quite fair to stress that the role of the wife who would produce citizens was taken very seriously in the democratic city. As has already been shown, the procreation of citizens was probably the only civic task that the city attributed to women.

This evolving picture rests on an a priori which has become a type of explanation in history. The move from wider family to nuclear family is a historical moment that historians find in each chronological period in which they specialize. In relation to the Greek city, and more specifically in relation to the explanation of women's status, this scenario does not seem to me to be adequate. The shift from tribal kinship to the *oikos*, from the wider family to the nuclear family, is not enough to give women a new status and strengthen the mechanism for keeping them under surveillance. I would be more inclined to stress the novelty introduced by the much stricter political definition of citizenship in a democracy, and if there is a change, to see this in the light of the emergence of the category of the politics of democracy. But above all, I believe that any attempt to explain women's status in terms of historical evolution is premature. We must first question the description of the division between the masculine and the feminine which is presupposed in all these studies.

APPENDIX 2: DIVISION OF THE SEXES, HISTORY OF CUSTOMS AND HISTORICAL CRITICISM*

The degree of criticism to which texts are submitted is not the same for all themes studied, and in certain areas historical criticism is hardly applied at all. No historian of ancient Greece would accept a statement about a political or institutional event in an ancient text without enquiry or discussion allowing the construction of the historical fact. The date of the end of a war, the content of a decree, the chronology of public office, are the object of assaults of philological and historical erudition. The division between the sexes, and everything else that comes under the 'history of behaviour', is approached in a much less critical manner. The same author, Xenophon, may be used in two radically different ways as a historical source – subjected to criticism of his texts relating to economic and political history, believed without the least hesitation when he deals, for example, with the question of sexual roles and the relationship between men and women. Ischomachos' speech to Socrates in the *Oeconomicus* on the division of roles in the Athenian *oikos* has given rise to many chapters on daily life in which the woman remains in the *gynaeceum* while the man is at the *agora*. Is this because the subject is the division between men and women? No. One could make similar observations in relation to other themes. In Greek history the positivist spirit which, as Le Goff says, 'expresses the naïve belief in the objectivity of so-called historical facts which can be gathered by reducing history to the faithfulness of a neutral recorder, and its desire to intervene in the area of history which we are simply describing' reigns without challenge in the history of behaviour, of daily life, the refuges of unchanging history. This also explains how fourth-century texts can be used without any caution to describe the condition of the Greek women of all times, although this penchant in studies of Greek history has often been denounced in other domains, as, e.g. Claude Mossé does with regard to Solon.

We need therefore to be critical in two areas when drawing up any history of Greek customs: (a) The study of the type of documents used: some texts (treatises, histories, apologetics) escape the criticism applied to other forms of literature (e.g. by Loraux on Thucydides); (b) The study of themes that do not arouse the historian's inquisitive procedures because they do not appear to concern the mainstream of historical knowledge.

* Reference is made here to J. Le Goff's 'Présentation' in C. V. Langlois, *La Vie en France au Moyen-Age* (1981), p. viii; C. Mossé in *Annales ESC* (May–June 1979), 425–37; N. Loraux, 'Thucydide n'est pas un collègue'.

8

Masculine and Feminine:
The Historiographical Use of
Sexual Roles

Jacques Revel

In this chapter I propose to consider the use of a set of categories –
sexual roles – in historical analysis on the basis of a small number of
written works. More precisely, I should like to try to define the historiographical circumstances in which historians of ancient societies began to
use these categories or divisions; the manner in which these historiographical circumstances left their mark on the formulation of questions
about the subject and the elements of reply that have been put forward
up to now. Finally, I should like to consider the relevance of these
categories, and, without attempting an appraisal, to show from a
few examples how their very use – in other words the work of historians – has raised new questions.

I am aware, in doing this, that I am venturing onto very uncertain
ground. First, because the works to which I refer, which serve as a basis
for this argument, are almost all very recent – for the most part, less
than ten years old. So I do not have the benefit of distance in time to
help me to appreciate the historiographical evolution I am attempting to
study. Nor do I have the benefit of serenity; the re-emergence of sexual
roles as an object of historical analysis has not been simply an academic
innovation, the annexation of an additional province to the already
enormous territory of professional historians. Rarely has the invention
of a theme been so clearly associated with the ideological changes and
clashes of contemporary society – at least in the case of European
societies. I shall return in a moment to this aspect. For the present, let
us remember that if sexual roles are a fashionable subject, the various
approaches that have been used in considering them are also very visibly
marked by the current period.

It may seem paradoxical to state from the start that, until very recently, historians appeared to be unaware that the societies they were studying were divided into sexes, in the same way as they were divided, in the historians' view, into classes, age groups, professions, nations, ethnic groups, etc. Yet one only has to open any of the great French works of social history to see that the social individual studied is not in fact endowed with any sex: one often feels that this individual is male, but I think that he is more generally *neuter*.

It may be objected that the spectacular development of research in historical demography has radically changed this picture, since demography cannot avoid a problem that is at the heart of its preoccupations. But when dealing with the distribution of ages at marriage according to sex, different mortality rates for men and women, or even fertility, the demographer is for the most part laying greater emphasis on the biological than the social. The reduction of categories of sex to their biological determination is no doubt the single factor that has, more than any other, prevented us from thinking about their existence and social functions. Only when demographical analysis opens its eyes to social history or anthropology – when it rather belatedly becomes interested in matrimonial strategies, for example – does it recognize the sexual division as an influential social fact. Even then, for obvious reasons, it does so essentially in the context of the family, in other words the 'social grouping that expresses best of all the institutionalization of the biological'.[1] It would be ridiculous to try to minimize the role of the family as a social expression, particularly when we are talking about western societies. But it would be dangerous to forget that there are other areas in which sexual roles are expressed, in terms that can be profoundly different and are in any case revealing. On this last point the approach of historians has changed considerably over the last few years.

In France, and no doubt more widely in the rest of Europe, the dominant form of social history since the 1950s has been serial, quantified history, reflecting on the largest possible statistical aggregates permitted by the sources. This approach, which in France could be simply identified by reference to the name, work and school of Ernest Labrousse, remains the most widespread even today. And yet a certain number of factors would seem to indicate that it is not the only possible approach and that, on its own, it no longer satisfies historians' demands. The spectacular success of case studies in the United States or in Britain and the argument in favour of micro-history in Italy,[2] together show that development is taking place. This development can, in the first analysis, be characterized by a change in the scale of observation. In place of the macro-social objects favoured up to now, the new trend is to focus on micro-social objects (a community, a group of families, an individual life), arguing that magnification of our findings will allow us to see realities (and in amongst these realities, systems of relations) that have so far not been grasped. Let us not enter further into a debate that might take us too far. But let us retain its explicit preoccupation, which is to bring to light other forms of the social. More widely, one might reasonably form the hypothesis that the same preoccupation underlies the increasingly close rapprochement between anthropology and history. The historian does not borrow only concepts, references and techniques from the anthropologist, but also suggestions about a terrain that most often falls outside the frameworks within which we are used to thinking of the societies we call historical. And in this area the sexual division is present at all levels of society, even if it assumes very diverse forms. There is thus no way of avoiding it. And without doubt it is as a result of the contact with the work of anthropologists that this particular social relation, which confronts the two sexes within each group, has become the object of history.

But there is more to it than this. At the same time – in France, broadly since the end of the 1960s – a new sensitivity has arisen, which goes far beyond the academic domain, but whose repercussions have not failed to influence the work of university historians. I am referring, of course, to the feminist explosion since 1968. Alongside much militant work, it has been the starting-point for militant scientific research work, or simply scientific work, and for a whole series of unpublished research projects that have had a profound influence on our perception of social history.

This influence cannot be considered simply anecdotal; first because its effects have been very strongly felt in the very treatment of sexual roles (and because it explains much of the resistance encountered); also because it has brought about a striking dissymmetry. All the work has been done in the direction of the feminine pole, while the masculine pole has seemed to fall into the oblivion of lost causes. It might be objected that this is a fair turn of events after women's long absence from historiography, if not history. Nevertheless I think that the dissymmetry that is so apparent today may explain a certain number of recent failures, and may help us to understand why sexual roles remain so difficult to think of as an active historical category. It may be useful to dwell on this for a moment.

Let us recapitulate. For some years, fresh attention has been paid to the study of sexual roles, and it has without exception emphasized feminine roles. This questioning has fallen within the twin frameworks of feminist claims (which are as diverse in their modalities as in their ends) and the historian's evident fascination with the very long span of 'traditional' societies before the industrial revolution. In the area that interests us, these two frameworks overlap to some degree. At the point where they overlap, we find the novel figure of what we might call 'traditional woman'. It was as if the history of this new object that was being attempted at the same time filled a gap and answered the needs of nostalgia; as if within the 'world we have lost' we were trying to find a world even more lost.

But of course such a rediscovery raises more questions than it provides answers. In an extraordinarily voluntarist way, a historical object was produced. My hypothesis is that the conditions of its production determine the rules that govern its functioning and its possible uses.

As is the case with many other minorities (if I may dare to use that term) in the twentieth century, women's history has had as its primary function to restore a memory to those women (and sometimes men) who felt themselves dispossessed of memory. The subject matter of history has therefore been examined in order to find women's place in it. But, quite naturally, this has been done on the basis of the promptings of the immediate present, and first and foremost the aims and objectives of the feminist struggle. In western countries, the Women's Liberation Movement has, over the last twenty years, started with the affirmation of feminine specificity, and the repossession by women of their own bodies. These militant priorities have, by and large, defined the topics that were to occupy the women historians of the 1970s. It is no small paradox that these topics are the very ones that, from the classical age up to the nineteenth century, inspired debates on 'feminine nature'.[3]

It is remarkable that the examination of feminine roles in history has very often begun with an examination of the body and its functions, as if, in keeping with the oldest notions of the clerics, moralists or doctors, feminine identity was primarily the product of a particular physiology. The themes identified in research seem to me very revealing in this respect: sexuality, procreation, childbirth, breastfeeding, women's illnesses and care of the body. Let us be clear: this list of themes in no way prejudges the investigations or methods of treatment that they have in fact received. In many cases, the work carried out has been able to give us entirely fresh perspectives, on childbirth, for example, or on female ailments and the woman–doctor relationship.[4] Nevertheless these themes, although arising out of a spontaneous sensitivity and the desire to break with the traditional social perception of women, do suggest an image of them that remains very close to the old stereotypes.

I find confirmation of this in a second group of studies, which are concerned not with the body, but with women's social functions.

Thanks to these pieces of work, we are beginning to have at our disposal a certain amount of data and hypotheses on the place and the role of women chiefly in the eighteenth and nineteenth centuries. But what place, and what roles? We find nursemaids,[5] midwives,[6] housemaids,[7] witches (here the bibliography is enormous in all languages), prostitutes,[8] middle-class women, nuns, washerwomen, seamstresses, and, most recently, mothers.[9] From this very incomplete list we may reasonably conclude that it is after all natural that women should have fulfilled feminine functions, and that historians should have looked for them in history in the place where they were. Obvious as this reply may be, it does not seem to me to be quite acceptable: for it is surely clear that by wishing to define the specificity of feminine roles by means of a catalogue of specifically feminine activities one in fact runs the risk of becoming trapped in a vicious circle. Other lines of research would, I think, suggest similar findings.

For these approaches seem to me to pose a twofold problem. On the one hand, they presuppose a definition of feminine identity, whereas it is the study of feminine social roles in history that should allow us to construct this identity. We cannot be content to consider as feminine the sum of the traces left by women, and the sum of the points at which they are mentioned. On the other hand, these works seem to me to have in common the fact that they fall within a 'feminine domain', as if this could and should be constructed outside society, like a closed world or a reserve (even if it is fair to point out that these are the terms in which the feminine condition has existed historically, at least in western societies). Although today historiography is written, for the most part, by women (or, perhaps, because it is written by women), it seems in its way to repeat the constraints and divisions within which women's history – by which I mean real history – has for so long been trapped.

One might then imagine approaches other than the one that seeks to find in the past the convictions of the present. For example, an approach that might seek to identify different forms of masculine and feminine roles in historical experience and might set itself the task of describing the relations between them.

Opening the presentation of an excellent special edition of *Mouvement social* devoted to 'Women's work',[10] Michelle Perrot asked ironically: 'Must we make the point that women have always worked?' Of course women's work is work, and it is useful to remind oneself of this after 150 years at least during which 'productive' work has been valued almost exclusively – 'productive work' meaning paid work outside the house, which was, of course, for the most part men's work. But at the same time, in order to give women's work the status of work like that of any other, we must not begin by describing it as exceptional or different from all others. On the contrary, we must compare it with all forms of women's work, and also with men's work, so as to understand how these types form a hierarchy and are related to one another, and so as to recognize the conflicts, similarities and interdependence of the different types of work. Further, if we want to define the problem more broadly, it may be desirable that the history of women's roles should cease to be written as a separate history, precisely in order that it may find a status and a place in an overall social history in which feminine practices (like masculine practices) find their true meaning. I shall give as examples here two illustrations borrowed from two recent books, which are incidentally very different in their approach, and in the proposals they put forward.

The first is Martine Segalen's study, *Mari et femme dans la société paysanne*.[11] This ethnographic research is based on a large corpus of 'popular' French traditions collected by folklorists, then by ethnologists, for the most part since the middle of the nineteenth century. One of its chief merits is that it compares feminine and masculine functions, but also feminine and masculine roles across a very varied range of social relations, from betrothal or marriage rituals to the sexual distribution of tasks within the framework of a peasant family. This wider approach has the advantage of showing how far the distorting framework of the nineteenth-century middle-class nuclear family, often implicitly super-imposed by observers, has affected what we have been able to understand about relations between husband and wife in former peasant society, and has been the, often fallacious, basis for a good many of what we hold as certainties today.

Let us take as an example the problem of the distribution of work, approached here in the context of the peasant household. The premiss is often, even nowadays, that marriage introduced the spouses to an immovable division of tasks, whereby the woman held responsibility for the management of the domestic sphere (children, housework, kitchen, water, farmyard, garden), while the man controlled all work in the fields and the farm livestock, and held sole responsibility for the family group's relations with the outside world. We cannot reject the idea that there was a distribution of tasks, for the sources attest this so often. But must we ignore the whole range of activities in which husband and wife were interchangeable, for example in work, where if it was urgent or appropriate, the wife might be required to help outside the house, and the husband might collaborate within the domestic sphere? Is it always legitimate to analyse at the level of the couple (in other words, a social unit not always necessarily relevant in the functioning of the traditional

rural family) the distribution of work between men and women? It is
rather as if the folklorists and ethnologists has wished at all cost to find
in the object of their study the rules they were used to in daily life,
which, more deeply, obeyed the dominant ideological models of the
society in which they lived. The forced opposition between domestic
work and work outside the house is a good example of this. It was in the
industrial and middle-class society of the nineteenth century that the
'domestic' sphere and the tasks associated with it became so many
proofs of the minor importance of the married or dependent woman. In
the peasant family, the hierarchical relationship between masculine and
feminine clearly existed, and was supported by a very great deal of
symbolism in marriage rituals, as in the control that the group thereafter
exercised over the functioning of the couple. But it was doubtless not on
the level of the work process that it was the most decisive, and in
particular not in the exclusive distribution of tasks.

The advantage of a 'vertical' analysis of relations between masculine
and feminine, like that proposed by Segalen, is that it reveals behind the
apparent simplicity of oppositions, and the very conformity of the way
in which the old peasant society spoke of itself, a whole series of shifts,
overlaps and compensations that indicate a redefinition of statuses,
functions and roles.

Yvonne Verdier chose a 'horizontal' analysis when she set out to study
collective feminine culture in a little Burgundy village in the twentieth
century. These women's *Façons de dire, façons de faire*[12] are pieces of a
symbolic code which links feminine customs and gives them their true
meaning. By following the analysis of three central feminine functions
in community life, the ethnologist restores not only the coherence of
the feminine sphere within village society, not only the distribution of
specific traits between men and women, but, more decisively, the way in
which feminine culture – feminine reality – fits into the collective existence. The woman who washes newborn babies and the dead presides
over human beings' passage at the two extremities of life. The seamstress manages all relations with the outside world and initiates adoles-
cent girls. The cook holds sway over alliances and guarantees social
mixing within the group. All three enable customs to be maintained by
doing what is necessary in order to ensure the cohesion and reproduction of the group, by symbolically restating the rule on each major
occasion, by watching over 'the nodes through which destinies pass'.

The unity of feminine culture does not serve here to prove the existence of another culture which is at the same time a counter-culture,
alternative to the dominant masculine culture. Instead, it shows that
across the specificity of women's actions and speech, women are present

everywhere and necessary where the group defines itself and symbolically plays out its existence. Of course the women are giving their version
of the social meaning, but it is a version that affects the community as
a whole. From the biological rhythms of women's bodies to the techniques for which they are responsible, from the spheres they appropriate
for themselves to the meanings they alone know how to give and understand, they express one of the systems of intelligibility that the group
needs in order to perpetuate itself, and they express it for every member
of the group. The feminine role here is no longer simply half of an
irremediably divided social force. Rather, through its embodiment of a
savoir-faire which is also a *savoir-être*, it testifies to the existence of a
wider order and the possibility of a collective hold over this order.

But it is the system of symbolic oppositions that has most readily
captured the attention of researchers, in that it has allowed them to
make clearer comparisons between masculine and feminine. An attempt
has been made, in particular, to understand the reciprocal relations
across a whole series of mechanisms that represent their inversion,
through a more or less thorough exchange of the symbolic properties of
sexual identities. For a long time, anthropological literature has made
us familiar with such symbolic mechanisms. At certain moments in the
existence of the group, either at particular times of year, or on occasions
considered to be exceptional or decisive for the future of the community, the exchange of sexual roles becomes a means of representing publicly the way in which the society functions, of expressing the
collective truth, but in reverse. In most of the cases studied, these rituals
have a protective or propitiatory function, whether or not they are
associated with rites of passage (at the moment of birth, adolescence or
death). By simulating the overthrow, item by item, of the social order,
by questioning the fundamental distinctions on which it is based (and
sexual identity is obviously one of these), by portraying its own death in
the form of a representation – and sometimes as a game – the group in
fact ensures its continuation. In a time of greater fragility, it supports the
established order by the very device of appearing to subvert it radically.

Here too, the anthropologists' lesson happens to coincide with
social-libertarian imagination, present throughout the western countries
since the end of the 1960s (and the events of May 1968 in France
provided a good illustration of this). Taking up some of the elements
of this movement, women's struggles for emancipation have often been
perceived by them (and, perhaps, even more by men) as the world
turned upside down (or indeed finally put to rights). Here too, attempts
have been made to find comparable situations in the past.

There is no shortage of these. But what do they tell us? Do they suggest a possible way of organizing sexual roles, a redefinition of status and power? Or do they simply, despite changing the signs, repeat an unchanging order of things? We cannot be sure of the answer.

If we confine ourselves ourselves to western tradition, woman has, at least since Greek antiquity, been at the same time a figure of disorder and of submission; or, more accurately, it has been important that she should be submissive because she has represented an extraordinary power for social disorder. On this point theologians, moralists, pedagogues, politicians and doctors have been in agreement: hence the importance of procedures for social control that refer specifically to women. The development of the nuclear family, characterized by the strengthening of paternal power, from the end of the Middle Ages on, is one of the most recent, but also most revealing, illustrations of this.[13] Tighter controls over women within the couple have been clearly associated with the aim to make society work better, as is recalled explicitly in the preamble to the order which, in the sixteenth century, regulated the new forms of paternal power: 'marriages are the seminaries of the State'.

But the figure of woman was not drained of its power by being forced into submission, nor were the terrors it inspired appeased. The image of the wild woman, of the still untamed shrew, haunts the European imagination at the end of the Middle Ages and the start of the modern age. Brueghel's *Dulle Griet* symbolizes this irruption of female violence in the collective conscience of a Europe in turmoil in the sixteenth century. It was as if the political, religious and cultural upheavals of the old world had found a favoured means of expression in this notion of a redistribution of sexual status and roles. Well before Brueghel, Erasmus had put into the mouth of a female character of the *Colloquies* (1524) an erudite woman exasperated by the derisive self-importance of a stupid clerk, this calm and devastating comment: 'If you continue as you have begun, the geese will preach rather than suffer any longer the mute pastors that you are. *You see clearly now that everything is upside down on the world's stage. You must take off your masks or else everyone will say his piece.*'[14]

More regularly, complex rituals come to represent, in the old society, the exchange of roles and statuses, principally in connection with the Carnival cycle. Do they represent a true questioning of the social order, and does the Carnival game change in any meaningful way the distribution of positions and roles, which might be redefined at this time? Among the authors who have carried out historical studies of this festive culture, Mikhaïl Bakhtine and Natalie Zemon Davis[15] think, in rather different terms, that they can reply in the affirmative. The first sees in

Carnival culture an explicit questioning of the order and representations authorized by the people (and thus also by the subgroup of the people that women constitute). The culture of the 'material and bodily lower orders' uses the values of derision which, periodically, recall the precariousness of legitimate values and powers. The second, while noting the limits of these models of inversion, considers that they could, by the sole device of representation, offer women the opportunity and means to become aware in a tentative, but relentless, fashion: So it would be understandable that through these ritual games of inversion, the image of the enraged woman should have remained, throughout the modern age, one of the incarnations of social protest.

This is not entirely convincing. Carnival does indeed correspond very closely to the complex rituals described by anthropologists. It is the limited, predetermined time during which a group mounts the spectacle of its own death in order to be reborn stronger – after the putting to death of the Carnival King. As for the exchange of sexual roles, it is remarkable how far the representations are codified and controlled. Whereas literary sources offer the elite several versions of women dressed up as men, while iconography does not hesitate to show daring representations of this in which women scandalously combine virile attributes and the physical properties of their sex, the public rituals allowed to the masses in general only tolerate men dressing up as women. This frequently noted dissymmetry raises the problem of what is acceptable in the way of social protest, even if it is protest in the form of make-believe. It recalls the fundamental link between sexual symbolism and the structures of order and hierarchy in which societies organize themselves, and still more, think of themselves.

I find further confirmation of this in the analysis of a series of pictures which were common in Europe between the sixteenth and nineteenth centuries, and which illustrate, in a generally popular style, the motif of the world turned upside down. In these engravings, the reversal of sexual roles holds a relatively important place. The husband spins at the spinning wheel, while the wife, pipe between her lips, sets off to the hunt or to war; the wife scolds her spouse; the trousers, the symbol of authority in the family, are exchanged for a dress. Is this popular protest, or, at least, an image of protest likely to be received and understood by the masses? The answer is doubtless yes, at the level of dramatic expression. But we can be less sure of the answer if we consider that, on the same stage, sexual inversion is portrayed alongside natural inversions (the sea changing places with the sky; the sun shining at night; things being shown upside down; lambs chasing wolves). By these means, the images shown tend to portray as natural the relations governing sexual status and roles, suggesting that any change in sexual values (and indeed more generally, in social values) is as unthinkable as a reversal of the properties of the physical world. The world in reverse is deliberately situated in Utopia; and it is no mere chance that it is closely associated, even in the printers' workshops, with the figures of the land of plenty.

From the imaginary game of the reversal of sexual roles I shall draw one last example from the work of the Italian historian, Roberto Zapperi, devoted to a study of the motif of the pregnant man.[16] This theme is found in very ancient works, and has at least two traditions. The first, rooted in the text of Genesis, is the origin of a vast iconographic production throughout the West from the eleventh and twelfth centuries onwards. It presents the image of Eve being born from Adam's side in the form of childbirth. Occurring at the same time as a new theology of marriage, recently studied by Georges Duby, it reminds us that Adam appears before Eve in the creation, that Eve is therefore subordinate to him (since she who is engendered comes from him who engenders), and attributes to a man the primary social power of women, that of giving life.

The second tradition is much more ambiguous. From the ninth century to at least the nineteenth century, fables, stories and also the oral tradition carry accounts, usually intended to make one laugh, and always constructed on more or less the same model. A man, credulous and/or stupid, convinces himself (or allows himself to be convinced) that he is pregnant. This unusual situation, which is impossible to handle, exposes him to ridicule and social misery; the hero will only extricate himself from his predicament, most often in burlesque way, after going through all the stages of anguish and humiliation.

Zapperi is less concerned to retrace the genealogy of this motif than to describe its social use. Since we are talking about a clearly polemical theme, what is its use and by whom and against whom is it used?

The reply varies according to the period, and, in particular, according to the socio-cultural level at which use is made of the theme of the pregnant man. The author thinks that he is able to identify an authentically folkloric and peasant vein, in which the motif supports the protests against the powerful (husbands and, above all, priests). This is the case, for example, in the fable collected by Giuseppe Pitrè in Sicily in 1888. A priest, who tyrannizes his village, so exhausts the patience of his parishioners that they decide to take revenge; they slip a scarab into his bed which, via the priest's anus, reaches his stomach and convinces him that he is pregnant. The priest is panic-stricken and thinks that he must arrange for an abortion. Since he doesn't know how to proceed, he is forced to seek advice from the women from whom he usually extorts confessions about their sexual behaviour so that he can condemn them. It is easy to appreciate the sexual inversion in this story, which puts the priest temporarily in the position of a woman and makes him an object of derision to those he oppresses in everyday life in the name of the privileges of knowledge, religion, rank and sex.

But if we assume that the popular version is the original one, the theme is often turned on its head to serve anti-feminine or anti-peasant satire. The pregnant man may then be, like Boccaccio's Calandrino, a country bumpkin lost in the town, his natural innocence making him the butt of the the town-dwellers' mockery.[17] But there is more to it than this: Calandrino thinks that he is pregnant because he agreed to make love underneath his wife, thus renouncing the male prerogative and in a sense making himself his wife's wife. His pregnancy is thus a punishment for a twofold transgression, the socio-cultural (the peasant in town) and the sexual (the man agreeing to be a woman). The theme of the pregnant man is no longer serving to question the established order: it is propping up the values and certainties of those who benefit from it. In other examples the motif allows clerics to show off their superiority by denouncing the credulity of the common people. It may also, as in a sixteenth-century short story by Nicolas de Troyes in *Le Grand Parangon des nouvelles nouvelles*, serve to inspire the subterfuge of a husband who, with a doctor's help, pretends to rid himself of the burden of his own pregnancy by transferring it to his servant (whom he has of course really made pregnant) in order to allay the suspicions of his wife.

The mockers and the mocked thus change roles according to the needs of the case. Nevertheless these different, even opposing, versions have a certain number of features in common, at least one of which marks the limits of the social imagination of which the theme in all its interpretations is the expression. Men and women, bourgeois and peasants, learned and illiterate, all seem to accept that pregnancy, a fundamentally female domain, is a social defect and that it may become a degrading punishment; that the man who is no longer entirely a man (Calandrino, but also the priest who borrows the characteristics of both sexes) must be punished by mockery; and that the hierarchy of sexual roles is a basic rule of all social life. Here again, the presentation of a temporary inversion of roles seems to me to reinforce the hierarchical organization that it appears to question.

If we seek to understand how sexual roles were constructed and observed in the societies that predate industrialization, the scenarios of inversion seem singularly limited – at least where western representations are concerned, because they generally only repeat the 'normal' order of things, but with the signs reversed. More generally, they seem to be less important in themselves than in the ways in which they are manipulated and put into use – and this is where Zapperi's work is so interesting. But, as we have seen, these uses, based on a relatively coherent imaginary world, can turn out to be very dissimilar, and even entirely opposite. Clearly, then, we cannot deduce social conduct from a symbolic device. Above all, contrary to what fashion and the ideology of emancipation seem to suggest, it seems to be less easy to understand sexual roles in the representations that simply mirror them than in forms that resist, or appear to form an obstacle to, representation itself. For example, from at least the sixteenth century up to the imagery of Epinal in the nineteenth century, a whole range of images shows the struggle for authority within the household between husband and wife, and it does so most often through two motifs: a fight for the trousers and the wife who beats her husband. This iconography is not very original, and is often extremely repetitive. Whether the woman is shown as such, or dressed up as a man is obviously of some relevance, but this does not basically alter the distribution of roles that the image seeks to convey. But when the representation hesitates as to the distribution of characteristics between the two partners, or when it makes this distribution complex, it reveals an attempt to organize a different system of representation. See, for example, the German engraving by Martin Treu, which dates from the 1540s, in which the woman who is beating her husband with a club is wearing aggressively male breeches and, at the same time, has clear signs of her femininity – her hair down and her breasts bared.[18] It is as if the engraver had created this complex androgynous figure (punishing a man who is incidentally just as indeterminate) to show what seems to be too often forgotten by current historiography of sexual roles, namely that these roles are constructed and not given. This construction, which fights against the threat posed by a lack of differentiation which endangers all social organization, is continuous and artificial. Perhaps historians should begin by seeking to identify and understand its variations, its hesitations and its implementations.

From this viewpoint, recent historiography has perhaps allowed its view to be too easily clouded by contemporary cultural patterns. It has also perhaps too easily accepted the idea that traditional civilization, the very long Middle Ages, which J. Le Goff sees as extending right up to the middle of the nineteenth century, contained a block of representations and practices that were relatively stable (because they were traditional?). For this twofold set of reasons, analysis has tended to focus on masculine–feminine opposition, and in doing so has too often taken this opposition for granted. I think that the history of a period further removed from our own, and also the suggestions contributed by anthropology could help to shed some light. I shall conclude by considering this briefly.

Let us look at history first. If masculine–feminine opposition is present in all human societies, it is organized according to symbolic codes which are new each time, and it tolerates forms of adjustment and transgression that are very different. Following the development of sexual and conjugal relations between the end of the Roman Republic and the reign of the Antonines, Paul Veyne has shown how, well before the intervention of Christian moralization, accepted bisexuality (where the division was not between man and woman, but more fundamentally, between active and passive) gave way in aristocratic society to a strictly conjugal sexuality wherein roles were controlled and any transgression punished.[19] Because in our culture the representation of sexual roles has gradually become rigorously binary, we have ended up becoming unable to imagine that there might once have existed in the social imagination a place (or several places) for those who are neither men nor women, or who, at least in the collective perception, display characteristics of both sexes. Of course we can think of homosexuality, the history of which, caught in the logic of dominant cultural models, has unfortunately only been written from the angle of repression, with very few exceptions.[20] But there are other phenomena which have become less obvious, and which have scarcely been studied up till now, such as the couvade (which has been attested – though in what forms? – in a certain number of medieval texts); or the old fascination in classical culture and medical taxinomies with the hermaphrodite. In its way, the hermaphrodite can serve as the emblem for a social game in which neither the identity of roles nor the predominance of one over the other could be as assured as they are in representations that have become dominant in the West. The hermaphrodite expresses a fascination for the undifferentiated which was able to coexist (though in very changing forms) with the fundamental requirement for differentiation which is a part of all social organization. Is it a coincidence that in societies that, like ours, claim to be libertarian as well as based on conflict, the figure of the hermaphrodite (or, as we say today, the unisexual) is beginning to find new favour? The status and function of these imaginations of the intermediate, of these surfaces in which the identity of roles is questioned and redefined, is yet to be analysed.

Now for anthropology. Françoise Héritier has reminded us, with the aid of a few monographed studies, that the distribution and allocation of sexual roles were not simply carried out according to sex, but also according to age and social status.[21] Among the Piegan Indians of

Canada, for example, a strictly patriarchal society, some women 'with a man's heart' enjoy the same social and cultural prerogatives as men. These women are almost all either menopausal or sterile. Among the Nuer of the Upper Nile, Evans-Pritchard noted that a woman recognized as being sterile returned to her family of origin and was thereafter considered a man: she would have a man's economic and familial powers and even had wives (a slave carrying out the sexual side of the relationship in her place). In both cases, it is significant that the transgression is not only accepted, but institutionalized by the group. In a sense these women have ceased to be women by losing their fertility. The dividing line is no longer between men and women in the morphological sense, but between fertile and infertile. Once again, it is differently constructed. Have these remarks taken us too far from western cultural models? Are they simply pure homage to the useless charms of the ethnographically exotic? I am not so sure. For in our societies too, such mechanisms can sometimes be identified, even if not easily – and almost furtively. Between the seventeenth and nineteenth centuries, a whole body of medical literature justified the necessary, measured exercise of conjugal sexuality in terms that suggest that with sperm a man brings a woman the means whereby her nature is transformed so that she becomes a 'real' woman; if she is deprived of this she is threatened with an aggravation of her femininity which leads her to get out of control and calls into question her identity. If she abuses it, like those women who make a profession out of love, she runs the risk of becoming virile. The effects of prostitution are a harshness of the voice and often excessive hairiness. Do we need to be reminded that in European societies too, the question of the transgression of sexual roles has been considered and sometimes organized? We find traces of this, without any real surprise, at the two extremities of 'normal' life: in the liminal period of adolescence, when, in the rituals of a propitiatory celebration, it has long been possible for girls and boys to exchange roles; and in the sterility of the old woman, the age usually attributed to witches and the point at which there is an awesome reversal of powers.

NOTES

1 Nicole-Claude Matthieu, 'Homme-culture et femme-nature?', *L'homme*, XIII (1973), pp. 101–13.
2 C. Ginzburg and C. Poni, 'Micro-histoire', in *Le Débat*, 1979.
3 Y. Knibiehler, 'Le discours médical sur la femme: constances et rupture', *Romantisme*, nos 13–14 (1976), pp. 41–55.

4   J. Gélis, *L'Arbre et le fruit. La naissance dans l'Occident moderne (XVIe–XIXe siècle)* (Fayard, Paris, 1984); *La Sage-femme ou le médecin. Une nouvelle conception de la vie* (Fayard, Paris, 1988). M. Laget, *Naissances. L'accouchement avant l'âge de la clinique* (Seuil, Paris, 1982). Rousselle, *Porneia*.

5   F. Faÿ-Sallois, *Les Nourrices à Paris au XIXe siècle* (Payot, Paris, 1980).

6   Gélis in *Annales*, 1979.

7   G. Fraisse, *Femmes toutes mains. Essai sur le service domestique* (Seuil, Paris, 1979), and A. Martin-Fugier, *La Place des bonnes. La domesticité féminine à Paris en 1900.* (Grasset, Paris, 1979).

8   A. Corbin, *Les Filles de noce. Misère sexuelle et prostitution au XIXe siècle* (Aubier, Paris, 1978).

9   Fouquet and Knibiehler, *Histoire des mères*.

10 M. Perrot, Introduction to the special issue of *Mouvement Social*, 'Travaux de femmes' (Paris, 1978).

11 M. Segalen, *Mari et femme*.

12 Verdier, *Façons de dire, façons de faire*.

13 Cf. Accati-Levi, 'Masculin, féminin'.

14 Quoted by N. Z. Davis, *Society and Culture in Early Modern France* (Stanford, Calif., 1975), p. 127; my emphasis.

15 M. Bakhtine, *L'Œuvre de François Rabelais et la culture populaire au Moyen-Age et sous la Renaissance* (Russian edn, 1965; French trans. Paris, 1970); Davis, *Society and Culture*.

16 R. Zapperi, *L'uomo incinto. La donna, l'uomo e il potere* (Rome, 1979 and 1982).

17 Boccaccio, *Decameron*, IX, 3.

18 Illustration in Davis, *Society and Culture*, plate 8b.

19 P. Veyne, 'La famille et l'amour à Rome sous le Haut Empire romain', *Annales ESC*, 1 (1978), pp. 35–63.

20 Cf. J. Boswell, *Christianity, Social Tolerance and Homosexuality: Gay People in Western Europe from the Beginning of the Christian Era to the Fourteenth Century* (Chicago, 1980).

21 F. Héritier, 'Maschile/femminile' in *Encyclopaedia*, (Turin, 1979, viii. 797–812).

9

'A Sex in Mourning': The History of Women in the Nineteenth Century

Alain Corbin

Women's history is like an echo, perceived with the help of a whole range of male data, despite the efforts of historians (both male and female) to seek out women's words more directly. Almost all the documents in the public archives were written by men in positions of responsibility. The accounts of the feminist struggle, the large body of pedagogical or edifying literature, the rare correspondence and the few personal diaries, interesting as they may be, will never restore the balance. This inevitably indirect approach, this sexual dyssymmetry in the creation of images is enough to make it a necessity to understand the male mentality.

A study of the feminine condition implies, as a precondition, the analysis of the motives behind these pronouncements from clerics, doctors, magistrates, policemen, administrators or writers. It is not enough to detect simplistic strategies, to show that women are removed from the public stage or to emphasize the silence imposed on them. What we must do is to identify the systems of representation, the network of fears, the kernel of anxiety that govern male language and behaviour.

In this context, it would also be too simple to be content with the old excuse of misogyny referred to as 'Judaeo-Christian'. Trotting out the anathemas of the Fathers of the Church, quoting with relish the terrible words of Tertullian or the cold admonitions of Saint Augustine certainly sheds light on the mentality of a period strongly influenced by the moral realism that sprang from this distant source. But patristic literature is then no more than a convenient mould in which to pour the new anxieties of a century haunted by Juliette de Sade and fascinated, on the other hand, by diaphanous angelism and the calming image of the Immaculate Conception. Fear of women has grown over the decades; contemplation of the hieratic female sphinx of *Modern Style* will mark the climax of this increasing phobia.[1]

There is no shortage of examples of successful pieces of work based on a fruitful investigative method. Martine Segalen has very skilfully deciphered the a-priori assumptions of the folklorists of the end of the nineteenth century. She has shown how their observations, distorted by the image of the middle-class servant girl, long misled the historians of rural France.[2]

If we do not undertake an initial analysis of this sort, we run the risk of constructing a history of women that is incomplete, and indeed of falling into traps set by male discourse. Three examples, for the most part borrowed from the history of sexuality, will allow us to perceive the danger.

The study of writings on feminine nature, as developed at the end of the eighteenth century and carried on since then, perhaps constitutes the fullest chapter of women's history today. One might, nevertheless, reproach those women who have devoted brilliant books to this subject[3] with not having taken sufficient note of doctors' attitudes to their own sexuality. The conviction of male sexual inferiority haunts the learned vision of woman. This sentiment, which inspired the members of the *Société Royale de Médecine*, the observers of hysteria,[4] led to the coital arithmetic that was in vogue throughout the nineteenth century. The boastful tales of brothel exploits or, more simply, the anxious counting of conjugal sexual activity,[5] the rise of the fear of failure,[6] the interiorized need for careful management of sperm, closely linked to the fantasy of depletion and loss, reinforce, or attempt to exorcize, the image of the excessive, devouring female.[7] If we do not take these feelings into account, we cannot fully understand the language, on the fringes of delirium, that arouses fear of the telluric forces whose strength is revealed by the nyphomaniac, the hysterical woman and the lesbian. We fail altogether to understand the anathemas pronounced against the sterile or menopausal woman, insatiable figures whose excesses are unappeased and unchecked by pregnancy.

The supreme value attributed to virginity, the necessity of initiation by an experienced man, and the responsibility devolved on the husband by the medical profession for controlling female pleasure while avoiding any excess, all flow from the same anxious source. The worried images of male sexuality contribute to put a brake on the exaltation of female pleasure, to obstruct hedonistic practices and to confine them within a hell of degradation, essential to the maintenance of sexual order which hangs over most women.

Another example, linked with the last. Since the peremptory affirmations of Michelet, of Jules Simon, Zola or Charles Benoist, everyone accepts that in the nineteenth-century town a woman, and in particular a working-class woman, could not live without a man. The specialists in industrial history, as well as those in women's history or the history of prostitution, claim to be convinced of this. In their view, the social practices of the time widely attest the validity of this observation.

Yet we must never forget that this is a masculine topic. For a woman to be able to live without a man would mean that she had the ability to dispose freely of her sexuality. The peremptory tone of the witnesses corresponds too closely to male anxiety and the subtle eroticism of the nineteenth century not to arouse suspicion. We may be fairly sure that this interested view has to some extent influenced the sources used by historians. Marie-José Bonnet[8] has shown that doctors have built up an extremely inaccurate picture of the female homosexual; they cannot bear to think that two women could give one another pleasure without a man or without one of them taking on masculine appearances and roles. For the observers of this period, as Jean-Pierre Jacques has pointed out,[9] lesbian relations could only be disordered, excessive, immoderate, for there was no man to control female desire. The same convictions govern the interminable medical chapters devoted to 'manualization' – masturbation – in young girls. They led to the cruel treatments sometimes used in this domain.

For the same reason, we need to re-examine the precise position of the 'old maid' in nineteenth-century society. Literature describes her as an incomplete woman, sallow, dried up, defined by what she lacked.[10] Was the misery of the girl without a man so intense? Adeline Daumard was surely right to stress the prosperity that was the widow's revenge.[11] Maurice Agulhon, moved by the same desire for a critical approach, has shown the gap between the debilitating image of the bachelor, as portrayed so magnificently by Jean Borie, and the happier realities of social life.[12]

To conclude this point, I should like to mention another trap, created by polymorphous male discourse – by clerics, medics and the police. The documents that give us information about venal love fall within the Augustinian tradition. The prostitute is, more or less explicitly according to the text in question, associated with filth, stench, disease, death. This system of correlations structures her image; it inevitably seals her fate as a woman doomed to misery and an early death. Once again, this image fulfils the male wish to subordinate to venal relations everything that is orgiastic in female sexuality. The woman who abandons herself to excesses must be guided by need, thrown onto the streets by the most abject poverty, stalked by death. Women who 'had madness in their bodies'[13] would be a dangerous threat to male sexuality and a terrible example to virtuous wives. If prostitutes acted out of financial greed, fortunes and social hierarchies would be in danger. In 1879, Nana could only end tragically.[14]

Historians, at least in my view, have to some degree allowed themselves to fall into this trap. There is no question of denying the existence of poverty-driven prostitution any more than of exalting the success of flattering courtesans, who were undoubtedly in a small minority. The problem lies in judging the condition of these prostitutes as accurately as possible. Were the street-walkers really unhappier than the 'honest' women of their milieu, who were condemned to the factory, the workshop and then to work in the home? Was their life expectancy objectively shorter, or as Alexandre Parent-Duchâtelet would have us believe, did they enjoy a normal lifespan?[15] Was their social function so negative as to deny them any happiness, any satisfaction?

Two types of presupposition can distort our view of the past in this area and make it subservient to the dominant prejudices. In this domain the historian is strongly influenced by philanthropy. Those researchers – for the most part women – who have chosen to devote much attention to places of refuge cannot help overemphasizing failure, distress and unhappiness, since the sample they are studying is exclusively composed of repentant or defeated women.[16] Obvious puritanism has, until very recently, heavily influenced university research. Misery or remorse is still often the only justification for the researcher, who is also a teacher, to speak of vice or, if we prefer, of the satisfaction of Dionysiac impulses. Only the image of Mary Magdalen succeeds in forestalling criticisms of smuttiness. This then is the basis for the dolorism on the part of historians who do not dare to speak of prostitutes, or more widely of sexuality, except under the headings 'hospice', 'disease', 'birth-rate', 'death-rate', 'prison', 'public highways', and 'sin'.[17] The word 'pleasure' remains absent from the contents list of university theses,[18] unless in the context of the pleasures of the table. One can only agree with Michel Maffesoli when he reproaches the historians of contemporary society with having studiously avoided any examination of the Dionysiac functions.[19]

But it might be objected that in the nineteenth century a woman's modesty, the fragility of the dressmaker's apprentice and the poverty of the prostitute were realities. Once again, I am in no way seeking to deny them a priori, but rather to invite scholars to re-examine them in order to avoid exaggeration. Such research is all the more necessary since historical analysis not only runs the risk of being distorted by male writing, but is also hampered both by the interiorization of the models put forward and by the proliferation of female scenarios. Dramatization of the attitudes imposed by the rigour of social control and by the rigidity of rituals is likely to lead credulous historians astray, just as the simpleton witness of former times did.

Clearly, naïve dramatizations, which would be without impact today, were cleverly exploited when the need arose. The ambiguity of manifestations of feminine modesty, which arouses and heightens the threat as much as it repels it, is today unmasked. But fragility can also be an invitation to seduction and provocative poverty can be an ingenious appeal for charity. All these tactics play on pity, a motivating sentiment whose forms and mechanisms deserve a systematic historical study.

It goes without saying that a relevant, comprehensive history of women must not restrict itself to the analysis of the obsessions, the preconceived ideas, and fears that run through its sources of male origin. It must never separate the study of the fates of the two sexes, since they shed light on one another to so great a degree. We might add that this disqualifies all specifically masculine history as well.

It has become clear, from debates at symposia and also from the best work of ethnologists, that today we must place the accent on solidarity, complementarity and the subtle distribution of roles, both in the domain of social practices and in that of symbolic interventions.

But it is also necessary to take into account the role of images. Representations of others and the self-image are not constructed independently. We cannot escape this truth, and since it is now clear that the study of women's past has been carried on with reference to men, we might as well bring men openly into the ambit of a sex-differentiated history which links its analyses rather than treating the sexes in isolation.

There have been many successes in this area: Anne Martin-Fugier[20] has brilliantly shown how the figure of the bourgeoise at the turn of the century was defined with reference to her waiting for a man. Martine Segalen has been able to describe and explain the condition of the peasant woman because at the same time she has set out to understand that of the male peasant.[21] The analysis of the functioning of the bourgeois household in the Paris of the property-based monarchy, to which Adeline Daumard devoted herself,[22] has led unexpectedly to a new and surprising account of the real condition of the married woman.

Something along these lines is particularly necessary in the history of sexuality. A study of the flawed relationship with desire, which characterizes the nineteenth century, cannot be carried out unless we take both sexes into account. The feelings of the female partner, whether wife or mistress, cannot be isolated from the forms of expression or inhibition, of satisfaction or frustration of male desire. Only if we analyse the whole relationship and abandon the eternal diatribe against male egotism, shall we be able to shed light on the emergence of the new couple, more united and more equal, which has taken place in the last third of the twentieth century.

In the same way, the history of the prostitute must give way to that of the prostitute couple. The roots of the desire inspired by the woman who offers herself venally, the nature of the relations she builds up with her partners, the social function of the woman who repairs the social fabric are all fields of investigation that have barely been touched.

Solitary pleasure itself, about which we have heard so much, must also be studied. For both sexes, it derives from tactics and implicit agreements that are based on the delayed satisfaction of impulses. More generally, we need to have a better grasp of the complementarity of the images of desire that arise in the absence of the other. In this context, Marie-Véronique Gauthier's work[23] appears very interesting. She tries to identify the origins and forms of expression of bawdiness, as seen at the heart of male sociability and through representations of the erotic.

All these considerations lead us now to want the historiographical balance redressed in one particular respect. The male symptoms of the unsatisfactory relationship with desire, to which we have referred, and, more generally, the signs of male suffering in the nineteenth century seem to me to be paradoxically shrouded in mystery. This silence, which is hardly in keeping with the dominant trend towards seeking out cases of misery, constitutes a major obstacle to women's history.

There are now any number of successful works on the female symptoms of frustration and repression that characterize examples of hysteria.[24] Historians are beginning to revel in signs of unappeased desire. The suffering this leads to allows them to speak without danger about desire on the part of the other sex. In the nineteenth century, of course, hysteria was long considered a specifically female affliction, a fact that was confirmed by clinical observation. It remains to be seen whether this outward display of female suffering, which was doubtless desired, sometimes dictated, and always observed with fascination by men, is not itself a symptom, perhaps with therapeutic effects, of male suffering,[25] which is more secret because it is less easily dramatized.

We are beginning to touch on a difficult kind of history, but one that is essential, namely that of the manifestations of emotion. It this context, nuance is everthing. Men's private diaries from the first half of the nineteenth century are one long lament. The unhappiness of the author surfaces on every page, but these confessions, written up at night in the privacy of the writer's room, are not intended for publication. The diary played the role of an absolutely discreet confidant. It may be said that poetry and romantic literature constantly convey male grief, to the point of taking refuge in the dream of the impossible androgyne. Indeed the reader finally becomes tired of the problems of the novice, the ups and downs of the initiation into affairs of the heart, the pangs of 'never-more'; but it is revealing that fiction is our only means of access to this subject.

On the public stage, men's suffering, and I stress this point, finds less and less scope for expression. Within the dominant classes, where behaviour patterns are formed, the male gestural vocabulary has become more refined over the decades. Theatricality in the style of Greuze soon fades, while tears go out of fashion.[26] Photographic poses accentuate men's calm, seriousness and dignity, and tend to keep the dramatic atti-tude for portraits of actors.[27] Tobacco, Philippe Perrot notes,[28] 'rarefies discursive verve', 'gesture becomes slow, dignified and measured.' The stroller, and the pedestrian in a hurry, absorbed by their private con-cerns, avoid any exhibition of the personal suffering which is tormenting them.[29] The person contemplating suicide must henceforth refrain from disturbing anyone.[30] Self-control, carried to its extreme limits, becomes a criterion of a good upbringing.

A man in good health and in the prime of life can no longer use any of the signals that would move an observer. Perhaps one indication of this strict dichotomy of images is the gradual disappearance of the rituals of inversion during the nineteenth century.

Women gradually gained the monopoly over tears, moans and vapours. Fainting and manifestations of nervous disorder underline the pertinence of medical pronouncements on the different natures of the two sexes. Lack of control proves fragility and authorizes pity. This ambiguous feeling links woman to those beings who are immature or defenceless, and who share with woman the benefits of such a condition: children, the sick, crippled beggars, the old and in due course animals.[31]

Nineteenth-century man – and this is one of the essential aspects of the distribution of images and behaviour which is disappearing today – had to fit in with the model of warrior-like virility, even, or indeed particularly, in the lower classes. In this sphere a boy's upbringing was tough and punctuated by punishments.[32] The brutality of the fights between friends, the prestige of muscle in the country, the ever-present, dark violence of the building workers in Paris[33] are so many signs of the power of force. Up until the Second Empire, the bourgeoisie preferred to keep its daughters at home,[34] while it confined its sons in cold, dark and stinking boarding schools, imposing on them a physical training whose severity contributed so greatly to the formation of the male mentality.

The lack of signals means that we have to listen all the more attentively in order to appreciate the depth of male suffering in this century of repression. This collective malaise constitutes one element of historical explanation that must not be neglected. It is already becoming clearer since historians have begun to examine accounts of private life into which is poured this pain, henceforth inexpressible in the *theatrum mundi*. In this context there are doubtless no better examples than the 17,000 pages of Amiel's diary[35] and the sad, disillusioned confidences of Maine de Biran. Increased awareness in this area has come about at the same time as the historians of the nineteenth-century economy have been representing male fatigue as the motive for growth.[36]

Although we must not be tempted to overestimate its extent, social mobility creates a sense of insecurity, a new anxiety in the face of the imprecision and instability of one's position.[37] In a society in which birth is gradually ceasing to be a clear, decisive criterion of belonging, the individual is begining to question his or her own self-image. Other people's views of one arouse new worries and suffering, and an anxiety increased by the incompleteness, the precariousness and complication of the signs indicating position. Furthermore, the individual obligation to situate oneself and one's conjugal unit on the status ladder falls almost exclusively on the man's shoulders.

The horrors of the battlefield have been transposed to civil life, and the image of the social mêlée has become more striking. This no doubt explains in part the increase in male suicide and the increase in what Durkheim calls individualist suicide and anomic suicide. The wounds caused by active life make necessary the warmth of the home, the tenderness of the nurse-wife, the faithfulness of the woman who could never add to one's wounds. The growth of social mobility, the advent of the importance of privacy, the relegation of the wife to the home cannot be isolated from one another.[38]

But there are other symptoms. Some arise out of the social tendency towards hysteria which we have already mentioned. Thus Théodore Zeldin stresses the growth of melancholy in the nineteenth century, then of neurasthenia and psychasthenia,[39] all considered essentially male disorders. One could also, with all due respect to Louis Chevalier,[40] bring in the concepts of sexual misery and the sexual ghetto.[41] The increase in the age of men on marriage and the postponement of patrimonial strategies, often more imperative than in former times, frustrates the satisfaction of impulses. The signs of this distress are the emergence of the literature of the unmarried, the growing terror aroused by attacks on morality,[42] the brutal behaviour of the peasants of Gévaudan,[43] the abusive sexuality of foremen and the regulation of prostitution. Women's misery is here a result of men's misery.

I shall conclude with the clearest indication of this historiographical dyssymmetry, which can be so misleading. While good bookshops abound with shelves devoted to the history of childbirth and maternity, nothing is being published on the trooper, the simple soldier of the nineteenth century. The only military histories available are about officers, deserters, anti-militarists, and, more recently, those who fought in the First World War.[44]

Have we forgotten the carnage of the Empire, the battlefield amputations performed by the surgeons of Napoleon's armies, the charnelhouse of Solferino, the 140,000 dead of the war of 1870-1[45]? What is the meaning of the disdain shown by historians for this warrior-like century? Why, as the metaphor has it, are we studying the 'soldier of work'[46] and not the soldier himself? In a word, why are we more or less consciously refusing to examine the dominant model of virility and the theatre in which male suffering is greatest?

Could it be that we are afraid of finding that the men of the nineteenth century, haunted by the fear of woman, were already bearing the burden of the ancient image of virility? Are we afraid of discovering the unhappiness and weakness of this 'sex in mourning',[47] whose suffering was in large measure precisely the result of the repression and silence imposed on women?

NOTES

1 See in this context, M. Perrot, 'Les images de la femme', *Le Débat*, no. 3, 1980, and Claude Quiguer's work, *Femmes et machines de 1900. Lecture d'une obsession modern style* (Klincksieck, Paris, 1979).
2 Segalen, *Mari et femme.*
3 An allusion to Yvonne Knibiehler's work on this subject, and in particular to *La Femme et les médecins.*
4 J.-P. Peter, 'Entre femmes et médecins. Violence et singularités dans les discours du corps et sur le corps d'après les manuscrits médicaux de la fin du XVIII siècle', *Ethnologie française*, 1976.
5 See, e.g., the attitude of Vigny, Michelet, Flaubert, Hugo and others.
6 Noticeable in Stendhal.
7 On this subject, see Y. Knibiehler, 'Les médecins et l'amour conjugal au XIXe siècle', *Aimer en France – 1760–1860* (Presses Universitaires de Clermont-Ferrand, 1980), and A. Corbin, 'La petite bible des jeunes époux', *L'Histoire*, no. 63, 1984.
8 M.-J. Bonnet, *Un choix sans équivoque* (Denoël-Gonthier, Paris, 1981, publication of a doctoral thesis presented at the University of Paris VII, under the supervision of Michelle Perrot, 1979).
9 J.-P. Jacques, *Les Malheurs de Sapho* (Grasset, Paris, 1981).

10 M. Perrot, 'De la vieille fille à la garçonne: la femme célibataire au XIXe siècle', *Autrement*, May 1980, pp. 222–31.

11 A. Daumard, *La Bourgeoisie parisienne de 1815 à 1848* (Sevpen, Paris, 1963).

12 M. Agulhon, 'L'Historien et le célibataire', *Romantisme*, 1977, no. 16; and J. Borie, *Le Célibataire français* (Le Sagittaire, Paris, 1976).

13 The title of Judith Belladona's work, *Folles femmes de leurs corps* (Paris, Recherches, no. 26, 1977).

14 The heroine of Emile Zola's novel, *Nana*, dies disfigured by smallpox. She has become monstrous. When the author published the novel (1880), he could not end it any other way. To describe a successful end to the career of a courtesan of lowly origins would have scandalized his readers.

15 Cf. A. Parent-Duchâtelet, *La Prostitution à Paris au XIXe siècle* (Seuil, Paris, 1981).

16 In this context, Frances Finnegan's work, *Poverty and Prostitution. A Study of Victorian Prostitutes in York* (Cambridge University Press, 1979) is revealing.

17 The result of a poll carried out in relation to higher doctoral theses presented in the years 1960 to 1977.

18 We find this reticence in literary historians, even those who specialize in Sade. See, in contrast, the courageous work of Jean-Marie Goulemot in 'Beau marquis parlez-nous d'amour'. Cérisy symposium: 'Sade, écrire la crise'.

19 Reproaches made, to the author in particular, at a conference on prostitution held in 1983 at the university of Tours.

20 A. Martin-Fugier, *La Bourgeoise* (Grasset, Paris, 1983).

21 See n. 2 above.

22 See n. 11 above.

23 M.-V. Gauthier, *Chanson, sociabilité et grivoiserie au XIXe siècle* (Aubier, Paris, 1992).

24 Cf. in particular, G. Wajeman, *Le Maître et l'hystérique* (Paris, 1982); G. Didi-Huberman, *Invention de l'hystérie. Charcot et l'iconographie photographique de la salpétrière* (Macula, Paris, 1982); G. Swain, 'L'Ame, la Femme, le Sexe, et le Corps', *Le Débat*, March 1983, and no. 8 of *Pénélope*, 'Questions sur la folie', Spring 1983.

25 This is the working hypothesis followed in Jann Matlock's research into hysteria in the nineteenth century.

26 Cf. Anne Vincent's Diplôme d'Etudes Approfondies thesis, 'Les transformations des manifestations de l'émotion. Projet d'une histoire des larmes – XVIII–XIX siècles' (Université de Paris, 1981).

27 Gisèle Freund, *Photographie et société* (Seuil, Collection 'Points', Paris, 1979, p. 65).

28 Philippe Perrot, 'Quand le tabac conquit la France', *L'Histoire*, no. 46, 1982.

29 On this point, Walter Benjamin, *Gesammelte Schriften* (Shurkamp Verlag, Frankfurt, 1972–7, 4 parts in 9 vols), part I (3), ed. Rolf Tiedemann;

French trans., *Charles Baudelaire, un poète lyrique à l'apogée du capitalisme* (Payot, Paris, 1983): 'Le flâneur', pp. 55–98

30   The account of the suicide of the Count of W . . . in 'Sentimentalisme', one of Villiers de l'Isle-Adam's *Contes cruels*, sheds light on this.

31   A woman's pity for animals is also perceived as a lesson in tenderness directed at men; cf. V. Pelosse, 'Imaginaire social et Protection de l'animal. Des amis des bêtes de l'an X au législateur de 1850', *L'Homme*, Oct.–Dec. 1981 and Jan.–March 1982.

32   Michelle Perrot illustrates this well in her article: 'Sur la ségrégation de l'enfance au XIXe siècle', *Psychiatrie de l'enfant*, 1982, no. 1.

33   Maurice Agulhon, Introduction to *Mémoires de Léonard, ancien garçon maçon*, by Martin Nadaud (Hachette, Paris, 1976).

34   F. Mayeur, *Histoire générale de l'enseignement et de l'éducation en France*, vol. 3, 'De la Révolution à l'école républicaine' (Nouvelle Librairie de France, Paris, 1981).

35   The interest shown in the text by Emmanuel Le Roy Ladurie is revealing, cf. *Parmi les historiens* (NRF, Paris, 1983).

36   François Caron stresses this in his *Histoire économique de la France – XIXe-XXe siècles* (Colin, Paris, 1981).

37   Alain Girard develops this idea in *Le Journal intime* (PUF, Paris, 1963).

38   On this correlation and the theses of Talcott Parsons, see Richard Sennett's *Families Against the City: Middle Class Homes of Industrial Chicago 1872–90* (Harvard University Press, Cambridge, Mass, 1970), and Philippe Ariès's Preface to the French translation of this work (1980).

39   *Histoire des passions françaises – 1848–1945* (Seuil, Collection 'Points', Paris, 1981, vol. V).

40   Chavelier criticizes this notion in *Montmartre du plaisir et du crime* (Robert Laffont, Paris, 1980, p. 29).

41   An expression used by Jean-Louis Flandrin about young peasants, in *Les Amours paysannes (XVIe–XIXe siècles)* (Julliard, Paris, 1975).

42   Cf. J.-P. Aron, *Le Pénis et la démoralisation de l'Occident* (Grasset, Paris, 1978).

43   Elisabeth Claverie and Pierre Lamaison, *L'Impossible Mariage, violence et parenté en Gévaudan* (Hachette, Paris, 1983). The Gévaudan is a region to the south of the Massif Central, where, in the nineteenth century, the 'Oustal' system operated. In order to get round the *Code Civil*, which had abolished the rights of the eldest child and provided for equal sharing of an inheritance between offspring, peasants wishing to avoid having to divide properties designated one of their children who would inherit the property and compensate his or her brothers and sisters, if necessary keeping them on the land as labourers. This practice led to all sorts of arguments and violent family conflicts, and even to murder. The authors of the book studied these conflicts as recorded in the files of the Assize courts. (Editor's note)

44   Cf. in particular the works of W. Serman, B. Schnapper, J. Vidalenc, R. Andréani and J. Maurin.

45 An exhibition in 1983 devoted to the works of Gustave Doré by the Musée Carnavalet and the Forum des Arts reminded us of the terror aroused by the war of 1870–1, and in particular the siege of Paris.
46 See L. Murard and P. Zylberman, eds, *Le Soldat du travail* (Editions Recherches, Paris, 1978), on the working-class world and the risks of industrial work.
47 A phrase borrowed from Baudelaire. In 1983 a radio presenter asked a number of French historians the following question: 'What was the male sex in mourning for in the nineteenth century?' An interesting enquiry.

10

A Consideration of the Trousseau: A Feminine Culture?

Agnès Fine

Like history, ethnology was, during the 1970s, subjected to the new questioning inspired by the emergence of the women's movement. A number of works in France and abroad, particularly in Britain and the United States, bear witness to this.[1]

Three works on rural French society all raise the question of women's powers. Yvonne Verdier's *Façons de dire, façons de faire*, published in 1979, analyses the importance of women's symbolic powers at significant moments in the individual's life – birth, marriage and death – through the knowledge and skills possessed by three women who supervised these transitions: the woman who washed the bodies of newborn babies and of the dead; the seamstress; and the cook. Martine Segalen, in *Mari et femme dans la société paysanne*, which appeared in 1980, considers the sexual distribution of economic tasks and stresses their complementarity. In *Paysans, femmes et citoyens*, Susan Carol Rogers examines many aspects of the social life of Grand-Fau, a village in Lorraine, and believes that she has found a society in which men are not dominant. In her conclusion, she seems to question the issue of feminine power as it was previously outlined, and streses the complexity of the notion of power.[2]

These three approaches are so different in terms of their method and analytical tools that I don't think that we can compare their results. I have decided, therefore, in this chapter, to approach the questions posed by ethnological work in a concrete way by presenting my own personal research on the subject of the trousseau.

The starting-point was a study of rural families in south-west France in the nineteenth and twentieth centuries. An analysis of the modalities of marriage seemed to me essential to an understanding of the status of women. In our societies the main elements are the wedding ceremony, the dowry and the trousseau. Although the dowry and the trousseau were at first considered subjects for anthropology (e.g. by Jack Goody[3]) or sociology (e.g. by Pierre Bourdieu[4]), they have now become fully fledged historical subjects.

The same cannot be said of another type of approach used in ethnology which sets out to analyse the symbolic. Yet this approach is essential if we wish to attempt to explain the many aspects of a social reality and at the same time take into account the coherence of representations. The trousseau is a good example of this.

Where does classic historical analysis lead us? Based on written documents, in this case on the analysis of notarial contracts, it enables us to analyse the composition of the trousseau and its value. It is an excellent indication of the economic level of a social group, and it also sheds light on what we call the material civilization of a period: objects, their form, their quality, their material. All this is important. But what do we do when these sources disappear along with the custom of drawing up a contract in front of the notary at the time of marriage? Where the most recent period is concerned, oral enquiry can fill the gaps and we can rely on the precious memories of old women. But oral enquiry does more than provide supplementary information, it changes the scope of the initial questions. For what the old women questioned tell us so strikingly is not simply the composition of their trousseau, still less its economic value. As we listen to them, we realize that the trousseau represented something essential in their lives as women, something that went far beyond the few ritual objects of which it consisted. It is this investigation of the popular representations of the trousseau that I propose to present in this chapter, although this poses two problems. First, the study seems rather long, and secondly it is of necessity too succinct, since there is not space to illustrate all the points fully enough.[5]

But perhaps this detour will help us to formulate a few questions more concretely. If a woman's trousseau represented something specifically feminine, what is the basis for this definition in the society we are studying? In so far as its acquisition involved certain practices specific to women, can we speak of a feminine culture?

NO TROUSSEAU, NO WEDDING

A wedding is inconceivable without a trousseau. This was confirmed over and over again in different ways by our elderly interlocutors. 'You always gave a girl everything she needed for a bedroom, her furniture, or else you had to be really very poor! Even the poor always had a trousseau; everybody had a trousseau.'

Not to give a girl who was getting married a trousseau would be like 'letting her go naked!' A mother would 'rather go without things herself!' In a word, it was unthinkable.

If one could not give the girl all her bedroom fittings, one gave some furniture, and if one could not give furniture, one gave at least six sheets. That was the minimum, below which the parents could not sink without dishonour, however poor they were in the rural society of the south-west in the 1930s.

The relationship between marriage and trousseau seems so close that a wedding could not take place if the girl's trousseau had not first been made up. This happened in 1907 to a sixteen-year-old girl from Ariège, the eldest of a family of five children whose father was a very poor tenant farmer. She had, at a very early age it is true, been seeing a neighbour, the son of comfortable small landowners, who was twenty-five. Her parents refused to allow the marriage, although it would be a step up the social ladder, because their daughter had no trousseau and they could not give her one. 'You can't get married, because we can't give you a trousseau.' This argument would have been final if it had not been for the young man's parents. They pleaded with the girl's parents to consent to the marriage, and offered to buy the girl's trousseau and have it embroidered with her initials. Their offer was accepted and the obstacle removed.

The custom seems an ancient and very widespread one, judging by the folklorists' accounts of practices in many areas in the nineteenth century. When girls who were orphaned and poor reached marriageable age, they would go round to every house, accompanied by a few women from the village, and ask for linen and hemp to make their trousseau. As was the case with a number of ritual requests, there was an obligation upon neighbours to respond positively. To refuse to give to these girls would be to condemn them to celibacy.

If a girl found herself without a trousseau when she was ready to get married, the moral blame would fall on her mother, whose duty it was to provide for her. In order to meet any eventuality, and especially in case of economic difficulties, mothers began their daughters' trousseaux very early, generally when they took their first Communion. Girls would still be at school when their mothers bought their first sheets. By saving and obtaining credit, the poorest families were able to fulfil this duty. Village grocers would provide linen on credit and would be paid after the harvest. They sold sheets, towels and table linen. The son of one of these shopkeepers, who was very active in the 1920s, remembers that fathers would say: 'I have made a sacrifice that is rather more than I can afford', but little by little they would pay off their debts. The larger commercial establishments set up a system of home sales, employing travelling salesmen. They would travel through the villages and visit especially those houses where there were girls of marriageable age.

It took really serious circumstances, such as the Second World War and the Occupation, for the situation, seen as tragic, to arise in which girls of marriageable age had no trousseau because there was a shortage of cloth. A farming woman from the Lot-et-Garonne still pays tribute to the foresight of her mother. When she was married in 1942, this allowed her to escape the awful fate of some girls of her generation.

The girls who didn't have a trousseau had to go to the black market, or else you had to be on good terms with a linen merchant, you had to be related to them or be well known; you had to swap it for food on the black market. Otherwise, the girls didn't have a trousseau if their mothers hadn't started before the war.

Those girls who could not manage something like this, had to be content with 'a few old rags', which was quite contrary to the custom that insisted that the trousseau should be new.

A woman who was to be married was so closely linked to her trousseau that even if parents and children were not on good terms, this link still operated. One account tells of a very serious conflict between parents and their daughter about her choice of husband. The parents threw their daughter out of the house and 'threw the trousseau after her'! A second case concerns one of the ritual abductions that were relatively frequent in the Languedoc when the parents opposed a marriage. The fiancés would go off together, telling a few friends or relations, who were asked to inform the parents. After about three days, the couple would return and the parents would then be obliged to agree to the marriage. About the year 1920 a girl from Bessède-de-Sault (in the Aude region of the Pyrenees) went off with her fiancé, after telling her aunt. Quickly, the aunt passed the trousseau secretly through the window to her niece! Sixty years later, the old people still loved to repeat this story.

The law sanctioned this privileged link between marriage, the woman and her trousseau. In southern France, the law of the dowry was the only matrimonial settlement from the early Middle Ages up until the Civil Code. Thereafter, it was chosen by the majority of country areas as the matrimonial settlement and when it passed out of use towards the middle of the nineteenth century in some southern regions, it was replaced by other matrimonial settlements which still observed its spirit. According to the dowry settlement, the father is obliged to give his daughter a dowry. This obligation is recorded by the notary when the marriage agreement is drawn up. To comply with this law, the father would give his daughter a dowry in the form of a sum of money in the best cases, but in all cases what the southern notaries called the *dotalices*, which consisted of furniture, clothes and linen, in a word, the trousseau. Even if she received no dowry in the form of money or land, a woman would, in the presence of the notary, receive at least a trousseau. In 1787, in the country areas of the Lauragais, although out of 271 marriage contracts there was no gift of money in sixty-nine cases, there was always a trousseau, whose composition and value the notary detailed.[6]

Thus there was no legal marriage without a trousseau being given to the girl. This trousseau, whose value was estimated by the notary, remained the woman's exclusive property. No one else had power over these possessions, as was the case with regard to the dowry in relation to which the father, the father-in-law, the husband and the girl herself all had specific rights. The girl was the sole owner of her trousseau, which consisted of belongings intimately related to her person such as a bed, sheets and clothes. All the items were described in minute detail in the contracts, right up to the most recent contracts. Her possessions were marked with her initials – that is, the initials of her maiden name – to record this as a personal right within the shared domain of the household. The trousseau was the only thing the wife owned and kept for the rest of her life.

This acute awareness of the ownership of the trousseau was maintained in the face of the husband's power. As an old Sicilian woman expressed it so well when questioned by Nonna Nedda, (some time between 1952 and 1960),[7] 'The husband is the master of the whole house, including his wife. The woman only remains mistress of the trousseau which she brought to her marriage.'

Furthermore, the bride's trousseau, which was so essential to marriage, would follow her if she were widowed and remarried. If the gift of a trousseau was not considered a legal obligation in the period under study (1900–60), it was seen as a moral obligation on the part of the parents. One might think that, with the profound social changes that have taken place in the second half of the twentieth century, this feeling would have changed, but nothing of the sort, particularly in the rural milieu where different cultural models combine in a unique way.

In the Pyrenean country areas near to Montréjeau, Maguy, who was married in 1973, bought her trousseau little by little from a travelling grocer. When her fiancé went off to begin his military service, she realized the urgency of the trousseau. From that moment on, she said,

'Ouh là là! Time to get the trousseau ready.' She bought her trousseau piece by piece, using a system of credit and savings developed by the Épargne company, putting aside sums from her modest earnings as a child-minder. The system used stamps, to the value of 10 francs, which had to be stuck on to sheets of fifty. When these sheets were completed, the saver had earned one 'savings parcel' which she could choose from a catalogue: 'parcels of linen, of crockery, or complete trousseaux'. The travelling grocer was the middleman. In this way Maguy built up her trousseau, in a particular order: 'I began with the sheets, oh yes, the sheets first! Then I went on to towels, then tea towels, and then to table linen.' The eighth child in a family whose father was a labourer, Maguy built up her own trousseau, but with the close collaboration of her mother, who advised her, placed the orders and even bought her a few pieces using the same system of stamp books.

Very often today the building up of a trousseau is justified as the expression of individual taste, a particular liking for linen. 'For the sheets I decided to go for the four seasons. Spring, summer, autumn and winter, with flowers . . . And then I took the 'You and me' collection, with modern hearts! That one really caught my eye, so I bought it!'

It is a question of individual taste or 'family tradition', as a seamstress from the Lot-et-Garonne, married in 1958, explained, giving the example of her own family. Her mother, married in 1930, embroidered her own trousseau. The woman herself, who was working as a seamstress in 1958, had had a very large trousseau which was shown to the notary in Agen item by item. Her sixteen-year-old daughter, she thought, had inherited this taste. 'For her birthday she likes me to buy some linen that will go towards her trousseau.' She presents her family as a line of women 'who appreciate the trousseau', as opposed to those who 'are completely uninterested and think it quite normal to get married without having any linen put by.'

These days the norm is often expressed in individual terms in this way: 'I like'; 'There are women who think it normal'. But in fact it is the latter phrase that expresses the norm: one does not get married without having a little linen put by!

This custom is not seen as contradicting or going against the changes in girls' status. Mireille, a postgraduate student form La Cadière (in the Var region), was married in 1982. Her mother's foresight and the family's relatively comfortable financial position meant that she and her sister Evelyne found themselves in possession of an enormous trousseau.

Before we were married, even before we talked about marriage, my mother would buy two towels for one of us, and then a month later she would buy two towels for the other. Sometimes she bought sheets from the 'Trois Suisses' or 'La Redoute' catalogues. She would say: 'That's for Mireille, because last month I ordered some for Evelyne.' I have so many things I don't know what to do with them all! It's terrible, I have a whole cupboard full, a chest full, and boxes full of tea towels! I got so many tea towels, handkerchiefs, towels, little ones, middle-sized ones, big bath towels, face towels, foot towels, it's too much!

'It's too much'. Abundance itself reveals the multiple functions of the trousseau which cannot be reduced simply to its economic utility any more today than it could in the past. The custom of the trousseau in La Cadière relates to all marriageable girls, even if it is affected by the young generation's new matrimonial customs. The practice of young people living together, which involved 10 per cent of French youth in 1977, has spread into the villages. It consists of settling down little by little as a couple, without marking the change of status by the public rite of passage constituted by marriage. There are two opposing maternal attitudes towards the trousseau. Sometimes the trousseau built up by the mother does not move from the linen cupboard. Some mothers punish their daughter's marginality. 'No wedding, no trousseau' declares one mother, in a logical inversion of the normal custom. But other mothers have a more flexible attitude. Often the trousseau passes gradually from the mother's linen cupboard to the new couple: a few towels, a few dozen tea towels are given as Christmas or birthday presents.

The trousseau, not referred to by that name so as not to offend the innovative sensitivities of the young couple, follows the girl discreetly. But mothers rarely go so far as to give their unmarried daughters sheets; this would be seen as full approval of the young couple's sexual life. It is significant that women who are always very willing to talk about their trousseau hardly ever give its value in financial terms. They speak of a 'fine trousseau', 'a rich person's trousseau', and they stress the quantity of items of linen, the quality of the material, the beauty of the embroidery. The trousseau, more than a material contribution, is a sign of a woman's social position, and also a sign of her womanhood. It is as if a girl without a trousseau was not complete, as if she did not possess all the attributes necessary for marriage, as if she was not fit to be married. What does this fitness consist of? With what symbolism are these material possessions invested to the point where their absence at the time of marriage seems inconceivable? An analysis of the composition of the trousseau allows us to form a few hypotheses.

THE BEDROOM

The French language has no word for the personal belongings brought into a marriage: the word *trousseau* is used here for convenience, but not in a restrictive sense. According to dictionaries old and new, the trousseau is 'the linen and clothes that a mother gives her daughter when she is married' (Furetière). But in the sense in which we are using it, it means, on the one hand, not just linen, but also furniture (bed, cupboard or linen chest), and on the other, it is not specifically feminine. Men too have their trousseau when they enter a house as son-in-law. Catalan has one word for furniture and linen: *l'aixovar*,[8] which corresponds to the Occitan *noviatge*. Whereas the Catalan word is frequently used, 'noviatge' is rarely used in south-west France. We prefer the word 'dowry'. Southern notaries of the *Ancien Régime* use the term *dotalices*, but only when it is the girl who brings the possessions to the marriage. These details of vocabulary are important. The existence of a single word for furniture and linen shows that these apparently disparate possessions share a functional identity. What are these possessions?

The composition of the trousseau varies a great deal according to social group, the region and the period.[9] Here we are relying on the analysis of marriage contracts in several regions of the the south-west (in particular the country areas of the Lauragais[10] and the Aude region of the Pyrenees)[11] between the sixteenth and twentieth centuries. The bride always contributes a bed with an eiderdown, a cushion, a bedspread (white in the Lauragais in the seventeenth century), a *bourasse* (a kind of mattress), and a few sheets and a chest with ornamental hinges, and a key, if possible. She also brings a black dress, and probably her wedding dress, which will be used on Sundays and feast days. Dresses disappear from marriage contracts around the beginning of the nineteenth century, but table linen (tablecloth and napkins) increases in importance. Items of clothing appear only in the last quarter of the nineteenth century, but became an important element of the trousseau right up to the Second World War. Furniture also varies, the number of items growing and their quality revealing a progressive change in lifestyle. The bed valance appears in the eighteenth century. New items of furniture begin to appear: the wash-stand and the bedside table. Some very wealthy brides, like the miller's daughter from Belfort-sur-Rebenty in 1910, bring a set of bedroom furniture described by her daughter as 'very, very pretty': 'a chest of drawers, a wash-stand with jug and marble top, with a marble and wooden shelf, a full two-door wardrobe and an inlaid bed'.

Despite the apparent diversity and the historical evolution of the furniture (which we have barely hinted at here), we can see the astonishing stability of the composition of what was customarily contributed. The bride brings her own bridal chamber and her wedding dress (and later her personal clothes). The historical depth of this custom and its wide geographical spread (covering at least the whole of Europe) show how old it is. It is not surprising to see that it was extremely widely observed in the south-west right up to the 1960s. It still is, in certain social milieux. The bride brings 'the bedroom' (*la chambre*) according to the old expression.

In different regions the bedroom suite would be paid for by the wife or the husband, sometimes by both, but in any case it would consist of the bed and its linen and the cupboard and would be brought by the bride. But it was the bed, and above all the sheets, that became the essential element of the bridal suite. Perhaps this is why French vocabulary has kept the word *trousseau* as meaning 'linen'. 'In a trousseau first of all you have the sheets.' In this way their symbolic importance is often stressed. In the Sault, in the eighteenth century, sheets were brought in threes or in fives, then by sixes in the nineteenth century, and finally the dozen appears to be the rule in the twentieth century. But to have less than four pairs would be an admission of poverty. In any case, there is no trousseau without sheets.

The young man also brings his trousseau when he comes to live 'as son-in-law' with his wife's family. In earlier times this would mean his bed. Today it means his sheets and personal clothing. But women stress the insignificance of their husband's trousseau as opposed to the abundance and beauty of their own: 'All right, my husband brought his half-trousseau!', a woman from Albi, married in 1950, concedes condescendingly. In principle, the young man's trousseau should amount to half that of the girl he is marrying. It does not include household linen, appart from a few sheets. However, in the twentieth century it does include an impressive number of handkerchiefs!

It is essential that all these items – bed, bedroom cupboard, clothes, linen – be quite new. However the couple's house is furnished, it is the girl (if she is at all able to do so) who contributes the bed and the cupboard. 'Nòra' cupboards (which take their name from the Provençal word for daughter-in-law) furnish all good houses, each one recalling a name, a person, a generation. An engaged girl is never given a cupboard that has already been part of a trousseau. Nuptial furniture cannot be passed on. It remains attached to the person who brought it. 'When the marriage was in sight, the cupboard was ordered, and the cupboard went from the carpenter's to the new home. Newly-weds never slept in an old bed. It was brand new.'

Those girls who could not bring new things expressed their regrets. The decision was not theirs. Sometimes it was the result of poverty: 'Don't think that the sheets we were given were new!' said one former farm servant from the Lauragais. Or else it was the mother-in-law who had departed from the norm in the name of economic rationality: 'My mother-in-law said that there were beds. We didn't need a bed. We only bought the cupboard. I would have liked to buy the bed as well.'

It is possible that this is a relatively recent requirement. We find used clothes and linen mentioned in marriage contracts between poor peasants in the seventeenth, eighteenth, and even nineteenth centuries. But in principle the trousseau should not have been used others. It should be new, like the newly-weds themselves, who were called the 'nòvi'.

During the wedding celebrations, young men and women twice intervene, manipulating the objects of the trousseau in ceremonial phases whose sexual significance is obvious. First of all, the day before the wedding, or the day before that, in a custom attested in a large part of France in the nineteenth and early twentieth centuries, the ceremonial transportation of the trousseau took place.[12] This marked, in symbolic fashion, the transfer of the bride herself, which would take place the next day. At the end of the day the happy band would go into the bedroom, set up the bed and the cupboard with a good many songs, jokes and puns referring to the forthcoming sexual union between the newly-weds. While the men set up the bed, the girls would put the linen in the cupboard. Only a few traces of these vanished festivities remain. In the Landes in the 1930s the bedroom would be visited the day before the wedding by the neighbouring women. They would admire the furniture, and in particular the linen of the trousseau, which would be attractively displayed in the cupboard. There is another, more recent, example of the manipulation of the trousseau before the wedding (Var, 1982). The young couple's bed must not be made by the fiancée or her mother, but by two young girls who are virgins, chosen one from each of the two families.

After the consummation of the marriage, young men and girls would burst into the bedroom again for the ritual of the carrying of the *tourain* (a cake). This very widespread custom is still alive in the region. Young men and girls go into the bedroom, wake the couple and with many songs and games of explicitly sexual content shake the bed and show everyone that the sheets have been well used.

The meaning of the trousseau is becoming clearer. It is the bedroom, the bed, the sheets in which the sexuality of a new couple is to be expressed.

While the sexual symbolism of the bedroom, the bed and the sheets is evident, why does it concern women more than men? Why do they identify so much with their trousseau to the point where they say that 'a woman without a trousseau is nothing'? The relationship between women and their own trousseau, particularly their sheets and personal linen, is the product of time, work and a personal initiation.

These links are ancient. In contrast to the furniture of the trousseau, the cupboard or the bed, which are bought by the parents when the couple become engaged and when the marriage is imminent, the accumulation of the trousseau linen is a long process that involves mother and daughter. It begins when the young girl has left school and taken her first Communion. At this point, the mother begins to buy her a few sheets. These purchases are made solely with money earned by women. Women in rural society are mistresses of the garden, the farmyard and the small-scale breeding of animals. Proceeds from sales of eggs, chickens, ducks or rabbits are immediately reinvested in linen. Linen is the feminine form of building up capital *par excellence*. The accumulation of her daughters' trousseau is a mother's major duty. The wife of a day-labourer from Belpech (in the Ariège region) used to raise ducks. When the ducks were big enough, her daughter would take them on her bicycle and sell them at the market in Mazères. The mother kept the money, put it aside and when she had enough, bought two sheets; 'Once a year, there we were, we would take our time.' The time it took to accumulate twelve sheets was the time it took to raise ducks, and also for the girl to grow up. The remarkable thing is that this conversion of small livestock into linen seems to have gone on imperceptibly. 'I don't know how we managed it. We had no money, we were poor, but we managed to buy what we needed.' In a smallholding in the Landes in the 1930s the mother would sell a few rabbits, a few chickens. Mother would say: 'Right, when these chickens are ready, I'll buy you some linen.'

They never used the money earned by the family's farm work, the rare and precious cash that the father would make from selling grain and livestock. 'The household money never went on the trousseau.' This was a way of affirming the exclusively feminine origin of the trousseau. If linen was bought, it must be bought with women's money.

The mother had to build up a trousseau for each of her daughters in order of their birth.

'My mother built up trousseaux for both of my sisters because there was little age difference between them. So she built up both trousseaux at the same time. Then mine was next. When my sister was married, she began on mine, and bought it little by little.' The mother's role was thus to build up her daughters' trousseaux as she brought them up, the progress of the trousseaux keeping strictly parallel to the daughters' growth. This was as much part of her duty as a mother as feeding and clothing them. It was also necessary that this should take time and be done gradually.

As soon as the daughters were able to do so, they contributed to buying their own trousseau. The poorest were found jobs keeping animals, as early as twelve years old. Sometimes as early as seven years old, they would look after geese or pigs. The money they earned, which was insignificant at that age, was taken by the parents. From a certain age on (fifteen or sixteen years) the parents had to let the girl keep part of her wages so that she could begin to build up her trousseau. It was recognized that she had a right to this money, and if the parents did not respect this, it was accepted that she could keep back the money to which she was entitled. Towards the age of eighteen, in principle the girl kept all her wages. She would seek every opportunity to earn money. 'I went out to do washing, to prepare a pig, to do cleaning to earn a bit of money to buy myself chemises.'

One girl earned 6 francs for each telegram she delivered during the 1914 War. Another mended her neighbour's stockings. 'We always found something to do.' To this legitimate end, young girls were permitted to work in factories. In the region, many small textile factories employed young girls for a miserable wage, and girls generally looked on this period of their life as essentially temporary. They would keep it up just as long as it took to build up their trousseau and meet their future husband. In the silk mills of the Cévennes, girls would work a precious thread that was not destined for them.

It is fascinating to see how, by working as a seamstress, an embroiderer or a textile worker – all crafts in which one handled linen, needle and thread – girls would earn their trousseau. These feminine tools and manipulation of cloth reinforced the girl's links with her trousseau, as Yvonne Verdier has shown so well (see below).

Girls would mark this new linen, which they began to receive at puberty. At school they would learn, around the age of twelve, to do this marking. An analysis of this leads us to link it with a girl's biological destiny. 'Marking the linen meant having periods. The expression clearly suggests the biological event, and girls would literally mark their linen that year with their blood. As soon as girls began to mark their linen with their blood every month, they would, having achieved this, go on to mark their trousseau in red cross-stitch.'[13]

The marking of the linen would soon be followed, in the winter when they reached fifteen, by another initiation, the period with the seamstress. In the course of one winter girls would not learn a great deal; they would 'pass the pins', but in fact they were being initiated into the 'feminine world of linen' by sewing dresses. Later, when a girl was ready to get married, it would again be the pin that was her privileged tool, and sewing would be the technique that would allow her to attain womanhood.

All her life as a young girl would thus be marked by her special relationship with linen. 'On a bit of material a girl inscribes her nubility.' In this way, on the basis of her analysis of the customs and sayings of the women of Minot, Verdier emphasizes the essential relationship between sewing and a girl's nubility.

This relationship takes on slightly different forms in our area. In the south-west, and not as in Minot, linen is no longer marked with red cross-stitch. This is thought to be too crude. It is kept for coarse linen, under-sheets and tea towels. Young girls use painstaking embroidery, white on white. Alongside initials come ladders, grilles, and openwork borders for sheets, and blanket stitch for chemises and pants. Girls are invited to carry out really artistic work. They make it a point of honour to compete with specialists. The fashion for embroidery has penetrated the countryside of Ariège as well as the areas of the Tarn, Gers, Lot and Lot-et-Garonne. Only in the poorest milieux of the Aveyron does simple marking still exist. Of course, this art demands a considerable amount of time. 'It never took me less than two weeks to do one sheet, with Nice hemstitch and embroidered initials. I would work in the evening until 1.00 or 2.00 in the morning. I had a little table and I would sit by the fire with my little petrol lamp, which my father had bought me for this' (1930).

In the year in which she was to be married, parents would excuse their daughter from outside work so that she could get on with her trousseau. That year she would be allowed to work at home without interruption and would manage to finish six really fine top sheets! It is an art that takes so much time that it is necessary to begin early. 'You had to start young, as soon as the girl left school, because, sometimes if she didn't hurry, she hadn't finished when she got married!'

Embroidery replaced the simple mark, which was thought suitable only for coarse linen, when fine industrial linen reached the country areas. Preferred for its quality, and also perhaps for its price, it brought to a sudden end the long involvement of girls with the working of their own linen. For centuries, the making of linen had been the exclusive province of women, from the growing and picking of hemp right up to the spinning of the cloth. Because of the length of time it took, embroidery then spread, thus renewing girls' traditional link with their trousseau. This change took place around the 1900s.

But this art, which demanded a great deal of time, also necessitated an apprenticeship. In the years between 1900 and 1940, nuns became the cultural intermediaries of this middle-class art and spread it through the country areas. Whereas girls had all learned the few basic stitches – stem-stitch and cross-stitch – at school, they generally left school without knowing how to embroider. This they would often learn in a sewing room, where they would spend one, two or three winters. Girls would continue their education in these sewing rooms. As they learned embroidery stitches, they would take in moral and religious principles, while some edifying text was read aloud to them. Dotted throughout the country towns (Quillan, Tonneins, Vic-Fezensac, Mazères, Beaumont-de-Lomagne), the sewing rooms would attract girls from the surrounding countryside. This was, of course, only possible if the farm work allowed it. The sewing rooms were real training centres for young girls, and tried to compete with the frivolous seamstresses' workshops. In some, which were open to boarders, girls would pay for their keep by embroidering for others. Some sewing rooms kept going by embroidering trousseaux. Everyone was satisfied in this way: the nuns, but also the girls, to whom, when they had worked enough, they gave a piece of material to embroider on Sundays for their own trousseau. Techniques spread very quickly. Girls who had learned from the nuns showed their neighbours, 'taught' their cousins and 'all the girls boasted that they had embroidered their trousseau entirely by hand in *petit point*.' Embroidering the trousseau became the fashion, according to some. It was undoubtedly the norm in the region at this period. 'We all tried to learn how to embroider a bit.' But it was difficult, and professional embroiderers were often called in.

If girls 'all tried to learn how to embroider a bit', some admit that they never knew how to – for example, the girl from Mirepoix who was married in 1933. Her mother had had her daughter's trousseau embroidered by embroiderers, but she herself 'had done all the grilles' and was proud of it. Another girl, a seamstress in Agen, admits she didn't have time to embroider her own trousseau herself. She had a workshop, customers and a great many orders, so she gave part of her trousseau to a sewing room and the rest to her mother. But she had done some – 'napkins, the edges of the table linen' for every girl must put her mark, in some way or another, on her trousseau. As this young middle-class girl, brought up before the War of 1914 by the Ursulines in Port-Vendres, explains, 'I didn't embroider my trousseau, just a few sheets, but not much, because you had to do something!'

'You had to do something.' It is clear that the forms differ, but the need to mark the trousseau was felt as much here as in Minot.

Trousseau linen is white. This was obvious in a period when coloured linen did not exist in the trade. As soon as it appeared, the requirement that trousseau linen should be white became all the more manifest. 'I got married in 1932. Coloured linen arrived in 1936 . . . My life spanned the two.'

The girl who said this loved linen so much that, despite having an enormous trousseau, after her marriage she bought some coloured linen. But even though it might be permissible to buy and use coloured linen, trousseau linen had to be white! And embroidered white on white! 'Red? Oh! shameful! tea towels were embroidered in red.' All the linen had to be white, even towels. Very gradually pale-blue or pale-pink nightdresses began to appear and would be embroidered blue on blue or pink on pink. But today, many older women still think that trousseau sheets must of necessity be white and refuse to buy the fancy green or yellow sheets mentioned on the anonymous wedding lists chosen by the young couple. This requirement that the trousseau should be white is reinforced by the fashion in embroidery, which ruled out red. White could not fail to recall the wedding dress, symbol of a girl's virginity.

The trousseau, in former times kept in a chest, is kept in the cupboard, in the new bedroom cupboard given to the bride. The cupboard and everything in it is thus her exclusive property – often, along with her bed, the only thing she possesses in a house in which she is a stranger. A girl would use her linen as sparingly as possible. The daughter-in-law's art is to use her mother-in-law's household linen as much as possible so as to preserve her own. Bitter arguments sometimes arise between mother-in-law and daughter-in-law. There is a story of the extreme avarice of one mother-in-law who, every time a bed had to be made, would only give her daughter-in-law one sheet, thus forcing her to get the other out of her own trousseau. In any case, the sheets were often so fine that they came to little harm from being used. In theory, the trousseau was kept for several reasons. A girl who had worn out her trousseau 'would be considered a spend-thrift – someone who couldn't keep house.' Sheets were taken out on special occasions: to hang on the barn walls at a wedding; tablecloths and napkins to be used for meals to celebrate threshing or a feast after a pig had been killed. 'We don't use those things in our house! We have them because mother wanted to give me a pretty trousseau – otherwise we don't use them!'

The second argument against using the linen is its impracticality. The sheets are stiff, heavy, and hard to wash or iron. One sheet fills a washing machine nowadays.

For this reason, the trousseau is hoarded in the cupboard; and women are proud to be able to say that they received so much linen that 'their sheets have never seen the bed' or else 'have never been touched by water.' One adds: 'I'll never use it. My trousseau is there in the cupboard; I've never touched it, everything's there, brand new, marked with my initials. They're all there; I haven't touched them!'

Even if the trousseaux marked with their various initials accumulate in the cupboards from mother to daughter, and girls inherit items from the trousseau, they must always have their own trousseau. For a trousseau cannot be handed on. It is unique, attached to each girl, marked with her initials. It is the story of a girl's body, made by herself and her mother. It is the history of nubility acquired and passed on. The treasure stored in the cupboard is seen in a very special light. The white trousseau is certainly the young girl's treasure, the equivalent of her new sexuality and virginity, part of which she tries to keep intact, despite her sexuality as a woman. These sheets, which 'have never been touched by water' have never seen the blood of the girl's periods, of defloration or childbirth, or the sperm of sexual relations either. Isn't this the secret of the trousseau, which old women hand on at the end of their lives?

A FEMININE CULTURE?

If this representation of womanhood, closely linked with sexuality, is shared by men and women, the way in which women see it is of course specific to their sex. For example, the world of linen and its manipulation remains specifically feminine. Isn't this a true culture of materials and embroidery stitches, which women will pass on to anyone who likes to ask about it? If by 'culture' we mean an ensemble of customs and representations shared by a group, it is perhaps wrong to speak of a feminine culture, for these representations of the feminine are shared by men and women. But there are specifically feminine practices. The question is how women see themselves in relation to these social norms. How is the problem of their sexual identification expressed in concrete terms?

Every girl is submitted some day to the duty of the trousseau. We can see how this social modelling of her status as a woman works both as a constraint and as a means of affirming her sexual identity, her social identity and her identity as an individual in her family.

The trousseau, like any norm, is a constraint. Coming after the knitting lesson – a real lesson in deportment, whose essential principle of ensuring a girl's submission to authority has been shown by Verdier – the making of the trousseau is a physical constraint. Spinning, and later embroidery, force one to keep still. At the age when bands of young men are roaming the village night and day, at the age when they are exploring the wilds by hunting, girls are sewing, with backs bent and eyes fixed on the threads to be counted, their attention held by their work. They are also restricted to visible space when, having set their work aside to go to the ball on feast days, they stay under the vigilant eye of their mothers. Unlike the young men, the only area they are allowed to explore is the village. They are never seen in neighbouring villages except when invited to votive feasts by relations. So they are controlled in space, but also in time. Girls must never be seen to be doing nothing; the occupation of free time is an important means of controlling them. Reading is one occupation that is particularly opposed, and girls had to escape out of sight of their parents to indulge in this pastime. One girl (in 1950) took the sentimental magazines *Intimité* and *Confidences* when she went off to look after the animals. Another climbed a tree in order to read novels. In former times, they were restricted by the immeasurable length of time they had to spend spinning, as the story of Penelope reminds us. Finally, the time spent embroidering was controlled: long winters, Sundays and holidays, whole evenings up until 1.00 or 2.00 in the morning. 'We embroidered in all our spare moments.'

In opposition to this feminine immobility, which kept girls under the constant watch of their relations, the girl who roamed was considered very suspicious. She had to be able to justify every movement in the village and reply to the question 'Ont vas?' (Where are you going?), which was the ritual equivalent to 'Good day'.

The trousseau, a constraint on the bodies of women, their space and their time, is even more a constraint on their future. By the symbolical linking of women's biological law to their marriage, the whole of their social existence was subordinated to this law. But our analysis would be at best limited, and perhaps even distorted, if it went no further than these observations. For at the same time as being a constraining norm, the trousseau is a stage in initiation which is filled with positiveness, creativity and pleasure.

In most cases, girls identify positively with their trousseau. What is involved is their social position, the recognition of their status in relation to an entourage aware of its function as social marker. When a woman is aware that it has played this role to positive effect, pleasure and pride are evident in what she says about it. They are expressed in the precise recollection of the quantity and variety of the furniture and items of linen, the quality of the materials, the handiwork and beauty of their embroidery. They are evident in her words, which are punctuated by exclamations, adjectives and superlatives and accompanied by laughter and volubility. There are two accounts, chosen from a much larger number, that bear witness to this. The first is as follows:

> When there was a wedding [in the Landes in 1935], the day before, the neighbouring women would come to hang up the garlands. They would look at the bedroom. The bride would provide the mattress ... I think my husband had bought the base, and we put the feather mattress on. I still have it, and the eiderdowns. My husband had had the room wallpapered. We had chosen pink – it was pretty! It was the prettiest bedroom in those parts! I had a lovely quilt in brocaded satin, with diamonds and a rose on it. My mother had bought it from a representative of the Galeries de Dax. How lovely and warm it was, this quilt, made of ewe's wool. The neighbours went home ... sick ... They said: 'That quilt is prettier than Irène's, the girl who made the best marriage.' We had to open the cupboards and show the linen, the embroideries. The handkerchiefs were tied with favours, pretty ribbons: three! four! five dozen! Whatever could be managed. Mother had bought me a lot at Aire in a shop that only sold trousseaux.
>
> And Valentine was there, in front of the cupboard, and she was peering at everything! I had chemises all hand made! And Valentine had an embroidered sheet which was full of scallops. Her mother said: 'It would be a pity if a peasant put his feet on it!' I don't know if she thought she would marry her off to an engineer. And she married a cattleman – such a peasant! I shall always remember Valentine peering at the linen.

The social importance of the trousseau was all the greater in this marriage, because the girl who was speaking came from a family of smallholders, much less well off than her husband's family, who owned a good farm. Mother and daughter were aware that their social status would be judged publicly on that day. As she said, 'The finer the trousseau, the more it paid tribute to the family it came from.'

The second account is not so much the expression of family respectability as the girl's pride in her own personal ability to acquire and embroider herself her own trousseau, despite the poverty of her social milieu (her father was employed by the railways, and her mother was a daily cleaner).

Oh Lord, the trousseau! I've still got it and I won't ever use it all! But I had embroidered sheets, my dear. I went to learn how to embroider. I could sew, because I liked sewing so much that I took an apprenticeship, but I already knew how to sew, I used to make little things for myself before I went, even as a little girl, because I had it in my blood!

If you could see the whole trousseau, which I've still got, and I'll never use! Imagine nightdresses all embroidered, chemises with straps, all embroidered down the front, the counterprane embroidered with embroidery all down the sides, linen pants, I even have linen ones! . . . One day when you come, I'll show you (you'll see!), with grilles and butteflies on them, *broderie anglaise*, everything . . . oh dear!

This pleasure in speaking of one's trousseau comes out in a number of interviews, especially when the girl has embroidered it herself. But it is also there when, although she could not manage this difficult art very well herself, she had been able to earn enough to buy lovely things and have them embroidered by a specialist, with her mother's help.

SOCIAL NORM AND IDENTITY

Reticence or silence, on the other hand, betray an anomaly. A certain number of very poor girls lack the means to live this period of initiation to the full. Their accounts are of a kind of failure. Three women who were young and poor between 1900 and 1930 told us of their experiences. The first was born in Aveyron in 1907, to a family of very poor farmers. The fourth of a family of eleven children, she was found a job as a farm servant at the age of seven. The account of her life is a series of positions with employers who are systematically associated in her memory with the amount of food they gave her. Her meagre wages, when she was a farm servant, were used by her parents to feed her younger brothers and sisters. This explains why she was unable to begin her trousseau even after she had reached eighteen. She had an illegitimate child at twenty-three, and any prospect of marriage seemed unlikely. Nevertheless she managed to get her wages out of her father's hands and put them into a savings bank. When, at the age of forty, she married a widower, who had seven children, she was able to bring with her a small trousseau, made up of a blanket and a dozen towels. But she immediately adds to her account what she was unable to have: 'Table napkins, those I didn't have.' And when she spoke of the sheets she brought, it was to compare the three pairs she managed to accumulate with the twelve pairs other women could afford. As for embroidery, she replied abruptly to the question: 'I did the letter, no more, and the grille.'

Material poverty and transgression of the norm (an illegitimate birth) together explain the impossibility of having a trousseau that was at least 'decent'. Her regrets are detected in the way in which she speaks of her wedding, the symbol of her social and personal lack of identity, with no white dress, no engagement ring, no wedding ring, no party. She even had to negotiate with her father to persuade him to buy her a coat and a handbag.

Again material poverty, the depth of which she feels incapable of conveying to her young interlocutor, explains the absence of a troussseau in the account of another woman. Born in 1899, she was the daughter of a wood-turner from Saint-Cirq-Lapopie. She became a maid servant at fourteen, and worked as one in Toulouse during the War of 1914. She earned 18 francs a month. 'A pair of shoes cost 17 francs, so how could you save anything? My parents had nothing. You understand?' Yet she married in 1919 and had a tiny trousseau, a little linen given her by some relations who had moved to Paris, a few brassieres she embroidered in her maid's room in Toulouse: 'something I made myself, I couldn't afford material, you understand.'

The absence of a mother increased her feeling of poverty. The youngest daughter of a family of seven children born to farmers from Aveyron, she too worked as a farm servant. She explains the smallness of her trousseau by the early death of her mother, who, despite the family's great poverty, had managed to build up trousseaux for her elder sisters Without this affectionate complicity between mother and daughter, she was unable to have an embroidered trousseau. She had to work extremely hard just to be able to afford the 'most basic' linen. How could she have found time to embroider it as well?

Alice, born in 1905 in the Lot, who was found a job by the social workers as a servant in a family of comfortable landowners, tells the same story: 'I didn't build up a trousseau. I didn't have anyone. I liked sewing and embroidery, but I needed someone to help me.' The absence of a mother was felt all the more keenly because there was no one around her to pass on to her what a mother usually passes on to her daughter; and the absence of a trousseau further increased her precarious status as a child who had been in care. Material poverty and emotional poverty went hand in hand.

Whereas for most girls the trousseau has positive social and symbolic significance, because they put ambition, creativity and affection into it, for some it is the sign of a painful failure, due to a material and moral poverty which is more than they can overcome. Having a fine trousseau thus represents an ideal to be attained, for all girls, and especially for the poorest.

But what is sometimes even more important than her social position is a girl's position within the family, in relation to her sisters, mother and father. This can have considerable bearing on the trousseau. In so far as it is the product of the combined efforts of mother and daughter, it becomes a favourite area of conflict between parents and children, especially when it comes to the children's choice of partner. Parental attitudes vary, as the two following cases show.

The daughter of a landowner from the Tarn was seeing a young blacksmith from the next village (in about 1950). The girl's father was against this relationship: 'They wanted me to marry someone from the countryside.' Clandestine meeting continued despite the combined vigilance of parents and brothers and sisters. The girl's stubbornness was such that in the end it was the parents who gave in. After the girl had gone on hunger strike, which produced a spectacular loss of weight, the father agreed to the young man making official visits to the house. But the parents showed their disapproval in the subtlest way, by treating the sister's fiancé and this daughter's fiancé differently in a number of ways. Whereas the sister's fiancé was treated like a lord when he paid his Sunday visits, because he was a comfortable landowner, the blacksmith was offered nothing to drink. The girl herself had to use her own wages to buy white wine to entertain her fiancé in the proper manner. And while all mothers made it a point of honour to give equal trousseaux to their daughters at the appropriate time, in this case the trousseaux were clearly unequal. Her mother bought her only a few sheets, while the father bought her sister a 'prettier' bedroom. We are hardly surprised to learn that she dug her heels in when it came to contributing the wages she earned as a shop-girl to the common family savings. Building up the largest and finest trousseau is a way of affirming one's value despite one's parents, and of affirming the value of one's despised marriage. It is also a way of affirming one's own will through a traditional activity to which one's parents cannot object.

The other account tells of a more violent conflict, to which the girl finally fell victim. A girl born in the Gers in 1905 was seeing a neighbour of whom her father did not approve. The boy was on the 'other side' in a village where two factions tore each other apart for apparently political reasons. The young couple saw one another in secret. To escape parental vigilance, they would meet 'in the lanes, in the fields, by the stream'. The narrator clearly enjoys recounting her disobedience. But in the end the father's anger and threats discouraged the suitor. The couple drifted apart. She 'missed him', she says, and admits to having kept his photo in a medallion worn over her heart all her life. The account, which is very detailed up to this point, accelerates from then on, as the girl evokes succinctly the series of misfortunes that came one after the other. She left to work as a maid servant for her aunt, became pregnant and was forced to return home, where she was shut up night and day, and then sent off to another aunt to have the baby. She finally abandoned the child. 'They made me abandon the kid,' she says. 'Then they made me go off and be a maid again.' She could not express more clearly the impression that she had been the passive plaything of external wills. Later, with the same passivity, she agreed to marry a café waiter introduced by her aunt. She agreed 'as long as he didn't get drunk. For the rest . . .'

When she had been given a job as a young maid servant in her aunt's house, it was on the aunt's advice, and in a way as a reaction against her parents, that she kept her wages instead of sending them to her parents, and saved up to buy herself things for her bedroom. She describes the pretty things she bought. Then came her illegitimate pregnancy. Her furniture and linen followed her back to her parents. Her younger sister married shortly after that and committed an act which sixty years later still aroused the narrator's indignation: 'My sister took my sheets, which weren't marked, because she got married before me. She took them. Do you think my father was reasonable then? He knew very well that they were mine. I was so angry! When I saw that, I was angry!'

This is the only point in her account when she expresses anger and indignation at her father's very hard attitude. Although she is only talking about two sheets, the theft of her trousseau, bought with her hard-earned wages, was symbolically a very serious act. It showed how little the parents valued a daughter who had lost her honour and who was therefore as nothing. Above all, it meant that in the eyes of her family she was no longer marriageable, so she no longer needed a trousseau.

The family's punishment through the affair of the trousseau was very hard. Not only did the parents not give her anything, they even went so far as to 'take' the linen she had bought. This is why, later, she was so adamant about recovering her bedroom furniture and everything that belonged to her a few days before her wedding. Her parents could hardly object.

Since the trousseau had such significance in terms of a girl's social place and the place within her sibling group *vis-à-vis* her parents, how could she not put all her energy into it? The only example to contradict this is that of a middle-class girl from Carcassonne, brought up by the Ursulines before the First World War and married in 1923. She was quick to compare her 'little trousseau' with the very large one possessed by her mother, the only daughter of a mother who had given her everything. Yet in the course of the interview she admitted to having had a considerable number of sheets, although she would not say how many, just as she would not give the number of chemises and undergarments she had. 'Oh yes, I was given sheets and napkins, and I still have them.' One has the impression that she did not consider her trousseau very important – she had not embroidered it herself. A maid servant had done most of it, although her mother insisted that she should embroider some of it herself: 'Oh! it was the fashion!' Her dislike of embroidery is clear in the story she tells of her twin sister, her mother and her sister-in-law.

> I remember, we were real children. We used to climb trees and take a novel, a book, and then no one bothered us. But I had a sister-in-law, the wife of my brother, who was at the front, and she said to my mother: 'Look at Elise and Mélanie, they aren't doing anything, they're always up in the trees reading books; and she would embroider and embroider and embroider! Then mother said: 'You'll never learn how to do anything, my poor girls.' 'Yes, Mummy, we will learn!'

These girls, like boys perched up in the trees, refused to fit into the constricting mould of female embroidery. But for them the trousseau had no social significance and did not constitute a personal battleground. Their mother, with whom they got on very well, was willing to ignore their attitude, and the marriage which followed took place entirely in accordance with the parents' wishes. The girls learned to embroider at the appropriate age. Another girl, from Normandy, born around 1925, also marked her trousseau tea towels with cross-stitch conscientiously, but without conviction. 'I thought it was stupid. Everybody knew the linen was ours and how much we had!' she says, pretending to believe that linen was marked so that it could be recognized. But she still did it, and was happy to prepare a trousseau which showed that she would be leaving the house where her mother ruled, a mother whom she says she did not love.

These two girls may have disputed the meaning of embroidery, and shown no interest in it, but in both cases they had a large trousseau and a big, stylish wedding. They still went through the necessary stages in the passage from puberty to marriage.

When this is not the case, and an illegitimate birth disturbs the normal course of a young girl's life, women try later on to relive the stage they missed. If they get married, they never tire of building up their trousseau afterwards, saving penny by penny in order to buy the things for the bedroom and the linen, in particular the sheets that they have embroidered or embroider themselves – either with the initials of both spouses, or even with the initials they had before marriage. It appears that even if circumstances turn out in such a way that the normal order of events is upset, such an essential stage cannot be missed out.

Nowadays, when they have a trousseau, girls no longer embroider it, thus showing that they are spending their youth on other things than the linen of their future marriage. For the girls of today, who more often go to school, and for longer, the way to womanhood apparently no longer takes in this stage or these techniques. The trousseau is no longer important, even if mothers sometimes insist on it, by regularly buying sheets to remind their rather passive schoolgirl or student daughters that they will be married one day, even if mothers and daughters often have a happy time together, when the time for the wedding finally approaches, choosing fine household linen in specialist shops and so on.

MASCULINE – FEMININE

In rural society, the period from puberty to marriage is marked for both sexes by a series of experiences through which girls and boys acquire femininity or virility. In parallel to the girls' experience of the trousseau (among other things), boys spend their youth in groups exploring a number of areas that are forbidden, but to which they still go – for example, the wild spaces. 'Being young' for a boy means earning a virile identity, as shown in the works of Daniel Fabre.[14]

At this point in life, the feminine and masculine domains have to be both separate and complementary in order for marriage to become necessary.[15] The masculine and the feminine are defined in a series of specific practices and are constantly coming up against each another.

It is this permanent confrontation, which occurs in the economic activities in which men and women each have their roles, that Claudine Fabre-Vassas[16] has considered. She shows, in relation to the domestic breeding of pigs, how men and women each use the powers they are recognized as having. This is particularly clear every year on the day when the killing of the pig is celebrated, thus marking the end of the breeding cycle.

The day the animal is killed, men and women have roles that are exclusive to their sex. A man, the 'bleeder', kills the pig, and once the blood is flowing, it is the women who start work collecting the blood and cooking it. The making of black pudding with pig's blood is full of ritual significance, from which men are excluded. If they were even present, the puddings would burst. The culinary practices, words, oaths, and even the comedy involved in the making of black pudding, constitutes a dramatization of gestation. There is conception, pregnancy, childbirth, and even baptism. At the end of a painstaking analysis, which we cannot even summarize here, Fabre-Vassas shows how in this activity women alone master the whole process of reproduction and symbolically appropriate the masculine element. They are able to do this in the making of black pudding because the animal's blood is thought of, in this society, as analogous to their own menstrual blood. Their physiology gives them specific powers over the animal's blood. In other places, such as Minot, black puddings are not made, but the meat is salted. This is a specifically masculine activity from which women are excluded. The salting is also a sort of gestation, controlled exclusively by men, who thus take over the feminine role. The fat is the opposite of the blood, and the meat to be salted must be free from blood. But in both of these opposite and symmetrical activities blood is seen as a feminine domain. We see how, in connection with the same economic production with similar elements, the categories of masculine and feminine cover the activities of men and women, how these categories are constantly manipulated and redefined, proof that the symbolic is an essential feature of the relationship between the sexes.

But it seems premature, at a time when this type of investigation of sexual symbolism is in the early stages, to make a synthesis of what is at the root of these categories in our societies, and even more premature to write a history of it.

It was said at the Saint-Maximin Symposium in 1983 that we can no longer write women's history, but rather the history of the relationship between the sexes. This seems to me entirely in keeping with current research in ethnology. But perhaps, for the sake of clarity in our debates, we must distinguish between different levels of analysis because they imply different methodological tools.

I would distinguish two: on the one hand analysis of women's place as a biologically and socially defined group – their place in the system of family relationships and production. Isn't the control of human progeny by a group as important a social factor as the control of the products of work? This is the problem that societies have solved by thinking out their family relationships, which are essential to an understanding of the status of women. The object of the anthropology of family relationships is to try to shed light on these questions, particularly in our societies. Women's history would then be the history of their place in the social relations of production and reproduction in different societies (ancient, medieval, modern, rural and urban).

The second level would be that of sexual symbolism, as seen by individuals of both sexes (and not only by the protagonists of political and ideological power). But analysis of the categories 'masculine' and 'feminine' implies a specific type of approach. It concerns both sexes, since men and women are constantly manipulating both these categories, even if they are seen in specific ways by each sex. It may seem artificial to distinguish these two levels, which are of necessity closely interwoven. But they have two different time-scales. Whereas the economic and social political conditions that have defined the place of women in our society for centuries have to be considered in a very detailed chronology, the symbolic link between a girl, her marriage and her trousseau, to take up this example once more, involves a long period of time. It is highly probable that the link described in the reminiscences of women married before the First World War was of the same nature as that of previous centuries. Of course it took different forms, as we have seen, from the spun sheets, the bed and the wedding garments found in the oldest marriage contracts up to the bedroom furnishings and household linen of more recent times. The most important thing is surely to appreciate the permanence of the importance of contributing the bridal bedroom rather than to note the detailed changes in terms of the individual items. We are talking about a long span of time which may, nevertheless, see various minor points of change.

If, since the 1970s, the feminine trousseau no longer represents something essential, shouldn't we see in this the sign of a fundamental change in the conditions of marriage and female sexuality and in their social representations?

1 It is not possible to give even a succinct bibliography of the very many anthropological works on women that have appeared in France and elsewhere, and still less an account of the questions involved. In France, a workshop on 'Anthropology of women and women anthropologists' was held in November 1981 within the framework of the First Congress of the French Association of Anthropologists. The reader may consult the report of this workshop, which appeared in June 1982 in the *Bulletin de l'Association française des anthropologues*, no. 8. See also my article, 'Linge de corps et linge de maison' in *Ethnologie française*, 1986, no. 3.

2 Verdier, *Façons de dire, façons de faire*; S. C. Rogers with Hugues Lamarche and Claude Karnoouh, *Paysans, femmes et citoyens* (Actes Sud, 1980); Segalen, *Mari et femme*.

3 Jack Goody and S. J. Tambiah, *Bridewealth and Dowry* (Cambridge University Press, Cambridge, 1973).

4 Pierre Bourdieu, 'Les stratégies matrimoniales dans le système de reproduction', *Annales ESC*, 4–5, pp. 1105–27.

5 This is no more than a summary of a much larger piece of work on nineteenth- and twentieth-century marriage in the south-west of France, and in particular on matrimonial ceremonies, the dowry and the trousseau. My research is based in part on a corpus of oral investigations consisting of some hundred interviews. Some I conducted personally, starting in 1978, in particular in the Sault area, others were conducted by undergraduates of Toulouse University as part of a credit system organized by Jack Thomas and myself. I must express my gratitude to those who were willing to talk about themselves, in particular Mesdames Clamens, Dutto, Huguet, Lignon, Marty, Puibuesque, Pous, Savy, and Messieurs Blanc, Pous, Vaysse. My thanks also to the students whose work is quoted here: MM Andreu, Baldecchi, Bayol, Benoffi, Birou, Borloz, Cabare, Casteran, Chataignier, Chong-Kee, Cochet-Jammes, Delesalle, Duneau, Françoise, Ginisty, Guillen, Larroque, Latger, Laverny, Leveziel, Marsan, Martinez, Monferran, Places, Query, Ravix, Souquet, Spierkel-Lasserre, Tournadre, Vareilles.

6 G. Sicard, *Comportements juridiques et société*. Les contrats de mariage avant et après la Révolution (Toulouse et pays toulousain). Annales de l'Université des Sciences Sociales de Toulouse, 1978.

7 D. Dolci, *Récits siciliens* (Einaudi, Turin, 2nd edn, 1963).

8 J. Amades, *Folklore de Catalunya, costums i creences* (Editorial selecta bibioteca perenne, 1980) p. 316.

9 R. Bonnain, *Trousseau et contrats de mariage dans les Pyrénées autour de la Révolution*, in Lavedan et Pays toy, no. 15, special edn, 1983.

10 Notarial contracts from Briatexte. Collected by M. R. Sabathier.

11 Archives départementales de Carcassonne. 3E, 6577–82, 6595, 6611, 6656, 6658, 6671.

12 A. Van Gennep, *Manuel de Folklore français contemporain*, Book I, vol. 1 (Picard, Paris, 1977). On 'le transport du trousseau', see pp. 352–9; on 'la coutume de la rôtie', vol. 2, pp. 560–72.

13 Verdier, *Façons de dire, façons de faire*, ch. IV: the seamstress, pp. 187ff.

14 See in particular the following works by D. Fabre: 'La voie des oiseaux. Sur quelques récits d'apprentissage', *L'Homme*, vol. XXVI–3, no. 99, pp. 7–34; 'Le garçon enceint', *Cahiers de littérature orale*, no. 20, pp. 15–38; with Charles Camberoque, *La Fête en Languedoc* (Privat, Toulouse, 1977); 'Juvéniles revenants', *Etudes Rurales*, no. 105–6, pp. 147–64; 'L'enfance d'un roi', *Ethnologie française*, no. 4.

15 Lévi-Strauss explains the division of work as the institution of a state of reciprocal dependence between the sexes. Cf. *Le regard éloigné* ch. III, p. 81.

16 C. Fabre-Vassas, doctoral thesis (Ecole des Hautes Etudes en Sciences Sociales) to be published in 1992: 'La Bête singulière: Juifs et chrétiens autour du cochon'. She developed this theme at a conference organized by the Groupe de Recherches Interdisciplinaire d'Etude des Femmes (at the University of Toulouse le Mirail) in June, 1983, entitled 'The death of a pig and women's blood'.

11

Feminist Singularity: A Critical Historiography of the History of Feminism in France

Geneviève Fraisse

By way of introduction I should like to draw attention to something that I believe to be specific to the French history of feminism. Born of the union between social history and the history of mentalities, it seems to me that it belongs to neither. It is too interested in private life for the first and too interested in political life for the second.[1] For this reason it has been given minimal recognition, if not ignored, by the professional historian, although the history of feminism has been of great importance in the early stages of women's history since 1970. This is certainly specific to France when we see how, moving in the opposite direction, the Anglo-Saxon countries, faced with the large number of works on the history of feminism, seem to be seeking to open the field to a history of women in general in order, no doubt, to compensate for a conception of the political history of women that has been too close to an abstract account of the winning of equalities.

There is a second point that deserves attention. Publications on the history of French feminism are mostly the work of foreign authors or authors outside the historical institution, whether they be scholars from another discipline or those who, whether historians or not, have chosen to produce militant writings or popularizing texts (or even both at once). If we examine the books produced,[2] in other words, those that make feminism the central axis of their analysis, we find something that is very much peculiar to women's history, something that is unknown to the professional historian who at once thinks of feminism if anyone mentions the history of women, thus dismissing the necessary distinction between the history of women and the history of feminism, between an analysis of condition and an analysis of subversion, a distinction which forces one to define one's subject clearly and to avoid making 'women's history' an ideological rag-bag denied any identity of its own. It is true that works on feminism encounter a twofold difficulty, that of being adopted and misrepresented by fashion and the media and that of being subjected to what might be called political superegos. Both of these factors, in their different ways, create an obstacle to the intellectual rigour that is usual and commonly accepted in university circles.

I have chosen to study here only the books written in this area, thus excluding articles in journals and unpublished theses.[3] This arbitrary division is, however, of little importance, for it is not the content or the scope of these works that interests me at the moment – simply their Prefaces, which I think are rich in clues as to the delimitation of a field: that of the history of feminism. Moreover, these Prefaces often reveal their author, and highlight the fact that in this subject he or she is almost always – and I include myself here – both judge and judged.

This reading of Prefaces or Introductions at once shows the importance of the relationship between present and past, a relationship of which we all know, of course, that history is made, but – and this is less common – a relationship expressed as such. It is very marked nowadays and certainly expresses a very contemporary sensitivity. Nevertheless it is not new, and in this sense it is perhaps fundamental. In 1926, Marguerite Thibert, who wrote at a time when feminism was flourishing, spoke of 'similarity of tendencies', of 'natural affinity' and 'gratitude'; Edith Thomas, whose work was published after the Second World War at a time when feminism was absent from the scene, is more restrained because she says nothing of the feminists of the 1848 Revolution, but presents Pauline Roland as a 'singular destiny' and 'significant'.[4] That was not the time for collective conscience. What does the feminism of today tell us about the feminism of yesterday?

OBSERVANCE OF THE DIVISIONS

This is the alternative. There are some men and women who place themselves in a unique relationship with feminism and some who only consider the relationship with feminism in relation to socialism. The link between the present and the past is thus situated either inside or outside the feminist struggle.

Permanence and distance

One may stress the similarities between yesterday and today. For Valentin Pelosse, a man, the modernity of Claire Demar's texts is a sign of the permanence of the oppression of women, the terms of which have not been changed by 150 years of history. Inversely, one may be struck by the positive aspect of this similarity, the repetition of the struggle and the will to win freedom. Women authors, in the main, underline the parallelism of claims, even at the risk of overstating this parallelism, as in Edith Taïeb's Preface to the writings of Hubertine Auclert (pp. 52–3).

In a warmer and more intimate way, women see in history a means of identification. Evelyne Le Garrec, a feminist and a journalist like her subject Séverine, explains that writing her biography was 'a question of sentiment'; Huguette Bouchardeau claims the author's subjectivity and assumes an 'aftertaste of revenge' in writing a book on the feminism of the years between 1918 and 1968, a period before the more collective renaissance and one that was her own, which Betty Friedan called that of the 'reticent heroines'.[5] Sometimes this relationship between author and subject goes hand in hand with an explicit value judgement: Maïté Albistur and Daniel Armogathe, in an attempt to avoid hasty identification, state that in the history of French feminism 'yesterday is more timid than today', but inversely Lydia Elhadad describes Suzanne Voilquin as a 'dissident', a superlative heavy with connotations in recent times. What is more, a value judgement can become a historical judgement: Laure Adler, seeking the similarities and differences between 1830 and 1970, concludes that the striking feature is one of similarity, that of the repeated defeat of feminism.

Other authors, particularly male ones, are more circumspect, and prefer to keep their distance. In the Introduction to his book, Jean Rabaut uses the image of the person who is aware of being 'on the inside' as far as erudite research is concerned, but 'on the outside' because he has a masculine standpoint, 'an observation which is both sympathetic and critical and does not exclude, where appropriate, either tenderness or humour.' Alain Dalotel wonders if he has really understood Paule Minck: 'Are men, however well intentioned, capable of listening to women and explaining their thoughts? The answer is doubtless no. But perhaps they can at least reject some of their masculine fantasies' (p. 11). One is calmer in his lucidity than the other; both reveal a strange and yet banal fact: the historian must treat himself as a subject, and the male historian of feminism is forced to do this more quickly than the female historian. And even if we are looking at a simple list of points rather than an analysis of the situation, it is clear that this historical subject, feminism, brings into play not just individual, but also sexual, subjectivity. The historian is not forced to take sides in quite the same way by the working class, the peasants, the proleteriat or the middle classes, which are of course not neutral subjects, but which do not compel a radical and definitive recognition of a difference, not to say opposition, between the sexes. This kind of history thus becomes a dangerous game, for it is in itself a kind of commitment. Witness the curious decision of Benoîte Groult. In order to talk of past feminism, she chooses (for what reason of prudence or justification?) to consider the feminist men of the nineteenth century. On the pretext of being on the inside, she prefers to remain outside.

The history of feminism certainly rules out indifference in analysis.

Feminism, socialism, trade-unionism

It is important that the history of feminism should not be an exclusive history, isolated from other political movements. Feminist life is often related to other things, utopias or socialist organizations, unionist practices and struggles. For this reason these relations of inclusion or exclusion are the starting-point for analyses and interpretations. Two authors have written reference works: Marie-Hélène Zylberberg-Hocquard and Charles Sowerwine.

The question of this relationship seems to be raised by an enquiry into the legitimacy of feminism as such, into its political validity. Zylberberg-Hocquard, in her first book on feminism and trade-unionism, draws on the history of mentalities rather than on political history, which seems to me a defensive position in the face of the political provocation the feminist struggle constantly arouses. The book on the relationship with the workers' movement at once places itself in a political context, but refuses to analyse the conflict between feminism and socialism in terms of structure, which is perhaps inherent in this difficult relationship. On the one hand, feminism today is validated on the grounds of its 'efficacity', as if the author is obliged to show gratitude to her own time, but on the other hand, the feminism of yesterday does not enjoy the same indulgence on the part of the (female) historian, because it failed to 'touch the working class'. One might, on the contrary, be struck by the similarity of the tensions between feminism and the workers' movement over almost the last hundred years. But that would commit one to another perception of feminist reality.

Charles Sowerwine is more nostalgic: he wonders why the women's socialist movement should be accused of failing, and why, since 1900, feminism and socialism have turned their backs on one another. Unfortunately, by the end of the Introduction, this examination of the relationship has become curiously unbalanced. What we find is that the socialists 'accept' the *theoretical* equality of men and women and that the feminists 'fail' to touch the working woman *on a practical level*. So he gives a plus point to the socialists and a minus point to the feminists in an unequal comparison, between theory and practice. We are surprised to see him putting forward judgements that are perhaps also prejudices. It is as if this question of the relationship of feminism to other political groupings, particularly those closest to it, were always raised from the outside and led inevitably to disappointment or even condemnation.

So it is amusing to see a militant female member of the CGT (France's largest trade union), of necessity outside the feminist movement, making a historical judgement that is less harsh towards feminists. Madeleine Colin speaks of the 'courage of the intellectual middle-class feminists', criticism which reveals a positive approach in which feminism does appear on the political battlefield, even if it is saddled with categories such as 'middle class' and 'intellectual', which are reproaches. In fact we need to examine these categories.

WHAT IS A HISTORY OF FEMINISM?

In general, the texts I have read do not answer this question; and yet, where does feminism begin and end? Should we have to define it in terms of progress or revolt, of sensitivity to a period or, on the contrary, of anachronism? Are the rules of legal or educational institutions or those of professional organizations appropriate measures for the analysis of oppression or emancipation, and of the rights allowed to, or recognized as being held by, women? Finally, if we know that the word 'feminism' appeared at the end of the Second Empire,[6] how do we define the phenomenon itself before the existence of the term? And then how do we use it to study the multiplicity of sometimes contradictory strategies or initiatives aimed at winning emancipation and equality?

The Prefaces and Introductions do not discuss these questions. Instead, their authors talk about categories of people. Who is a feminist? It is not so much a question of giving labels as of knowing which women are the feminists.

Uncommon figures

This expression was used by Olivier Blanc of Olympe de Gouges. In the same way Edith Thomas speaks of the 'significant singular destiny' of Pauline Roland. Uncommon figures: one thus avoids famous women like courtesans and princesses, as well as political heroines, who are often taken for feminists – for example, George Sand, Flora Tristan, Louise

Michel, even though they may have dismissed the feminist struggle of thier time or shown a theoretical or practical misogyny scarcely in keeping with claims for equality. These 'symbolic heroines'[7] do not convey a reality in which the exceptional has been misunderstood or mistreated rather than overemphasized, and in which instead the solitude of uncommon women, feminists, has, from the nineteenth century onwards, often been associated with the existence of collective networks which today we would call a movement. For this reason it seems questionable to marginalize them to the point of making them, in Zylberberg-Hocquard's expression, 'exceptional women' as opposed to ordinary women. They thus lose any power to represent anything, and become simply 'rare birds', lost in a social vacuum.

This 'uncommon' character might perhaps be further defined by Alain Dalotel's notion of the 'unclassifiable' when he discusses Paule Minck. On the one hand, this avoids a judgement of what constitutes the ordinary and the exceptional in every feminist, and on the other, it brings in what, to my mind, is the nodal problem for feminism – that of political classification. The unclassifiable is neither a republican bourgeoise nor an obedient socialist, two figures which reduce the importance of the feminist. Nor can the unclassifiable be strictly assimilated to one social class or one political party. Moreover, the three French heroines of the nineteenth century mentioned above are certainly more politically classifiable, besides the fact that their exceptional status is enough in itself. The fact that we cannot immediately put a tag on each feminist undoubtedly gets to the heart of this particular political and ideological commitment.

Uncommon, not exceptional, unclassifiable: this difficulty in describing the feminist individual is perhaps one of the reasons why feminism is always forgotten by the people and by historians. After the revolt aroused by this forgetfulness, we need to analyse and understand its causes. If misogynous history exists, we cannot content ourselves with the excuse that society itself is misogynous. The writing of history obeys obligatory norms and divisions produced by the very conception of history. The digging up of a suppressed history invites us to go beyond the gesture of claiming a memory and repairing an omission.

The category of female worker and feminist discourse

For a long time feminists were justifiably classed as suffragettes – in other words, middle-class and intellectual. Socialism helped greatly to create this image, for it was as necessary to maintain a contradiction between feminism and socialism, as between feminism and trade-unionism. This contradiction centres on the awareness of the existence of the female salaried worker. Thus for Madeleine Colin (and she is not alone in this), there exist on the one hand the 'courageous middle-class feminists' and on the other 'the essential struggle of female workers'. Apart from the fact that she is comparing a quality with an essence and individuals with a practice, she underlines yet again the fact that the problem of women, outside the world of work, takes us back to a secondary contradiction within the Marxist analysis of the contradictions of capitalism. But, looking at the problem the other way round, it emerges that the feminist is *ipso facto* ignorant of the problem of work. It does not concern her. Thus not only is the militant feminist an exception to the great mass of women, she is also the bourgeoise or even the petite-bourgeoise, shirking the first reality of earning and the cost of daily bread.

In reply to this reproach, both historical and contemporary, I would make two remarks, or rather I would suggest two directions for work: 'Does feminism ignore the question of women's work?' No. Certainly not, as far as interesting work is concerned (the opening up of the professions and careers), nor indeed at the level of industrial work, the point of contention. I shall give two examples taken from many others. Julie-Victoire Daubié (1824–74) was not only the first French woman to pass the baccalauréat, but also the author of a voluminous work, *La Femme pauvre au XIXe siècle* (1866), in which she gives a systematic description of all the jobs, working-class in particular, that women could do in order to avoid poverty. The poor woman is the woman who needs to be given 'means of subsistence' other than prostitution. Elisa Lemmonier, a former Saint-Simonian, was one of the founders, in 1862, of the first lay-professional school opened for girls with the exact aim of improving the situation of female workers. These two examples predate the moment when socialism and the trade unions took up responsibility for working-class work. Afterwards, if feminists did not submit to this authority, their work could only be viewed with suspicion, like the congress on women's work organized by Marguerite Durand in 1907, denounced by political and trade-union organizations. It looks as if the institutions of the left have shown a marked deafness before any precise discussions on the subject were possible.

The writing of the history of feminism forces a recognition of one dimension – in my view an essential one – of feminism: the use of discourse. Discourse has a dominant place in the feminist struggle, whether this is visible through that I might call 'the move to become heard' (the setting up of newspapers as the first militant act) or manifest in the demands, and in the urgency, of the feminist argument, the constantly renewed demonstration of the justification of the demands. Exploitation of the workforce is easier to recognize than exploitation of women, which some people deny altogether. Hence the repeated need to justify the revolt and the struggle.

So feminist discourse often takes the form of moralism, if by that we mean an expression that falls between the heritage of tradition and the desire for liberation, a reflection subordinate to the obligatory represen- tation of the opposition of nature and culture in women's lives. A study of the history of feminism can only be seen as an analysis of discourse if it is clear that this is not one method among others, but both a methodological and a theoretical necessity. This is why – and this is my point – feminism can cut through class and socio-professional categories, not because it ignores the female worker, but because the problem of salaried work cannot be isolated from a whole network of difficulties common to women as a whole.

THE METAPHORS OF THE HISTORY OF FEMINISM

Because it has been forgotten, this history jumps out when it is found again. We look, we dig, we explore this field, which is still so ill defined, and we see something that others had not seen, and we describe what we see as far as we can. We also get to know people – but whom, and how?

The privilege of vision

We must say at once that the notion of the vision is far from being specific to women's history, still less to the history of feminism. Indeed Edith Thomas cites Jules Michelet in order to stake her claim to history as vision. Nevertheless, we may note a certain insistence on the part of authors who write on feminism as they use the visible as the image of their objective or method.

The history of feminism has been forgotten and overshadowed; today we are seeing its emergence and unveiling: Maïté Albistur and Daniel Armogathe thus want to see an updating that might also 'shed light' on the present. The iconography proposed in their *Grief des femmes* runs counter to the 'opaqueness' of history for the images of yesterday, and their 'reflections' can be extended by the way we look at them.

This updating may be coupled with a clarification. Daniel Armogathe wishes to see Suzanne Voilquin's face more clearly because he 'needed a few more traits to clarify the contours'. Olivier Blanc, putting together the 'puzzle' of Olympe de Gouges's life, intends her biography to be a clarification, in this case in the sense of setting the record straight.

Updating and clarification – doesn't women's history invite us, as Pascale Werner says in her Introduction to *L'Histoire sans qualités*, to draw up a new 'geography', a 'historical landscape' in which feminist research leads us 'to people space in a different way' and 'to move the boundaries'?

This desire to make things visible seems to me to have a double meaning. We can of course ask ourselves if writing history is really 'making people see' what has necessarily been forgotten or inadequately remembered, but, above all, we need to analyse what this means in the new field of the history of feminism. The desire to see as much as to make visible arises out of a method that makes me uncomfortable today. Whether one takes one's place inside or outside feminism, and whether one is identifying or making a judgement (as in the positions described above), the result remains at the level of designation, almost of pointing one's finger. This search for a vision and the words with which to describe it are scarcely analysed as a *way of seeing*. Today we should be able to go beyond the immediacy of the first glance.

Seeing and knowing[8]

This might be our objective: to know, and not simply to see. But how are we to know, and whom or what are we to know? This applies as much to our process of working, our objectives, motivations and methods, as to the object studied – in this case, feminism.

First, on the level of the method of work, the history of feminism (and indeed feminism itself) is a history whose justification has to be established. Thus it is insufficient to state that history is lost and at the same time that it must be reappropriated. Not that this is completely untrue; simply that we have to understand precisely why it was lost, for this will give us clues as to how to go about rediscovering it. Otherwise, to continue to say that we must find what is hidden and excluded from misogynous history is to confuse cause and effect by being content with the presupposition of the misdeeds of patriarchal society and male history; and this is never an explanation, simply a denunciation. In terms of historical research, to speak of loss and reappropriation supposes that archive material is an object in itself. On the one hand, this is never true, and on the other, the history of feminism is peculiar in that it was denied at the very time when it came into existence. More than other struggles or revolts, feminism arouses, at the moment when it expresses itself, both lack of recognition and a ban on recognition. The loss is contemporary with the act, probably more than in other historical fields.

This is not the place to pursue this analysis, but we shall note here the need for work on the causes of forgetting. I was seeking, above, in the 'unclassifiable' nature of the feminist, one of the reasons for the fact that the history of feminism has been forgotten. Another reason probably lies in the immediacy of the neutralization of feminism.

The transformation of this double idea, of forgetting and reappropriation, requires new markers if we are to achieve a real updating of history. In particular, the fact that most of the time it is women who are carrying out research into the history of feminism gives a new status to this work: new, but dangerous on several levels, as much methodological as ideological. More than for the history of other political movements, the history of feminism, and indeed of women in general, excludes this usual minimal distancing between the subject and the object of research. Thus the forgetfulness of yesterday is replaced rather too easily by a process of recognition which involves a game of identification and opposition. Perhaps we might propose a relationship of 'interlocution' between the female historian and the feminism of the past, if by this we mean not so much an obligatory two-way movement between the positions and analyses of different periods as a constant process of distancing from this privileged position, which is both good and bad.[9]

These questions on the presuppositions of the processes involved in the history of feminism raise the problem of content. This whole study turns on the delimitation of the field of this history, but as in the texts quoted and used, it does not produce a definition of it. However, it seems to me possible, by way of a conclusion, to mark the history of feminism with a twofold dimension which distinguishes it from the history of women. Feminism allows us to represent women as a historical subject on the one hand, and a political subject on the other. I deliberately use this term 'subject', which is suspect in the eyes of contemporary philosophy. But perhaps feminism is anachronic, deaf to a contemporary thinking no longer troubled by this question of subject? Above all, feminism only affirms the subject as a paradox. The notion of difference (the difference between the sexes) being the very principle of feminist enquiry, it is not insignificant that the subject should be defined from the standpoint of the Other – Woman – whereas the philosophical subject is first of all a subject of the Same.

If feminist women are subjects for history, then analyses may be proposed, going beyond the sex or class struggle, where the choice is limited to an ahistorical representation of the struggles and a desire for the political reduction of an autonomous movement. Consequently, speaking of a historical subject enables us to see women outside a traditional, or exceptional, framework, and to see them as social or political protagonists.

If women are also political subjects, we must allow them something other than an evolutionary progression from private space to public space. We must place them in political life as a whole. What does a feminist do, once she has ceased to be perceived as a woman claiming equality in the most basic sense of the term, like a suffragette for example – in other words, a figure of political resentment? She thinks of the social entity as a whole, of public life as well as private life, but also of the place of the individual, whether male or female – in this case female – in the city as a whole. The political subject questions, but at the same time transcends, sex-based identification. To understand woman as a historical subject and a political subject is perhaps to call for new representations.

The notion of women's history often calls up that of feminism in the mind of the researcher, the reader or the teacher. Conversely, much is written in the field of women's history without the slightest reference to the historical reality of feminism. Over-defined or underestimated, feminism, like history, is still represented very imprecisely. We must not conclude from this that this history should be constituted as a domain closed in on itself, or as a subcategory of the history of women. Its political character gives it a place apart, but certainly not marginal status. Indeed feminism, even if it is the object of repeated misunderstanding, has a real relevance and precise consequences in the lives of men and women. So the history of feminism takes its place, of necessity, in an examination of both subversion and the condition of women, an enterprise that involves hunting down the facts and also putting them into perspective. The definition of the field of the history of feminism, which is lacking today, may emerge from this study.

NOTES

1 Cf. G. Fraisse, 'Les Bavardes. Féminisme et moralisme' in P. Werner, ed., *L'Histoire sans qualités* (Galilée, Paris, 1979).
2 Below is a selection of French publications since 1970 relating to the history of feminism in France:

Histories

Laure Adler, *Les Premières Journalistes* (Payot, Paris, 1979)
Maïté Albistur and Daniel Armogathe, *Histoire du féminisme français* (Des Femmes, Paris, 1977)

Huguette Bouchardeau, *Pas d'histoire, les femmes* (Syros, Paris, 1977)
Madeleine Colin, *Ce n'est pas d'aujourd'hui* (Editions sociales, Paris, 1975)
Paule-Marie Duhet, *Les Femmes et la Révolution 1789–1794* (Julliard, Paris, 1971)
Benoîte Groult, *Le Féminisme au masculin* (Denoël, Paris, 1977)
Jean Rabaut, *Histoire des féminismes* (Stock, Paris, 1978)
Charles Sowerwine, *Les Femmes et le socialisme* (Fondation nationale des sciences politiques, Paris, 1978)
Marie-Hélène Zylberberg-Hocquard, *Féminisme et syndicalisme en France* (Anthropos, Paris, 1978); *Femmes et féminisme dans le mouvement ouvrier français* (Editions ouvrières, Paris, 1981)

Biographies

Olivier Blanc, *Olympe de Gouges* (Syros, Paris, 1981)
Evelyne Le Garrec, *Séverine, une rebelle, 1855–1929* (Seuil, Paris, 1982)

Anthologies and new editions

Maïté Albistur and Daniel Armogathe, *Le Grief des femmes, anthologie de textes féministes du Moyen Age à nos jours* (Editions Hier et Demain, Paris, 1978)
Cahiers de doléances des femmes en 1789 et autres textes (Preface by Paule-Marie Duhet, Des Femmes, Paris, 1981)
Hubertine Auclert, *La Citoyenne, 1848–1914* (Introduction by Edith Taïeb, Syros, Paris, 1982)
Jeanne Bouvier, *Une syndicaliste féministe, 1876–1935* (Introduction by Daniel Armogathe with the collaboration of Maïté Albistur, Maspéro, Paris, 1983)
Hélène Brion, *La Voie féministe* (Introduction by Huguette Bouchardeau, Syros, Paris, 1978)
Claire Demar, *L'Affranchissement des femmes* (Introduction by Valentin Pelosse, Payot, Paris, 1976)
Maria Deraismes, *Ce que veulent les femmes, articles et conférences de 1869 à 1894* (Introduction by Odile Krakovitch, Syros, Paris, 1980)
Paule Minck, *Communarde et féministe, 1839–1901* (Introduction by Alain Dalotel, Syros, Paris, 1981)
Madeleine Pelletier, *L'Education féministe des filles* (Introduction by Claude Maignien, Syros, Paris, 1978)
Nelly Roussel, *L'Eternelle Sacrifiée* (Introduction by Daniel Armogathe and Maîté Albistur, Syros, Paris, 1979)
Séverine, *Choix de papiers* (ed. by Evelyne Le Garrec, Editions Tierce, Paris, 1982)
Suzanne Voilquin, *Mémoires d'une saint-simonienne en Russie* (Introduction, with annotations by Maïté Albistur and Daniel Armogathe, Des Femmes,

Paris, 1979); *Souvenirs d'une fille du peuple ou la saint-simonienne en Egypte* (Introduction by Lydia Elhadad, Maspéro, Paris, 1978)

3 Among the journals that have produced articles on the history of feminism might be cited first the political or historical journals (*Les Révoltes logiques; Critique communiste; Dialectiques; Le Peuple français*); more 'academic' or official reviews such as *Romantisme* and *Les Temps modernes*, and some feminist journals (although such articles are in fact very rare): *Les Cahiers du Grif; La Revue d'en face; Pénélope; Questions féministes; Le Bief*.

4 M. Thibert, *Le Féminisme dans le socialisme français de 1830 à 1850* (Paris, 1956); E. Thomas, *Pauline Roland, socialisme et féminisme au XIXe siècle* (Paris, 1956); *Les Femmes en 1848* (Paris, 1948).

5 Betty Friedan, *Ma vie a changé*, quoted by H. Bouchardean in *Pas d'histoire, les femmes*.

6 Cf. G. Fraisse, 'Droit naturel et question de l'origine dans la pensée féministe au XIXe siècle', *Stratégies des femmes* (Tierce, Paris, 1984).

7 G. Fraisse, 'Des héroïnes symboliques? Celle qui écrit et celle qui parle: George Sand et Louise Michel', *Les Révoltes logiques*, no. 6, 1977. We must, in spite of everything, allow Flora Tristan (1804–44) a more important place as a feminist in consideration of her writings on women. She was an important figure in the French working-class movement. Before Marx and Engels, she advocated the formation of a workers' union. She also considered that the emancipation of women, although secondary to that of workers, was a battle to be fought.

8 I borrow this distinction from Rosemarie Lagrave. Cf. 'Les paradoxes du féminisme: l'expérience de *Pénélope*', paper written for the symposium 'Femmes, Féminisme, Recherches', Toulouse, December 1982.

9 G. Fraisse, 'Des femmes présentes', *Les Révoltes Logiques*, nos. 8/9, Winter 1979.

RECENT WORKS

Françoise Blum, *Mouvement de femmes, 1919–1940* (Cedias-Musée social, Paris, 1984)

G. Fraisse, *Clémence Royer, philosophe et femme de sciences (1830–1902)* (La Découverte, Paris, 1985); *Muse de la raison, la démocratie exclusive et la différence des sexes* (Alinea, Aix-en-Provence, 1989)

Dominique Godineau, *Citoyennes tricoteuses, les femmes du peuple à Paris pendant la Révolution française* (Alinea, Aix-en-Provene, 1988)

Laurence Kleiman and Florence Rochefort, *L'Égalité en marche, le féminisme sous la Troisième République* (Presses de la Fondation Nationale des Sciences Politiques, Des Femmes, Paris, 1989)

Annelise Maugue, *L'Identité masculine en crise au tournant du siècle* (Rivages, Paris, 1987)

Elisabeth Roudinesco, *Théroigne de Méricourt, une femme mélancolique sous la Révolution* (Seuil, Paris, 1988)

COLLECTIVE WORKS

Stratégies des femmes (Tierce, Paris, 1984; trans., *Women in Culture and Politics: A Century of Change*, Indiana University Press, 1986)
Un Fabuleux destin, Flora Tristan: Symposium presented by Stéphane Michaud (Editions Universitaires de Dijon, 1985).
Les Femmes et la Révolution française: Proceedings of the Toulouse Symposium (3 vols, Presses Universitaires du Mirail, Toulouse, 1990–1).

JOURNALS

Corpus, Journal of the Collège International de Philosophie, no. 1 (devoted to Poullain de la Barre)
Revue du Ceres, no. 1, Université de Paris VII, 1989

The publishing house Côté-femmes Editions (4 rue de la Petite Pierre, 75011 Paris) aims to republish feminist works (e.g. those of Marie de Jars de Gournay, Olympe de Gouges, Maria Deraismes). It publishes a collection, 'Des Femmes dans l'Histoire', which includes many new editions of feminist works.

12

Women, Power and History

Michelle Perrot

Women's relations with power can be seen first and foremost in language. 'Power' is, like many other terms, polysemic.[1] In the singular, it has a political connotation and tends to suggest the central, cardinal figure of the State, generally accepted as being masculine. In the plural, it breaks down into many fragments, which are equated with diffuse, peripheral influences, of which women have a large share.

If women do not have power in the singular, they have, we say, powers in the plural. In the West today, women are to be found in the private sphere, the family sphere, and also in the social sphere and in civic society. They rule men's imaginations and fill their nights and their dreams. 'We are more than half of you. We are the life you lead when you are asleep. How can you claim to be in control of your dreams?', says the heroine of a novel from the nineteenth century which, more than any other, celebrated *The Muse and the Madonna*.[2]

AN AMBIGUOUS AND TOPICAL THEME

The representations of women's power: what an enormous subject for historical and anthropological enquiry. These representations are numerous and ancient, but often repetitive. They are reflected in the first lesson of Genesis, which presents the seductive power of the eternal Eve. Woman, the origin of evil and unhappiness, a nocturnal force, a force of darkness, Queen of the Night, as opposed to man, a creature of the day, of order and clear reason: this is a great romantic theme, particularly in opera, from Mozart to Richard Wagner. In *Parsifal* the quest for salvation 'consists in exorcising the threat that woman represents so that a male order may triumph'.[3]

In French nineteenth-century society, the prevalent images were those of a connective power, circulating in the social tissue or fabric, the hidden secret motivating force. According to an English traveller of the 1830s, 'Although legally women occupy a position greatly inferior to men, in practice they constitute the superior sex. They are the power behind the throne and, in the family, as in business affairs, they undoubtedly enjoy greater consideration than English women.'[4] This is, more prosaically, the widespread idea that women pull the strings off stage while men, poor things, dance like puppets on the public stage. The inspiration behind political decisions, often made 'in bed', woman herself, so far from being criminal, is the real instigator of crime. 'Find the woman', chorus Lombroso and Joly.[5]

But women are not solely a force for evil. They are also a civilizing influence, another very old theme,[6] which again came to the fore in the nineteenth century with the insistence on the educational function of a child whose value has been reasserted. Mothers hold 'the destinies of the human race' in their hands, writes Louis-Aimé Martin in a work with the significant title: *On the Education of Mothers, or The Civilization of the Human Race by Women.*[7] The obsessive figure of the Mother tends to overshadow all others.

But don't women possess real power? 'There is a sex that is called weak, which nevertheless exercises, whether over the family or over society, a sort of omnipotence for good and for evil', preaches Father Mercier, whose argument has been excellently analysed by Marcel Bernos.[8]

Note how modern this problem of reversal is. It is supported by the importance given to civilian society and its protagonists, and to the private dimension of life. In a period of privatization, to quote Albert Hirschman,[9] the feminine pole in society is becoming the stronger.

This is a common theme, echoed by men of very diverse political backgrounds. 'World change will come through women', said Giscard d'Estaing,[10] reusing the old myth of woman the redeemer. Hence the new – and formidable – responsibility that falls to women. Hence too the idea of women taking power and men being defeated, which underlies a number of male texts today or is explicit in works such as Fellini's *Cité des femmes* or Philippe Sollers's *Femmes*.

Furthermore, recent feminist research has sometimes contributed to this re-evaluation of women's power. In its desire to go beyond the *misérabiliste* language of oppression, to subvert the viewpoint of domination, it has sought to show that women are present and active, that they have full roles and a coherent culture and that their powers are real. This has been what one might call the matriarchal era, triumphing over American feminist anthrophology, the time of Françoise d'Eaubonne's Amazons, and Pierre Samuel's *Guerrières et gaillardes* (*Female Warriors and Wenches*),[11] a sympathetic, ardent demonstration of women's physical strength.

A number of ethnological works of fundamental importance have helped to bring about this reversal. For example, the fine books of Martine Segalen and, to a lesser degree, Yvonne Verdier.[12] Objecting, quite rightly, to the false vision of the oppressed rural woman, constructed on the basis of the preconceptions of nineteenth-century ethnologists such as Abel Hugo, Martine Segalen attempts to present a conflict-free society based on an even distribution of roles, tasks and space, on a complementary, rather than a competitive, basis. What has disturbed this balance, worked out over centuries, is current economic evolution which, through the development of the banking system, is reinforcing the impact of male authority in financial management. This is the thesis developed by Ivan Illich, in a much more systematic fashion, in *Le Genre vernaculaire*[13] in which he opposes the complementarity of recognized and organized differences in traditional societies with the singleness of economic 'sex' in industrial societies, which is disastrous for women.

Two studies by Susan Rogers[14] illustrate both this desire for demonstration and the subsequent awareness of the limits of this thesis and its variability. In the first monograph ('Female forms of power and the myth of male dominance'), based on work carried out in a community in the north-west of France, the author stresses the informal powers of women who in fact control the largest share of resources and decisions. In these circumstances, the perpetuation of the myth of male power serves the interests of both genders. Behind the fiction of this power, women can develop their own strategies at leisure. In a second enquiry, this time based on Sainte-Foy (in Aveyron), Rogers was led to draw much more qualified conclusions. Here, women have far fewer powers, even informal ones – the reason being, above all, a much more dispersed habitat, which makes communications between women much more difficult. It is also due to different rules of inheritance. So there is no general model valid for all rural societies and the author concludes that it is necessary to elaborate or draw up more sophisticated models, including several variables. This also invites us to be a little more circumspect in making generalized assessments of former societies.

A similar desire to overturn traditional historiographical perspectives and to show the real presence of women in everyday history underlies the efforts of female historians over the last few years. I offer three examples among many. The success of the books of Jeanne Bourin and

Régine Pernoud[15] has raised the question of the relatively privileged status of women in the Middle Ages. Georges Duby, in particular, has spoken out against an excessively rosy vision of this period. In *Le Chevalier, la femme et le prêtre*, he stresses the degree to which women remained an object of male power, a pawn in the matrimonial game, and, in the last resort, very silent. 'A great deal is said about them. What do we know about them?'[16] he asks in conclusion.

Bonnie Smith, studying 'the bourgeoises of northern France in the nineteenth century' shows the many forms of activity of 'ladies of the leisured classes'[17] who, excluded from business affairs, tried to recon-struct a domestic feminism based on the house and religion.

The same spirit runs through *L'Histoire sans qualité*, in which I wished to replace the dominant image of a lowly, neglected and negligible housewife, beaten and humiliated, with that of a 'rebellious woman of the people', active and strong, the guardian of the family's means of subsistence, in control of the family budget, at the very heart of the urban sphere.[18]

These texts all use the same procedure: inversion or reversal of the poles. Black becomes white (or red – it is of no matter). Sharing is preferred to conflict. The emphasis is on the existence of a sphere, a 'world of women', characterized by sociability, its own forms of expression, in short, its own culture. This doubtless corresponds to a phase of euphoric re-evaluation of women's history, and at the same time to the discovery of the pleasure of female company.

This procedure also has its dangers and its weaknesses. It is too systematic and dichotomous. It offers too much support for the thesis of women's social power, which is maintained by those who intend to leave matters there. Since women have these powers, what else do they want?

Thus the analysis of women's power is also part of the power game.

WOMEN'S POWER IN THE NINETEENTH CENTURY

Taking the example of the nineteenth century, I should like to show the links between the formulation of a question and the type of society that produced it, and in particular the type of relationship between the sexes that gives the question its structure. I must make it clear that I am not embarking on a history of origins. The nineteenth century invented nothing in this area. It only reformulated a very old, indeed an eternal, question and reappropriated it – perhaps with particular strength, in that the building of western democracies has been accompanied by, and has even relied on, a stricter definition of the public and the private, and of sexual roles.

It would be interesting to compare this experience with others. There are those societies in which the exclusion of women from political power goes without saying, others in which it is accompanied by justifications or compensations, and yet others in which it admits of degrees. Theory and practice need to be examined and compared. Women and politics: yet another vast field for common effort.

History and women's power in the nineteenth century: *Jules Michelet*

'Women! What a force!', Michelet wrote. As an individual and a historian, he was haunted by this question. He had a profoundly sex-based view of history, as Thérèse Moreau shows.[19] In Michelet's view, the opposition between man/culture and woman/nature dominates the history of societies and regulates the flow of events. The feminine principle, which is profoundly ambivalent, must be respected. Feminine nature itself has two poles: one maternal and beneficial; the other magic, red as blood, black as the devil and malefic. When they are mothers, women are a force for good: thus on 5 and 6 October 1789 they were fulfilling their traditional role as housewives. 'Women were in the forefront of our Revolution. This should not surprise us. They suffered more.'[20] Again, at the Fête of Federation, they cemented the union of citizens by making families think of the good of the homeland, by linking private and public:

> Whether or not they were called, they took the most active part in the Fête of Federation. In some village somewhere, the men had gathered alone in a vast building, to draw up an address to the National Assembly. The women approached, they listened, they entered, tears in their eyes, asking to join in. The address was read to them. They approved it whole-heartedly. This deep union of the family and the homeland filled all souls with an unfamiliar feeling.[21]

But if they step outside this role, if they try to usurp male power – like Catherine de Medici, the incarnation of evil and misfortune – if they allow violence to be unleashed, and give vent to their taste for blood and the nocturnal passion that lies within them, then history, like a wild river that has flooded its banks, carries all before it.

The course of collective events depends, like happiness and the peace of households, on this balance between the sexes. Michelet shows this in different phases of French history, particularly in the course of the Revolution. The fourteenth century, dominated by paternal law and royal authority, seems to him a era of decisive progress achieved by excluding women. In the fifteenth century the law becomes confused, the sexes are mixed, and this brings about intellectual disorder – the madness of Charles VI – and disorder in the kingdom. François I, a masculine figure *par excellence*, restores the situation; but on his death, with Catherine there begins a long period of inversion of roles and sexual aberrations. Thus woman 'distorts history for a hundred years.'

The feminization of the monarchy at the end of the eighteenth century is also a mark of decadence. By nature and by education, women are counter-revolutionary. They prefer the anarchy of the word to the order of writing. Aristocratic by nature, they are hostile to equality. 'Women can spell the sacred word of the New Age – *Fraternity* – but still cannot read it.'[22] Women bear the greater part of the responsibility for the unleashing of violence: the September massacres are a bloody Sabbath whose recurrent theme is women's pleasure, and the men who created the Terror – Marat, Couthon and Robespierre – are 'female men'. Marat in particular, 'by his temperament was a woman and more than a woman, very highly strung and very passionate'; his house, like his skin disease, was feminine. Danton alone was 'first and foremost a male' and therefore able to dominate women, the people – who were like a woman – and, perhaps, to save the Revolution.[23]

Never have sexual roles been defined with more normative and explanatory rigour. Political power is the prerogative of men – of virile men. Moreover, the patriarchal order must reign over all: in the family and in the State. This is the law of historical equilibrium.

The matriarchy: A myth of origins

The question of the matriarchy is at the heart of anthropological discussions in the nineteenth century. Françoise Picq[24] has shown that a broad consensus existed on this score. For Bachofen, Lewis Henry Morgan, Engels and Robert Briffault there was no doubt that women had established the law as a barrier to protect them from men's lubricity.[25] But for the most part, this is a primitive, barbarian stage. Maternal law is a stage in the establishment of the law in which patrilinear descendancy marks decisive progress. For Bachofen, Roman paternal law is a great leap forward for civilization. Engels alone stresses 'the historical defeat of the female sex', linked with the strengthening of private property, and sees in monogamy and in its modern form – middle-class marriage – the key to the oppression of women. Unlike Morgan, to whom he owes so much, he does not consider this development to be progress. In a sense, the golden age lies behind us. But, at the same time, in socialist theory and action, Engels subordinates women's liberation to the long-term collectivization of property.

All this is too well known for us to dwell on here. As far as women's power is concerned, there are several interesting features, which fit perfectly with the dominant ideas of the nineteenth century. First, the civilizing power attributed to the mother. Briffault, in particular, develops the theme of the settled way of life and of agriculture. Then the domination of the father figure, the ultimate end of this teleological progression, whose triumphs at the end of the century could no longer be counted and were justified by the general interest, both public and private. Finally, the writing into history of the relationship between the sexes. It is not rooted in a natural fixed order of things; it is the product of evolution. The subjection of women is the result of a process that might be thought to be reversible.

The passionate attention feminists have devoted to these theories is now understandable. In 1901 a French group for feminist studies put the question on its agenda and published a brochure on this theme. But it was mainly in Germany, in Heidelberg and Munich, in the progressive intellectual milieux so well represented by the Von Richtofen sisters,[26] allied to Otto Gross, Max Weber and D. H. Lawrence, that the matriarchy was discussed at the same time as sexual relations, madness and free love.

We can also understand the increased interest aroused by these authors among feminist anthropologists confronted with the asexual logic of structuralism. But matriarchy was found to be an impasse. Even those who studied the Trobriands lost some of their halo.

Nevertheless, as a representation of women's power and the relationship between the sexes, these texts retain their importance.

PUBLIC AND PRIVATE: WOMEN'S POWER IN THE NINETEENTH CENTURY

There have not always been dividing lines between public and private. They change with time. Their development, their delicate balance, and the overall tendency towards privatization, with alternate phases of 'public' and 'private' are one of the major themes of contemporary thought, illustrated notably by Jürgen Habermas, Richard Sennett and Albert Hirschman.[27] The liberal nineteenth century might be considered to mark a pause in this process, even though, between the State and the private individual, civilian society remains, in France at least, a rather vague concept.

What interests us here is the creation of a political space, broadly

consubstantial with 'public' space and with two exclusions: the prole-
tariat and women. The Fourth Estate knows how to enforce its rights
more effectively than the Second Sex does. Proletarian men, after 1848,
were only too ready to adopt the middle-class exclusion of women from
the political sphere.

This exclusion of women is scarcely in accordance with the Declaration of Human Rights, which proclaims the equality of all individuals.
Aren't women individuals? This is an awkward question, as a number of
thinkers, such as Condorcet, foresaw. The only possible justification was
to argue that the sexes were different. This is why the nineteenth
century restated this old argument with a new vigour, using discoveries
in medicine and biology to support it.[28] It is a naturalistic argument,
stressing the existence of two species, with specific qualities and
aptitudes. Men had brains (much more important than the phallus),
intelligence, clear reason, the capacity for decision. Women had heart,
sensitivity, feelings.

Are these the hackneyed stereotypes of the epigoni of antifeminism?
No doubt, as Anne-Lise Maugue has shown.[29] But they are also principles of political organization stated by the most respected philosophers. Fichte: 'Her femininity gives woman more practical aptitude,
but never speculative aptitude.' Thus, 'women can not take on public
responsibilities'. Hegel speaks of the 'natural vocation' of the two sexes.
'Man's real and substantial life is the State, science or another activity of
the same type. Let us say in general combat and work, which bring him
into opposition with the outside world and himself.' Woman, on the
other hand, is made for piety and the home. 'If we put women at the
head of government, the State will be in danger. For they do not act
according to the requirements of the collectivity, but according to the
caprices of their whims and thoughts.'[30] Auguste Comte goes even
further, since he speaks of the 'radical inaptitude of the female sex for
government, even of the family', because of the 'sort of constant child-
like state' that characterizes the female sex. The domestic sphere cannot
be abandoned to women without any control; but within certain limits
women can be trusted with the family and the house, the keystones of
the private sphere.

The nineteenth century stresses the harmonious rationality of this
sexual division. Each sex has its function, its roles, its tasks, its spaces,
its place, as it were predetermined, even down to details. There exists in
parallel a vocabulary of the trades that makes the language of work one
of the most sex-bound there is. 'Wood and metals are for men. The
family and material are for women', as one worker delegate proclaimed
to the universal exposition of 1867.

Political economy reinforces this vision of things, by distinguishing production, reproduction and consumption. Men take care of the first and women of the third; they deal with the second together. The notion of a female domestic economy emerges in the treatises written at the end of the eighteenth, and the beginning of the nineteenth, century. Madame Gacon-Dufour, for example, in her famous treatise on domestic economy, addresses the housewife, the steward of the household, whereas equivalent works of the seventeenth and eighteenth centuries addressed the 'housekeeper' (in the masculine) as the veritable head of a rural enterprise.[31] This language of the business, the 'science' of the household and the housewife as the woman in charge, was developed in the nineteenth century, in England and in France.[32] The control of the budget is the pivot of this new branch of political economy. Later, in the twentieth century, with electricity and domestic science, the mistress of the house was to become a kind of engineer at the controls of the machines of a kitchen-factory.[33]

But this power is also exercised in the city. In the autonomized sphere of merchandise, women, middle-class and also working-class, would be sovereign, deciding what to buy, diffusing taste, dictating success and fashion, the motivation behind the essential industry, the textile industry, and in control of consumption. The symbol of this power: the language of advertising, which addresses her first and foremost; the large stores, a female space *par excellence*, are her kingdom.[34]

Wife and mother, 'divinity of the domestic sanctuary', as Chaumette put it,[35] woman is also invested with immense social power,[36] for better and for worse.

These are the principles. This is what the norm is claimed to be. But the multitude of discourses on the subject, amplified by reciprocal fantasies, cannot hope to take account of actual practice, which is much more difficult (perhaps impossible) to pin down. What were the nature and extent of women's power or powers in the nineteenth century? How was decision-making shared between the two sexes? What battles, both open and hidden, were fought on this point? Only a detailed study, carried out at the level of family, local community and the State can allow us to form a clearer picture of this.

A movement on three levels can be seen to be at work in the nineteenth century: a relative retreat on the part of women from the public sphere; the constitution of a private family sphere dominated by women; and the overwhelming invasion of the male imagination and male symbolic world by female images. But we must make certain reservations. First, the public sphere is not entirely political, and the public sphere is not entirely masculine. Women's presence in the street was strongly felt in the eighteenth century,[37] and they continued to be present in the town in the nineteenth century, moving about as before, occupying mixed spheres and constituting their own space.[38] Furthermore, the private sphere was not entirely feminine. In the family, the major power remained the father's, in law and in fact. Political studies have even shown that the spread of the republican order in the villages was accompanied by a strengthening of the power of the father, the only citizen with full rights, over spouse and children. The triumphant Republic has a Roman aspect.[39] In the house there coexist places for representation (the middle-class drawing room) and spaces for men's work (the study, where woman and children may only enter on tiptoe). The borderline between public and private is ever changing, sinuous, and even crosses domestic microspace.

Nevertheless, the tripartite division sketched above covers the main zones of the exercise of power. Women's action in the nineteenth century consisted above all in adapting the private power, over both the family and children, for which they were destined. Bonnie Smith shows how the middle-class women of northern France, excluded, after 1860, from the management of businesses in which they had up until then been involved, confined to their fine houses, which were from then on removed from the factory perimeter, administered their households, their large families and domesticity by constructing a coherent domestic code, which gave meaning to their smallest actions. Faith as opposed to reason, charity as opposed to capitalism, and reproduction as fundamental justification were the major axes of this philosophy. These northern women were very conscious of themselves. They were not simply resigned or passive, but tended to erect their vision of the world as a judgement of things. This 'Christian feminism', in the author's words, was expressed by women novelists such as Mathilde Bourdon, Julia Récour and Joséphine de Gaulle, who wrote a kind of domestic epic in which good confronted evil. Women confronted men. With their taste for power and money, men engendered chaos and death. Domestic heroines, with their suffering, sacrifices and virtue, restored the harmony of the household and family peace. They had the power – and the duty – to do good.

In lower-class urban milieux, the strengthening of the mother figure, in the absence of a father increasingly taken up with his work, is attested by most of the autobiographies of the time, and also by Frédéric Le Play's family monographs.[40] Control of the husband's wage-packet was largely in her hands, and this was doubtless a female victory implying power, but it also increased responsibility, and, in periods of hardship, personal privation. And yet the persistence of this 'budgetary matriarchy' is confirmed nowadays[41] as a reality to which housewives are attached. Lower-class women have other forms of knowledge and power – in particular, medical, religious, and even cultural. Their role in the early education of children, including basic reading skills, is considerable. Female literacy increased rapidly in the towns in the nineteenth century, and the private reading of novels and newspapers shaped their imaginations.[42] The development of institutions – hospitals and schools – generally occurred in the spheres of their empirical knowledge, whence sometimes the impression of despoilment.

Outside the home, women were active in the city, and the list of cases in which they took some active role, whether formally or informally, on particular occasions or as a matter of course, would be long. Increasingly, middle-class women – society women – were encouraged to leave their homes and practise charity or philanthropy, like the women of the north, described by Bonnie Smith. But in this we see the limit of their influence. Encouraged when they became involved in the management of the social sphere, their works were criticized – even opposed – by northern employers who, confronted with the violence of the working-class movement, opted for a secular republican administration which was more suited to the circumstances, and condemned their mothers and their views as old-fashioned.

Criticism of the reactionary nature of women remains, indeed, a major theme of the period. It was the basis of the demand for a new form of education for girls, expressed at the end of the Second Empire by the republicans, in particular those of the Protestant persuasion. Around 1867, the Church and the Republic found themselves in opposition – on one side Monseigneur Dupanloup, on the other the likes of Ferry, Favre and Legouvé, the creators of secondary education for girls.[43] The breadth and violence of the conflict suggest the importance of what was at stake: the extent of women's social power, but also its lack of autonomy.

Non-existent on the political level, strong, but restricted, within the family, the space occupied by women in a public and private imagination in the nineteenth century, whether at the political, religious or poetic level, was enormous, almost to the point of becoming an obsession. The Church celebrated the cult of the Virgin Mother whose apparitions originated great pilgrimages. The Saint-Simonians dreamed of salvation through the Mother who came from the East. The Republic took the form of a woman, 'la Marianne'. Poets and painters sang of women, despite their everyday misogyny. Thus Baudelaire, for example, who was afraid of his mother, the terrible, pitiful Madame Aupick, despises the stupidity of the women of his period, while exalting 'the Muse and the Madonna'.[44]

The mother was the geometric centre of these diverse cults which, in the end, created an unbearable saturation, and fed the old fear that men felt for women, and above all for maternal power. Georges Darien, François Mauriac and André Breton are modern interpreters of this ancestral terror. 'Mothers! We experience Faust's terror, we are, like him, seized by an electric shock at the very sound of these syllables in which the powerful goddesses who escape time and place are hiding', Breton writes.[45]

Yet it was not primarily this source that fed the new anti-feminism of the early twentieth century, but women's victories, the suggestion, however timid, of a reversal of roles by the 'emancipated woman', who demanded equality of civil and political rights and access to the intellectual professions, and refused to be restricted to the maternal vocation. This 'new Eve' (to use Jules Dubois's words in 1896[46]) aroused the fervour of those few who dreamed of intelligent, free female companions, but far more widely the fear of those who dreaded being dispossessed[47] and saw in this threat of feminine power the risk of the degeneracy of the race and moral decadence.

The Otto Weininger case, recently analysed by Jacques Le Rider, shows the extent of antifeminist reaction around 1900 and the nature of its argumentation.[48] This led to vibrant appeals, from all quarters, for the restoration of the father figure and virile values. 'We want to glorify war – the only salvation of the world – militarism, patriotism, the destructive act of anarchists, fine ideas which kill, contempt for women. We want to demolish museums and libraries, fight moralism, feminism and all opportunist and utilitarian cowardliness', as Marinetti's futurist manifesto in 1909 proclaimed.[49] War was to put each sex 'back in its place' in the most dramatic fashion, the effect of wars on relations between the sexes being most often conservative, if not retrograde.

To conclude, we might consider the attitude of women themselves, in particular as regards political power, the kind of power that was really a problem. Isn't the attitude of women, in France, marked by a certain inhibition and a *de facto* acceptance of patriarchal society? Most Anglo-Saxon commentators[50] stress this fact, which seems to them to link France with Latin societies. Feminism in France, in their view, remains a social, not a political, fact. The idea that politics is not for women, that they have no place in politics, remained, until very recently, anchored in the opinions of both sexes. Women tend, moreover, to undervalue the political and to value the social and the informal, thus interiorizing the traditional norms. Once again, the whole problem of consent is raised.

In history and in the present, the question of power is at the heart of relations between men and women.

NOTES

1 I agree with Marcel Bernos's comments in his article, which directly concerns our subject: 'De l'influence salutaire ou pernicieuse de la femme dans la famille et la société', *Revue d'histoire moderne et contemporaine*, July–September, 1982, esp. n. 1.

2 Lassailly, *Les Roueries de Trialph*, 1833, quoted by Stéphane Michaud, 'La Muse et la Madone. Visages de la femme rédemptrice en France et en Allemagne de Novalis à Baudelaire', doctoral thesis, Paris III, 1983, ii. 559. Reference omitted from abridged edn (Seuil, 1985).

3 Quoted by Michaud, *La Muse et la Madone*, ii. 737.

4 Quoted by Théodore Zeldin, *Les Français* (Laffont, Paris, 1983), p. 403.

5 Famous criminologists of the nineteenth century.

6 Developed in particular by Jean-Louis Flandrin.

7 Louis-Aimé Martin, *De l'éducation des mères de famille, ou de la civilisation du genre humain par les femmes* (Gosselin, Paris, 1834, 2 vols).

8 Bernos, 'De l'influence salutaire ou pernicieuse'.

9 Albert Hirschman, *Bonheur privé, action publique* (Fayard, Paris, 1983). Hirschman shows in history especially since the sixteenth century, a series of cycles in which public interests alternate with private interests as the dominant element.

10 Quoted by Zeldin, *Les Français*, p. 410.

11 Pierre Samuel, *Amazones, guerrières et gaillardes* (Editions Complexe, Brussels, 1975).

12 Segalen, *Mari et femme dans la société paysanne*; Verdier, *Façons de dire, façons de faire*.

13 Ivan Illich, *Le Genre vernaculaire* (Seuil, Paris, 1983).

14 Susan Rogers, 'Female forms of power and the myth of male dominance: a model of female/male interaction in peasant society', *American Ethnologist*, vol. 2, no. 4, Nov. 1975; 'Rules of order: the generation of female/male power relationships in two rural French communities', paper given at the 76th meeting of the American Anthropological Association, November 1977.

15 Bourin, *La Chambre des dames*; Régine Pernoud, *La Femme au Moyen Age* (Stock, Paris, 1980, 1984).

16 (Hachette, Paris, 1981). Subtitle: *Le Mariage dans la France féodale*.

17 Bonnie Smith, *The Ladies of the Leisure Class. The Bourgeoises of Northern France in the XIXth Century* (Princeton, 1981).

18 See my paper in P. Werner, ed., *L'Histoire sans qualité*, a collective work.
19 T. Moreau, *Le Sang de l'histoire. Michelet, l'histoire et l'idée de la femme au XIXe siècle* (Flammarion, Paris, 1982).
20 Michelet, *Histoire de la Révolution française* (Gallimard, La Pléiade 1952), i. 254.
21 Ibid. i. 408–9.
22 Quoted by Moreau, *Le Sang de l'histoire,* p. 170.
23 Ibid., pp. 201–39.
24 Françoise Picq, 'Sur la théorie du droit maternel. Discours anthropologique et discours socialiste', thesis, Paris-Dauphine, 1979.
25 Johann Jakob Bachofen, 'Das Mutterrecht. Eine Untersuchung über die Gynaikokratie der Alten Welt nach ihrer religiösen und rechtlichen Natur' (1861) in Bachofen, *Gesammelte Werke*, ed. Karl Meuli (Basle, 1948, vol. II, pp. 293ff.).
26 Martin Green, *Les Sœurs Von Richtofen. Deux ancêtres du féminisme dans l'Allemagne de Bismarck face à Otto Gross, Max Weber et D. H. Lawrence* (Seuil, Paris, 1974).
27 J. Habermas, *L'Espace public. Archéologie de la publicité comme dimension constitutive de la société bourgeoise* (1962, French trans., Payot, Paris, 1978); Richard Sennett, *Les Tyrannies de l'intimité* (French trans., Seuil, Paris, 1978); Hirschman, *Bonheur privé*.
28 Stephen Jay Gould, *The Mismeasure of Man* (Penguin, Harmondsworth, 1983; Fr. trans., *La Mal-mesure de l'homme*, Ramsay, Paris, 1983), ch. 3.
29 Anne-Lise Maugue, 'La Littérature antiféministe en France de 1871 à 1914', doctoral thesis, Paris III (supervised by G. Fraisse), 1983.
30 Quoted by Michaud, *La Muse et la Madone*, ii. 815.
31 According to a paper given by Elisabeth Fox-Genovese at the EHESS, Spring 1982.
32 Katherine Blunden, *Le Travail et la vertu. Femmes au foyer: une mystification de la révolution industrielle* (Payot, Paris, 1982), a very pertinent demonstration of women's retreat from production and the construction of the roles of wife, mother and consumer in Victorian England. See also Anne Martin-Fugier, *La Bourgeoise. Femme au temps de Paul Bourget* (Grasset, Paris, 1983).
33 Martine Martin, 'Le Travail ménager des femmes entre les deux guerres', doctoral thesis, Paris VII, 1984.
34 Rosalind H. Williams, *Dream Worlds. Mass Consumption in the late XIXth Century* (University of California Press, Berkeley and Los Angeles, 1982).
35 Speech of 27 Brumaire, year II, quoted by Michaud, *La Muse et la Madone*.
36 According to the title of a book by a disciple of Auguste Comte, who thinks that this is their territory: Georges Deherme, *Le Pouvoir social des femmes* (Paris, 1912).
37 Arlette Farge, *Vivre dans la rue à Paris au XVIIIe siècle* (Gallimard, Paris, 1979).
38 Michelle Perrot, 'La ménagère dans l'espace parisien au XIXe siècle', *Annales de la recherche urbaine*, Autumn 1980, no. 9.

39 Christian Thibon, 'L'ordre public villageois au XIXe siècle: le cas du pays de Sault (Aude)', paper given at the symposium on 'The maintenance of public order in Europe in the XIXth century', December 1983. And more generally, Claude Nicolet's book, *L'Idée républicaine en France, 1789–1924* (Gallimard, Paris, 1982).

40 *Les ouvriers européens* (1855, 6 vols.).

41 Andrée Michel, *Activité professionnelle de la femme et vie conjugale* (CNRS, Paris, 1974). The study focuses in particular on 'decision-making powers within the couple' in relation to the woman's socio-professional status.

42 Lise Vanderwielen, *Lise du Plat Pays* (Presses Universitaires de Lille, 1983), an autobiographical novel constructed like the serialized novels which were the author's main form of reading, is a good example, for the twentieth century, of this influence of reading on the imagination.

43 In this context, see the works of Françoise Mayeur, and also Marie-Françoise Lévy's doctoral thesis, 'Education familiale et education religieuse des filles sous le Second Empire. L'enjeu du savoir', Paris II, 1983; the latter concentrates particularly on the 1867 crisis in the female education system, published as *De mères en filles. L'Education des Françaises (1850–1880)* (Calmann-Lévy, Paris, 1984).

44 It is Baudelaire's expression that gives its title to Stéphane Michaud's work, quoted above. Maurice Agulhon's *Marianne au combat (1789–1880). L'Imagerie et la symbolique républicaine* (Flammarion, 1979) and Claude Quiguer's *Femmes et machines de 1900. Lectures d'une obsession Modern Style* (Klincksieck, Paris, 1979) provide remarkable examples of woman in the imagination and symbolism of politics, advertising and novels, etc.

45 André Breton, *Le Surréalisme et la peinture*, quoted by Michaud, *La Muse et la Madone*, p. 373.

46 Jules Dubois, a novelist linked with the 'Amazones de Paris' (Renée Vivien, Natalie Clifford-Barney and others) in the Belle Epoque. He believed in regeneration through women, the new Eve who would save humanity.

47 Anne-Lise Maugue has made a remarkable study of the themes of this literature.

48 Jacques Le Rider, *Le Cas Otto Weininger. Racines de l'antiféminisme et de l'antisémitisme* (Presses Universitaires de France, Paris, 1982, Perspectives Critiques collection). Weininger's book, *Sexe et caractère*, published in Vienna in 1903 (*Geschlecht und Charakter*), is a survey of antifeminism which served as a reference work for a whole generation.

49 Quoted by Fanette Roche-Pézard, *L'Aventure futuriste, 1909–1916* (Ecole Française de Rome, Paris, José Corti distributors, 1983).

50 See also T. Zeldin, *Les Français*, ch. 25, 'Pourquoi la libération des femmes progresse lentement'; and also James McMillan, *Housewife or Harlot. The Place of Women in French Society, 1870–1940* (Harvester Press, 1981).

Index